Truth and Justice
in
Côte d'Ivoire:
French Scandals Revealed

Truth and Justice

Laurent Gbagbo
Talks with
François Mattei

Côte d'Ivoire:
French Scandals Revealed

*Passages in **bold** are the reconstitution of François Mattei's memories of various conversations he had with President Gbagbo over several years, from 2005 in Abidjan when Laurent Gbagbo was still in office, and later in Scheveningen prison, The Hague, in the Netherlands, where he has been imprisoned by the International Criminal Court, the ICC, since November 30, 2011. Indeed, Laurent Gbagbo is the first ex-head of state to be incarcerated there. François Mattei--not President Gbagbo--bears full responsibility for the content of this book.*

"As long as lions do not have their own historians,
Hunting stories will always give glory to the hunter."
African proverb

The Translators' Note

The story of Laurent Gbagbo is a story in progress. And it is a story that most in the English-speaking world know little about.

This book tells the story of how a University professor became a leading politician of the opposition and then president of a West African country, *Côte d'Ivoire*, otherwise known in these pages as *Ivory Coast*. It is a shocking story of how France, with the backing of at least some of the International Community, intervened militarily in a sovereign state, to bring to power their own candidate for president.

The story is also a complicated one. Within these pages the highly respected French journalist, François Mattei, author of numerous books and former editor-in-chief of *France-Soir,* tells what he has learned about the crisis which has rocked Ivory Coast for over a decade. He weaves his own analyses with verbatim quotes gleaned from conversations he had with President Gbagbo over many years, beginning from 2005, when he met with the then-sitting president in Abidjan until very recently, as he met with Laurent Gbagbo behind the prison walls of the International Criminal Court in The Hague, where Gbagbo has been held prisoner for three years as he awaits his trial for crimes against humanity.

Though at times the reader may find the transition from Mattei's to Gbagbo's words somewhat hard to follow, the task is made easier since Gbagbo's words are all marked **in bold**, while Mattei's narration and analyses occur in normal font. As noted earlier, Mattei takes legal responsibility for the entire book.

For the translators of this book (from French to English), the task has been a formidable one. Mattei speaks with much emotion and irony--never an easy thing to translate--but more difficult perhaps, are the many terms and context that will be new to most readers. The venue is West Africa, the actors mainly African and French, evolving in a judicial and political system quite different from its American or British counterparts. Hopefully the glossary and list of abbreviations of the many French acronyms will help orient the reader.

While some consider translator's notes in a translation as a sign of weakness or lack of skill, we the translators have deemed them necessary here, especially given that the themes, context, and terms will be quite foreign to most of the readership. Added in brackets are words not in the original but needed to fill out the thought. At the beginning of each chapter, the translators have also included a short "orientation box" which introduces the reader to what follows.

Due to pressures of time, and also because no translation is perfect, there will certainly be some errors here, but we hope they will not affect the very well documented and heartfelt presentation of François Mattei and the powerful words of Laurent Gbagbo.

The copyright of this English edition was acquired through a purchase from a French publisher, *Editions du Moment*, by *NextAfrika Inc.*, a company owned by a group of associates representing the Ivorian diaspora.

This story is ongoing; it is a story in progress. Only time will tell if **truth** will win and true **justice be** rendered.

For obvious reasons, we the translators, have worked anonymously, but with the belief that **if the truth is known, injustice can be stopped and true justice will "see the day."**

The Translators:
in Washington, D.C. and Abidjan, Ivory Coast.

Table Of Contents

Foreword

Door after door and still more doors... There is nothing else to be seen in Scheveningen. Over a period of two years, I returned there again and again, at all times of the year to pursue my regular meetings with Laurent Gbagbo. This long conversation, which began in 2005, was often interrupted but never completely broken off. I found him behind the walls of the *Penitentiary Inrichting Haaglanden, at 32 Pompstationswe,* the terminus usually reserved for those who have committed genocide, for bloodthirsty tyrants and those dictators who have shed so much blood.

The time has certainly come for a less biased version than the one set forth during the hottest moments of the political and military strife in Ivory Coast, when the media artillery kept thundering in our ears. The war is over, the media fog has dissipated, and the living demand to know why the mass graves contain so many dead.

For ten years, Gbagbo and his supporters were accused non-stop. It is difficult to imagine what more could be added now. The long list of those accusations is known in great detail. But listening to Gbagbo, and considering a number of facts concealed for far too long, we may gain a clearer and more complete picture of the narrative. Up to a certain point, Laurent Gbagbo was alone in the dock of the International Court. Later, he was joined by Charles Blé Goudé, the leader of the Ivorian Young Patriots, a legal move which surely saved this young man's life. At least in The Hague, he will hopefully escape death, an almost certain fate, had he remained in the prisons of Ouattara.

Despite all Gbagbo's lawyers have been able to bring as arguments to the ICC to allow investigations to cover the period preceding the post-electoral crisis, from the 2002 events which are at the very root of the crisis and the war, the judges of the International Court have still not addressed the abuses perpetrated by the rebels and their leaders in a global way. A true chronological narrative could reveal the causes and effects of the Ivorian crisis and help pinpoint the true responsibilities of each person: clearly no one is 100% innocent in the matter. If the International Court continues on its current path, despite its promises of fair justice and its declared commitment to fight against impunity, if indeed the ICC refuses to inquire into the crimes of the former rebellion and its leaders now in power, and if it is content to judge only the defeated, then the International Court will make clear to the entire world that it has allowed itself willingly to be manipulated by various countries and by various interests.

On February 26, 2013, in a report entitled *The Laws of the Victors*, Amnesty International criticized the so-called "justice" in Ivory Coast and The Hague. In its online publication the same day, RFI (the French Public Radio) quoted Stephan Oberreit, Director of Amnesty International in France:

> *"It has been widely recognized that there have been abuses on both sides, but only one side has been prosecuted, with Laurent Gbagbo at the International Criminal Court. In the Ivorian judicial system, only Gbagbo's wife, the former members of his government and others close to him are accused. This creates a sense of imbalance and partial justice that undermines any possibility of national reconciliation."*

Guillaume Soro, the current president of the Ivorian National Assembly, ironically remarks: *Who cares?* This man even shamelessly declared during an interview on Cameroon STV:

> *"Where have you ever seen justice exist for the vanquished?"*

According to him, it is common sense. For Guillaume Soro, the Ivorian rebel chief, it makes sense to send a lone woman, who was raped and who gouged out her attacker's eye, stand accused before a judge, standing alone in the dock while her rapist looks on mockingly as *she* faces justice.

In what follows, the reader will find a multifaceted version, that is, a snapshot "in reverse" of just a few moments of the Ivorian crisis. You will walk through a hall of mirrors which reconstructs another "reality," one different from the realities presented to the public up till now. You will have access to facts this young institution, the International Criminal Court did not bother to consider. Perhaps the ICC is unaware that outside its halls of justice, the wider world is populated not only by more than just a set of small deaf, dumb, and blind "little monkeys."

Chapter 1
"I am confident the truth will win out in the end"

This direct quote from President Gbagbo's televised address to the Ivorian nation on New Year's Eve 2011 shows his courage and confidence in a time of extreme crisis. The presidential elections held in October and November 2010 produced an extraordinary situation: both candidates, Laurent Gbagbo and Alassane Dramane Ouattara were declared the winner and on November 28, both were sworn in as president of the Republic!

In this chapter Mattei and Gbagbo give the background and details of these unusual events. Immediately after the elections, Gbagbo's team uncovered proof of incredible fraud on many levels. But as Gbagbo was in the process of lodging formal legal complaints, the French, UN, and American representatives were working underground to establish "their candidate" as president. While the Ivorian Constitution stipulates exactly how the election results are to be announced, suddenly the president of the Independent Electoral Commission emerged at the wrong place at the wrong time, at Ouattara's campaign headquarters, flanked by the French and U.S. ambassadors to declare Ouattara's victory.

The Ivorian Consitutional Council, removing fraudulent counts, later declared Gbagbo the winner and he was sworn in, in conformity to the Ivorian Constitution and protocol. However the International Community could barely conceal its displeasure. Though Gbagbo proposed an open and internationally supervised recount, this proposal was rejected by Mr. Young-jin Choi, the UN representative in Ivory Coast, with the French (led by Nicolas Sarkozy) and the Americans (led by Obama and Hilary Clinton) following suit. Together they manipulated the UN Security Council, who concocted Resolution 1975 which "urged" Laurent Gbagbo to step aside. From that day on, things went downhill for Laurent Gbagbo, as the following chapters will reveal.

Yet from his prison cell in The Hague, where he awaits trial for his purported "crimes against humanity," Laurent Gbagbo remains serene. "I am confident that the truth will eventually win out."

It was, after all, a simple dispute over an election: nobody goes to war if you've won an election. Laurent Gbagbo has been repeating this statement for three years. In Abidjan, it was late in the morning of April 11, 2011. The French "Sagaie" tank blew up the gate and the wall of the residence of the president of the Republic of Ivory Coast. The armored crews weren't asking any more questions. The last links in the chain of the French military command had been put in place. The armed men of the 12th regiment had finished up their job. Louis Ferdinand Destouches, better known by his code name, Céline, once brigadier, and later, sergeant during the First World War, describes in *Journey to the End of the Night* and in *To Kick the Bucket[1]*, similar events and similar gestures of the French cavalier ancestors who fought with the royal symbol of the "Dauphin" on their sleeves.

All around, the French battalion of the 4th regiment stood poised to launch the attack… The president of the French Republic, the ultimate chief of the French armed forces, gave the order to open the gate, so that the rebels renamed "the New Forces" and later "the Republican Forces of Ivory Coast," (FRCI) could penetrate inside. The goal of the French was to have these local troops--the Ivorian rebels-- capture and hand over Laurent Gbagbo, so that power could be passed to Alassane Ouattara, their chosen leader.

Ouattara claims to have been elected with 54.10% of the votes in the presidential run-off election held on November 28, 2010. The president of the Independent Electoral Commission, acting alone, tallied up these results without consulting the members of his own Commission. This figure would not be confirmed by the Constitutional Council, the only body with jurisdiction to rule on the validity of Ivorian presidential elections, indeed the sole authority with power to declare the winner of this presidential election.

Youssouf Bakayoko, the chairman of the Independent Electoral Commission, composed predominantly of Gbagbo's political opponents, announced the outcome in a very surprising way. The results were announced on the evening of December 2, 2010, after the three day limit stipulated by the Ivorian Constitution had expired. Moreover, the election results were announced, not by the Commission assembled, but by a single individual, even if he was the president of the Electoral Commission. What's more, this

---

[1] Translator's note: *Journey to the End of the Night* (Le voyage au bout de la Nuit) and *To Kick the Bucket* (Casse-pipe) are two French novels which depict the author's pessimism with regard to human nature, human institutions, human societies, and human life as a rule.

announcement was made at the Golf Hotel[2], the campaign headquarters of Alassane Ouattara! During this time, all the other members of the Independent Electoral Commission were elsewhere waiting to meet their president at the election headquarters. In the meantime Bakayoko was actually meeting with the ambassadors of France and the United States, planning their next move. As he was announcing the election's results, the president of the Electoral Commission was flanked by two foreign diplomats. The ambassador of France, Jean-Marc Simon, later told me with the utmost seriousness:

> *"I had gone by the hotel to see Soro[3], I don't know why... He told me that Bakayoko was in some room"* with the ambassador of the United States, Philipp Carter III.

While the Ivorian press was not invited to the announcement of the results of the Ivorian presidential election, the cameras of France 24, the international French TV channel, were rolling. Meanwhile all the other journalists were waiting for the results at the headquarters of the Independent Electoral Commission—where, according to the Constitution, the results were supposed to be announced.

Barack Obama and the special representative of the UN in Ivory Coast, Young-jin Choi, validated this unbelievable electoral procedure and outcome, which was immediately activated by Nicolas Sarkozy through a letter to Youssouf Bakayoko, the president of the Independent Electoral Commission. Immediately following this announcement, Bakayoko himself was air-lifted out of Ivory Coast by helicopter and eventually made his way to Neuilly-sur-Seine, France, where he took refuge, certainly fearful for his life and well aware of the illegality of his proclamation. Only in Africa could such a thing happen! Eighty coups d'etat in fifty years of independence! This clearly demonstrates that

---

[2] Translator's note: Gbagbo's government in yet another attempt at negotiating peace, allowed the Ivorian rebels to use this hotel facility as their headquarters following the Marcoussis Accords of January 2003. This hotel complex became the campaign headquarters of Alassane Dramane Ouattara before and after the two rounds of the presidential elections in October and November, 2010.
[3] Translator's note: One of the main leaders of the rebels during the civil war which began in 2002, Guillaume Soro, became Prime Minister under Laurent Gbagbo in a national unity government after the Ouagadougou Peace Agreement of 2007. He rallied behind Alassane Ouattara in 2010. He has been president of the Ivorian National Assembly since 2012.

elections in Africa are nothing but a puppet show, with the puppet strings being pulled from behind the scenes.

What good was it for Laurent Gbagbo and Alassane Ouattara to have signed a joint proclamation on November 27, 2010 addressed to all Ivorians, calling for calm and pledging to respect the constitutional directives, which stipulate that the Constitutional Council was to tally up, check, and validate the votes attributed to each candidate and to proclaim the winner of the election within three days.

Yet, surprisingly, on December 2, 2010, Youssouf Bakayoko "pulled out of a hat," with the blessing of Sarkozy and the United Nations, the name of Alassane Ouattara in contradiction to Ouattara's signed agreement concerning the electoral procedures and in violation of any provision in the Ivorian Constitution.

The following day, December 3, 2010, the Constitutional Council of Ivory Coast declared President Gbagbo the winner with 51.45% of the votes. In so doing, the Constitutional Council noted the massive fraud that had taken place in the northern part of the country under rebel control. The Ivorian Constitutional Council, the highest court in the country and the sole authority to determine and declare the winner in presidential elections had ruled and had given the name of the winner: Laurent Gbagbo was the victor of the Ivorian run-off election of November 28, 2010.

While this Ivorian presidential election was supposed to resolve the politico-military crisis which had started in 2002, instead, a long period of post-election turmoil and drama began. Albert Bourgi, professor of Political Science in Reims, France, an old friend of Laurent Gbagbo, an acquaintance of Alassane Ouattara, as well, and someone who knew quite a bit about political life on the African continent, made the following comment on African TV, TVM on June 8, 2012:

"[...] *I do not know many elections whose results were announced in comparable conditions to what happened in Ivory Coast. [...] Along with the Ivorian institutions, the UN [...] was apparently supposed to certify the Ivorian presidential election. This notion of certification had never before been applied in Africa. Thus, it is a completely vague notion, as vague as the official results of this election. Nobody knows the results in detail. We don't know the results of the polling stations. Neither you nor I, nor any other observer or researcher covering this Ivorian presidential election, know the details. We don't know the results, polling station by polling station. The abstention rate is a mystery [...]"*

It was not until the ousting of Gbagbo on April 11, 2011 that the Constitutional Council led by Paul Yao N'Dré proclaimed Alassane Ouattara president, without even formally reversing the decision of December 3, 2010[4]. To legitimize this new president, the Council relied on the decisions of the UN and certain African institutions. Through the weighty bayonets of the International Community, the decisions of the Ivorian Constitutional Council suddenly became respectable in the eyes of the West! By the end of March 2013, with Vladimir Putin, the spokesperson of the heads of state and members of the BRICS countries—(Brazil, Russia, India, China, South Africa, the emerging countries seeking to provide a counterweight to Europe and America in favor of a multipolar world order), declaring that, from now on, they would no longer tolerate the use of force against sovereign states. They had drawn their own conclusions from the military operations carried out in Libya and in Ivory Coast.

In Ivory Coast, since the death of Houphouët-Boigny, the first president of the country, there has never been a peaceful handover of power[5]. At Houphouët's death in 1993, Henri Konan Bédié, president of the National Assembly, became president of the country in accordance with the Ivorian constitutional provisions. He then "won" the 1995 presidential elections, but only after these elections were boycotted by a united opposition, who protested the new electoral code introduced by Bédié, which stipulated that candidates for president were required to be 100% Ivorian, born both of an Ivorian father and mother. Bédié was later overthrown by a coup d'etat masterminded by General Robert Guéi on December 24, 1999. It was against the then-sitting president, General Guéi, that Laurent Gbagbo won the presidential election in October 22, 2000. Guéi tried to challenge the outcome of this election, but this military coup was unsuccessful. Guéi later retired from public life. What an incredible song

---

[4] Translator's note: It was on Thursday May 6, 2011, that Paul Yao N'Dré proclaimed Alassane Ouattara president of Ivory Coast, that is to say, 122 days after having proclaimed Laurent Gbagbo president.
[5] Translator's note: Even the succession to the throne in the wake of Houhpouët-Boigny's death was not without conflict. Instead of respecting the orderly transition of power as outlined in the Ivorian Constitution, Alassane Ouattara, the then-Prime Minister, tried to gain control and take over as president. Such a move prompted Konan Bédié, the constitutional heir, flanked by armed men, to hasten to the Ivorian Radio and Television Network (RTI), to declare his own ascendency as president of Ivory Coast.

and dance to open up the post-Houphouët era. It was in fact the beginning of a very long crisis!

On December 4, 2010, Gbagbo and Ouattara both took the oath of the office, each in a different place and in a different manner. While Gbagbo proceeded to take the oath of the office according to constitutional rules, his opponent's swearing-in was a sham. After ten years, the long awaited election gave birth to two presidents. Only the naive were surprised. Some of the players on the scene, including France, had anticipated this outcome. Others said nobody could have desired or organized such a chaotic tangle, which opened the door for all kinds of political maneuvering. That following Saturday, the outgoing president, Laurent Gbagbo, was sworn into office at the presidential mansion, with the president of the Constitutional Council acting as the presiding officer. The challenger, in a letter dated the same day and addressed to the president of the Constitutional Council, proclaimed himself as president of Ivory Coast, addressing a body whose authority he suddenly and paradoxically recognized. The members of the Constitutional Council rejected the action of Ouattara as unconstitutional. Nevertheless Ouattara proceeded to "camp out" at the Golf Hotel for months with his French advisors, Ivorian warlords and soldiers. Despite his rejection by the Ivorian Constitutional Council, Ouattara appointed a counter-government. The Independent Electoral Commission, the Special Representative of the UN and finally the Ivorian Constitutional Council gave three different results, a fact quickly pointed out by Thabo Mbeki, the second president of the Republic of South Africa, after Nelson Mandela. He was very familiar with the Ivorian dossier for having officiated as a mediator during the 2004 crisis of the country.

On New Year's Eve, 2011, in his televised speech to the nation, Gbagbo proposed that there be a recount of the votes, with a general audit under international supervision:

> "We need to ask ourselves how, when our election year in 2010 was to signal the end of the nation's crisis, this year ends instead in confusion. Since the proclamation of the results of the election of November 28, 2010, Ivorians suffer violence from an armed rebellion inside their own borders, all the while being subject to international hostility from outside their frontiers. It's unfair.
>
> "We wonder what reasons are behind the International Community's attitude towards us, an attitude which has never been so manifest in an internal political crisis in a sovereign state. That is why I propose an

evaluation mechanism to determine the facts and to establish the truth about the election process in our country. I am confident the truth will win out, that truth will prevail in the end. We have the right with us; truth and justice are with us."

The recount of the votes as proposed by Laurent Gbagbo was refused by Young-jin Choi, the Special Representative of the Secretary General of the United Nations, who said he had already counted [the votes] three times. The proposal to recount was also rejected by France and by the United States. The fate of Laurent Gbagbo was therefore sealed. All speeches and appeals now appear out of the question and even illegal. These international powers preferred a military attack against Gbagbo, while, according to observers, a recount under international control would have ended the debate without causing a single death.

"If the end result had been a victory for Gbagbo, the rebels would have taken up arms against him anyway," Jean-Marc Simon, the former French ambassador in Abidjan, confided to me.

With these words, the kingpin of the operation, Jean-Marc Simon, shrugged off any possible twinge of conscience, even if a negotiated solution seemed possible to others…

On April 11, 2010, after ten days of bombing the presidential residence, the Puma and Gazelle helicopters of the French military contingent of the Licorne force, backed by UNOCI, carried out the final attack. Many believed that attack to be the end note, not only to the post-election crisis, but to the most tormented decade in Ivorian history.

Chapter 2
"I wanted to give meaning to the word *independence*"

This quote from Laurent Gbagbo summarizes the driving force behind the man. From the beginning of his career, as a teacher, leader of the opposition, and finally president of Ivory Coast, Gbagbo's main objectives have been democracy within the country and independence from those outside the country.

In this chapter, Mattei provides a lengthy background on the first Ivorian president, Houphouet Boigny, whom Gbagbo had opposed for years. It was this president who is responsible for Ouattara's entrance into Ivorian politics, when he appointed him Prime Minister on November 11, 1990, under pressure from France. Houphouët and Gbagbo are opposites, the first, coming out of the colonial era, doing all he can to preserve ties with France, even to the detriment of the Ivorian people. The second, Gbagbo, though not anti-French, wants his country to be free of economic and political dependence. Mattei reveals the important role cocoa and oil play in both of these domains.

Today with Gbagbo out of the picture and Ouattara at the helm, French companies, as well as former generals of the French army and former French ambassadors, continue to profit from the riches of Ivory Coast. The Françafrique which Gbagbo fought long and hard against is making a 'come back.'

Since the time Laurent Gbagbo had been elected in October 2000, no French president, neither Jacques Chirac nor Nicolas Sarkosy, has accepted him. As historical and economic anchor of the French presence in Africa, and representing 40% of the gross domestic product of the sub-region, Ivory Coast is the powerhouse of French-speaking West Africa.

Ivory Cost has always provoked the jealousy of the greedy Elysée. Yet clearly France has Ivory Coast "under its skin." To France, this land of affluence represents an exceptional financial and economic boon, with its cocoa, coffee, bananas, and palm oil, as well as its huge deposits of oil, gas, uranium, diamonds, magnesium, and rare metals, not to mention its ports and its markets in construction, transportation, and communication. The major French companies, that is, Areva, Castel, Total, Bouygues, Bolloré, Orange, Veolia, and the Anglo-Saxon Armajaro, namely the cocoa empire directed until 2013 in Africa by Loïc Folloroux, the son of Dominique Ouattara, and other chocolate giants, Nestle, Cargill, etc., have thrived for years in this country with virtually no any competition. These companies have monopolized all key financial sectors, not to mention Air France, with its prohibitively priced tickets, which has for decades had a monopoly on major African destinations.

Indeed Africa was responsible for putting the French airliner back on its feet. France enjoys a privileged position, an advantage gained by colonization and perpetuated by the Françafrique system, even if, in his "La Baule" speech delivered on June 20, 1990, François Mitterrand tried making people believe that all this was a thing of the past. With the help of his speech writer, Erik Orsenna, Mitterrand declared:

> "The wind of freedom that blew East will inevitably one day blow South [...] There is no development without democracy and no democracy without development."

Twenty-four years later, France is still the master of the game. The former colonial power has made this clear, making Ivory Coast its private, protected hunting grounds and one of the keystones of its edifice. Thus, until recent years, the constant imperative for France was to control Ivory Coast since, without that control, the whole French system in Africa would collapse. Clearly Gbagbo was not the one Jacques Chirac was hoping for. The head of the French state knew that Laurent Gbagbo would refuse to submit to Paris. He would not follow in the submissive footsteps of Félix Houphouët-Boigny, Ivory Coast's first president, but also, ironically, one of the founding fathers of Françafrique. When he fought in the opposition, Gbagbo called Houphouët-Boigny a dictator, fiercely criticizing his blind allegiance to France...

Thus Gbagbo threatened France and its political authorities felt targeted. Having become, in the 80's, the historical opponent to the "Father of the Nation" and his policy of French assimilation, Gbagbo was never seen in a good light. He was fought on several fronts, first, by Jacques Chirac and then by Nicolas Sarkozy, in a succession of tense episodes, with only brief lulls of calm. France was pitted against Gbagbo who was the new opponent of their own political allies. France had always favored its old friends: more understanding, more docile, more integrated into their system. Chirac adored Houphouët-Boigny, who had been raised in the inner circles of the French political system, serving as a Minister in the French government under the Fourth and Fifth Republics. Even Houphouët's successor, Henri Konan Bédié, was personally supported by Chirac through his political party, the RPR[6].

Félix Houphouët-Boigny is the product of the old French era: here was the nostalgic ideal African leader—but the mold has now been broken. Houphouët was a member of the French Parliament and a governmental Minister of the French Republic before becoming the first president of his country. His personal relationships with the men in power in France, or in today's terms, his "social networking," earned him their unwavering support. At every level of his administration and government, Houphouët-Boigny was surrounded by dedicated French public servants who served the interests of Paris before giving any thought to Abidjan. Houphouët's vision for his country and for Africa was to relegate it to the status of a prefecture of a French province. His real name was Dia Houphouët.

He adopted the first name "Félix" in 1915. In 1945, he then added the name "Boigny": "ram" in his Ivorian mother tongue. He sculpted his own destiny and molded his own stature. But he was a politician with two faces.

Abroad, Boigny knew how to distill messages of peace and humanism. In Africa, he supported French interests, and without batting

---

[6] *Rassemblement pour la République*, which reads Rally for the Republic.

an eye, he acted against all socialist-leaning regimes and even certain African "brothers." He did not balk at collaborating with those who spread propaganda, carried out military coups or civil wars. The man was convinced and convincing. Houphouët was a Black crusader for the White cause--an African--, he was more French than the French. In 1946, he introduced a law which forever abolished the forced labor White settlers had so strongly established in Africa. As France's "beloved" dictator, Houphouët's wildest whims were catered to and satisfied by the protective Western powers. The Basilica of Yamoussoukro, built according to his dream, "greater than the Basilica of St. Peter's in Rome," was of course erected in the middle of the bush by French companies. In one of the stained glass windows of this cathedral of Notre-Dame-de-la-Paix, Our Lady of Peace, Félix Houphouet-Boigny's effigy appears riding on a donkey entering Jerusalem. Gbagbo comments:

During **that time, everyone forgave Houphouët for everything**.

This is the backdrop in which Laurent Gbagbo appeared: he came on the scene and was immediately perceived as a troublemaker. He was accused of everything, including being a xenophobic nationalist, because he didn't want his country, the jewel of all neighboring countries, to be overrun by armed invaders, because he believed that it was the Ivorians' right to write their own history. It was a true culture shock. The break from the Houphouët model was too abrupt. France--struggling outside as well as within its borders to renew its status around the world and to project itself towards its "new frontier," Europe--could simply not accept the situation. France itself found it hard to change because its political leaders were more accustomed to managing their achievements of the past than to imagining the future.

How long ago and far away it is: the time of the "beautiful French colonies." Scarcely had France granted independence to Ivory Coast that it took with one hand what it had given with the other. France had put in place Félix Houphouët-Boigny, a worthy representative, in a travesty of presidential elections where he was the only candidate. The French gave him the nickname "The Old Wiseman," a flattering name they used to refer to him until his death in 1993. All this took place in a context where no one in the West even thought of questioning elections won with 100%

12

of the vote, with no abstentions, in a one-party system in place for twenty years (1965-1985). Nor did anyone dare to criticize the methods of such a zealous servant, even when he ruthlessly oppressed others, bringing about the death of thousands, provoking regional secessionist unrest and large student demonstrations.

One understands why the opposition in Ivory Coast was then non-existent or remained underground. Apart from a few pioneers of anti-colonialism, mostly communists, the situation offended no one. During the Cold War, Houphouët, the friend of the West, the bulwark against Marxist contamination in Africa, obviously was fully supported.

At that time, Laurent Gbagbo, the historical leader of the opposition, surrounded by just a few activists, formed together a new underground party, the *Front populaire ivoirien* (*FPI*). His mistake was clear: he disturbed the French political class. He broke the consensus which allowed the French to live so comfortably for so, so long.

In 2000 when Gbagbo was elected president, Charles Josselin, Minister of State for the Socialist Cooperation, took the same position. He condemns the "artificial exclusion of the most serious candidates," meaning the first choices of France, that is to say, Bédié and Ouattara. The Elysée was tremendously disappointed to see an intruder sneak in between the two favorites of Paris and swoop up the elections. Gbagbo comments:

The Elysée has always had these two irons in the fire, Bédié and Ouattara. The problem in Ivory Coast came from their rivalry at the death of Houphouët, which led to the exclusion of Ouattara by Bédié, who accused the former of dubious nationality. Bédié even launched an international warrant of arrest against Ouattara for falsifying administrative documents, a warrant that I expunged when I came into power. They are both today against me. I would not like to live with their consciences...

In the Parisian political milieu, this "prof" of history was well known. The author of speeches and books on democracy along with his critical analyses made everyone nervous. Even in Africa Gbagbo disturbed his fellow presidents, those hiding under the protective wing of France, fearing for their pensions and benefits, whose only desire was to stay in power. In 2010, Sarkozy naturally gave preference to his friend of twenty years, Alassane Ouattara, former Prime Minister of Houphouët, former senior official at the International Montetary Fund (IMF), someone familiar with finance and business networks and a *persona grata* in Washington, D.C. These advantages make Ouattara the undisputed champion in the new France-USA tandem in Africa. France is ready to ensure political stability in Africa for its ally, the United States, who would rather not get involved if its economic interests are not threatened. *"Probably we would have had another type of relationship with Ivory Coast,"* an American diplomat told me, *"but we are pragmatic, and since France provides the service ..."*

But even though he calls himself a francophile [one who is fond of anything French] and a francophone, Laurent Gbagbo had plans to free his country from its postcolonial yoke. And because of this, he was of course at odds with France. Not only does he not follow the usual reverent submissive policy towards Paris, but more importantly, his accession to power took place without the help of France! His long political experience makes him hard to handle. His journey follows in the footsteps of many Africans from disadvantaged backgrounds who have forged their own careers. Yet, he is among those who "do not fall in line," he is one who dreams of emancipation and progress for his country.

Gbagbo's high school degree, the French baccalauréat, was in philosophy; his BA in history. First, a teacher at the *Lycée Classique d'Abidjan*, in the 70's, he later became a researcher at the Institute of History, Art and African Archeology (IHAAA). He obtained his Masters degree in history from the Sorbonne, in Paris, and in 1979, defended his PhD thesis, entitled "Socio-economic Motivations of Ivorian Politics: 1940-1960." In the early 1970s, he entered politics and opposed Houphouët, calling for a multiparty system. He was imprisoned from March, 1971 to January, 1973, following demonstrations in which Ivorians, including many students, demanded democracy. Gbagbo, the fighter for democracy, became the undisputed leader of the protesters. In 1982, he created, with four other university colleagues, the FPI party, which fought for the end of the one-party system and for the establishment of true democracy in Ivory Coast. In 1982, to escape the repression against the advocates of democracy, he was forced into exile in France, where he stayed for four years. Upon his return to Abidjan, he was appointed to the direction of IHAAA, and he continued to campaign for a multiparty system.

In the first free presidential election in October, 1990, Gbagbo ran against the "commander-in-chief," Félix Houphouët-Boigny. In so doing, he was officially recognized as the leader of the opposition. In the parliamentary elections in November of the same year, Gbagbo was elected to the Ivorian Parliament as a representative for the region of Ouaraghio[7]. In February, 1992, he is arrested, as leader of the opposition, after student demonstrations called for democracy. He was sentenced to two years imprisonment. Alassane Dramane Ouattara or "Ado,"[8] as he was already known, had just prepared an anti-disturbance bill for the occasion and had it signed just a day before Gbagbo's arrest, providing a legal way to imprison the "trouble-maker" of the Republic.

The conditions for conflict were now in place... Gbagbo had not been selected by Houphouët, or by France, or by the international institutions. He owed nothing to anyone. From then on, he was considered anti-French and dangerous... Gbagbo comments:

Yet, in ten years, I went three times to France and once I was invited to China. Where is the problem?

Gbagbo provides his own answer to his own question by saying that his original "sin" was that:

I just wanted to give meaning to the word "independence."

More than fifty years after France granted "independence" to the Francophone countries in Black Africa, the term "Françafrique" is still alive and well, even though the media regularly report that its end is near. This term, believed to be invented by Houphouët-Boigny himself in 1960, refers to a financial, economic, and political system of influence, born under the facade of decolonization... In the beginning of the 1990's, Houphouët--France's strongman in Africa since independence--is still in

---

[7] In Central -Western Ivory Coast.

[8] This is a nickname of Alassane Dramane Ouattara then Prime Minister of Houphouët-Boigny.

power. In his book, *Act for Liberties*[9], Laurent Gbagbo gives the following analysis:

> *"In Côte d'Ivoire, the highest authorities of the state have very little confidence in the Ivorian people. All the real responsibilities are entrusted to the French. Ivorians only appear to carry titles of responsibility, while in fact they carry out second class duties. In each government cabinet, each minister has at least one Frenchman, and here I am not being generous with my words. The vital ministries of Economy, Finance, Planning, etc. are virtually flooded with the French. Hardly more reassuring, the French army is overtly positioned between the airport and the channel leading to the port [...] When one of those who has true access to the inner workings of the economy and politics of our country breaks the complicit silence by bringing to the attention of the world the slightest inkling of the actual political practices of the 'one who reigns and governs,' it is like a message or a symbol, it is like saying 'the king has no clothes...'"*

In 2014, nothing had fundamentally changed in Ivory Coast or in most Francophone African countries. Even if the networks of spies of the 1960s-1980s have disappeared, the three major founding principles of Françafrique endure: (1) a president chosen or at least accepted by France, (2) a military presence in territories supposedly independent for fifty years, and (3) a currency managed in Paris. It means these sovereign countries live "on credit" under the authority of the Bank of France.

The close collaboration between the French authorities and the Ouattara's camp during the Ivorian crisis of 2010 is now giving its payback, lucrative revolving doors which are reminiscent of the great years of Houphouët-Boigny. *La Lettre du continent* explains[10]:

---

[9] Laurent Gbagbo, *Côte d'Ivoire, Agir pour les libertés* [Ivory Coast, *Act for Liberties*], Paris, L'Harmattan, 1991.
[10] *La Lettre du continent* (The Letter of the Continent), n° 677, February 26, 2014.

"Parallel to the theaters of military operation [in Africa], the number of French military personnel being "recycled" in African palaces has not diminished. Experts in 'crisis management,' these informal emissaries, are extremely valuable to Paris. General Bruno Clément-Bollée, from 2007-2008, head of the military force known as Force Licorne in recent months, through re-activating his Ivorian network, was chosen to direct the complex restructuring of the Republican Forces of Ivory Coast (FRCI). He won a [juicy] contract as senior adviser to Alassane Ouattara. He works in duo with Claude Réglat, another general housed in the presidency in Abidjan since his appointment by Nicolas Sarkozy in 2011. [...] Other French senior officers preferred to join various companies or organizations. Wearing a second diplomatic hat, General Emmanuel Beth, Frédéric Beth's brother, former boss of the Special Operatgions Unit [...] was recruited by ESL & Network. Chief of the Licorne force from 2002 to 2003, Beth's job was to develop an African base for this firm dealing in economic intelligence, a group founded by Alexander Medvedowsky."

On the economic front, French companies own and operate a good portion of Ivorian ports, telephone systems, water supply, electricity and motor fuel companies as well as banks, airlines and railways: more than 30% of the overall economy. Behind this French flag of blue, white and red[11], the participation of the Anglo-Saxons in the Ivorian economy has gradually expanded. Alongside Swiss Barry Callebaut and Dutchman Continaf, they already dominate most of the cocoa trade, with Ivory Coast, at 40%, being the largest producer of this commodity in the world[12]. With Cargill and ADM, the Americans have also moved into position. They have won most of the oil contracts on the most recent production sites. Gbagbo comments:

---

[11] An image of the French flag.

[12] NB: The world chocolate industry has an annual turnover of 135 billion euros.

It's through Ghana that the Americans entered our oil market. I met with John Atta-Mills, the then-president of Ghana, and we reached an agreement on sharing 50/50, because it's the same oil deposit.

Towards the town of San Pedro, on the border with Liberia, our second largest port, there is also oil. The first oil company in Ivory Coast was a US-Canadian society. We sold blocks for exploration and exploitation. At the stage of exploration, I had never seen the French involved. One day, Pierre Fakhoury[13], who bought some blocks, came to see me, very happy to tell me that Total[14] wanted all of the blocks that belonged to him. I then understood that there was a lot of oil, and I sold the remaining blocks at three times the original price.

Is all this just happenstance? Since Laurent Gbagbo was brutally dethroned in 2011, Total keeps announcing the discovery of new oil deposits in off shore waters: in May 2014, one off San Pedro in south-western Ivory Coast, and a year before that, another at the Ghanaian border in south-eastern Ivory Coast. As for Bouygues, we learned in March, 2014 that he has recently launched into gas exploitation and production. Where? In Ivory Coast! Then there is the British company Armajaro, the world's leader in cocoa, who entered the Ivorian market thanks to Alassane Ouattara, when the latter was deputy director of the IMF. Loïc Folloroux, son of Dominique Ouattara's first marriage, became the Africa director of Armajaro. Gbagbo comments:

In recent years, in order to know whether we were on the verge of a coup d'état in Ivory Coast, you only had to watch the price of cocoa!

Various speculations, including the purchase and storage of huge amounts of cocoa, with a goal to driving up prices, curiously occurred in 2002 a month before the attempted military coup against Laurent Gbagbo, as well as three months before the 2010 Ivorian presidential

---

[13] Translator's note: Pierre Fakhoury is a Lebanese and Ivorian architect whose notable work includes the Basilica-of-Our-Lady-of Peace, in Yamoussoukro, the political capital of Ivory Coast.

[14] A French multinational integrated oil and gas-company.

election. In August 2002, Anthony Ward, commonly nicknamed "Chocolate Finger," figuring at the top of the Armajaro hierarchy, suddenly revealed their purchase of 200,000 tons of cocoa. The war launched by the rebels caused the cocoa market to soar. Armajaro pocketed nearly 70 million euros in profits.

At that time, while half of the Ivorian territory was held by the rebels, neighboring Burkina Faso, the rebel's haven, suddenly became an exporter of cocoa, a product that is not even grown there! They were putting on the market what had been stolen from Ivory Coast, In July, 2010, as the first round of the presidential election loomed, the English trader bought 240,000 tons of cocoa from the commodity exchange in London: 7% of the world production, 15% of the global stocks, purchased for more than 700 million euros, and made an unbelievable profit. Prices rose to the extravagant level of 3,264 euros per ton, the highest since 1977. Criticism came from all sides. The competitors suspected insider trading. The economic observers of several NGOs understood that this infernal roulette game could only hurt Ivorian cocoa farmers. But who could have cared? Thanks to Ouattara and his stepson, Loïc Folloroux, Armajaro had it made. Gbagbo comments:

In 2007, I launched a major investigation into the cocoa sector. There had been many arrests, a clean-up operation was in process, a serious judicial investigation and trials were being conducted. All revealed abuse and fraud of most of the exporters at the expense of the state and the farmers, along with the complicity of some of my government ministers. I know some who changed sides during the last election, passing into the opposite camp for their own security...

There was much to suggest that rebel funding weighed in on the cocoa sector, coming from a portion of the profits diverted to their advantage by Armajaro, in association with Alassane Ouattara and his associates. Cocoa is the gold and the blood of Ivory Coast. It has long served to feed speculation among foreign companies. Houphouët confronted this same problem during his own time: slush funds, illegal exports and arms purchases. On April 16, 2004, while investigating this gray area of economy where money flows so freely, the Franco-Canadian journalist Guy-André Kieffer disappeared, never again to be found. The accusations against the Gbagbo clan, in this case, against a brother-in-law of Simone Gbagbo, led nowhere. A former Minister of Laurent Gbagbo, Ahoua Don Mello told me that, in 2002, in an article published under a pseudonym, this journalist, gone missing, had revealed an imminent military attack against Ivory Coast funded by the cocoa industry. This possible lead in the case was never explored, a very surprising fact given the involvement of Ouattara through Loïc Folloroux in the cocoa sector and his secret dealings at the highest level of this global industry. Close to Ouattara, Adama Bictogo was, in 2004 and 2005, busy exporting huge quantities of cocoa diverted from Ivory Coast. He passed cocoa through the port of Lomé, Togo, using commercial bases in Burkina Faso, Luxembourg, and a French bank. We will never know what Kieffer discovered, but it is certain that his investigations threatened specific and numerous commercial interests.

Indeed, the rebel zone in the northern Ivory Coast allowed all kinds of traffic, with no customs or fiscal taxes, and with no customs control. Bictogo, a rebel and a businessman, began to focus on "all that glitters": gold traffic, biometric passports, bogus compensations to victims in the toxic waste fiasco (when fatal toxins were dumped in Abidjan in August 2006 off the ship Probo Koala, run by Trafigura). Promoted to the post of Minister of African Integration by Ouattara, Bictogo was fired in May, 2012, without being prosecuted for the many successful schemes that benefitted him alone.

During the post-election crisis, on January 24, 2011, Guillaume Soro's appeal to stop the export of the cocoa was naturally the first step in the economic paralysis of Laurent Gbagbo. Anglo-Saxon operators were slavishly loyal to their friend from the International Monetary Fund (IMF). Armajaro chose that moment to unlock and sell its 240,000 tons of cocoa, purchased seven months earlier, at a very high price, due to the artificially created scarcity. This operation did not escape the vigilance or the criticism of the Anglo-Saxon economic press.

Chapter 3
"My father landed in France in January, 1940"

In this chapter, Laurent Gbagbo talks about his father Koudou who was born in 1912, in what is now Gagnoa, in the only region of Ivory Coast which had not yet been "pacified" by the French colonialists. Koudou was sent to Catholic school and was christened "Paul."

At twenty years of age, Paul Koudou travelled to Tabou, in the extreme south-west, where he boarded and worked as a seaman's apprentice on a ship going to Matadi, in the Democratic Republic of Congo (DRC). Upon his return, he quit his job and joined the French colonial army as a volunteer, the only option offered to him as an African. He served as a corporal, then a sergeant in Ivory Coast and Senegal. During World War II, Paul Koudou was recalled from retirement and travelled to France in January, 1940, where he served as sergeant. In Germany, he was taken prisoner of war, but he eventually escaped. In homage to his commander, Captain Laurent, who was killed before his eyes, Paul Koudou named his first son "Laurent."

Besides presenting information on Gbagbo's family life, Mattei provides historical background on de Gaulle's post-war for Africa— plans--which were anything but altruistic. He surveys the many African presidents who, over decades, have been raised up to--and pulled down from power, seemingly at the whim of the French authorities. While the details of Laurent Gbagbo's life and origins show he is not, as some claim, anti-French, his understanding as a historian of Francophone Africa's past only makes his anti-colonial fight for Ivory Coast's true independence all the stronger.

After Algeria won its independence in 1962, in the aftermath of a long and bloody war--people say there were more than one million dead and more than a million exiled Europeans--, Metropolitan France was left without a source of gas and oil. De Gaulle found the magic formula enabling France to retain its rank as a major power between the eastern and western blocks: the raw materials of Africa and the allegiance of African heads of state chosen by the Elysée. Françafrique is not, in fact, an ideology. It's the product of pragmatism and state interests. The dogma is simple: the superiority of France and its interests. The stakes are huge, and the goal is to maintain France's place among the Great Powers and save the country from decline. The means of carrying this out is like a lock which can be opened by three different keys: a political key, a military key, and a financial one. First, what is needed is a head of state under Paris's command, well surrounded by intelligence agents, next, the presence of a permanent military contingent, backed by defense agreements and, finally, control of the currency, in this case, from 1945, a currency issued in France, guaranteed by reserves stored in the Bank of France. With these three keys, Françafrique is completely "locked up."

Understanding the Franco-Ivorian crisis--whether it pleases extremists or the non-repentant or not--, requires understanding and knowing the main principles behind the Françafrique policy and its current ramifications.

At the end of the Second World War, after the humiliation of the German occupation and the weakening of the French Republic with respect to its Anglo-Saxons allies, de Gaulle decided to establish Françafrique, a model of imperialism peculiar to the French culture, in order to ensure France's own independence in matters of energy, military and politics. It was an attempt to force the states in Africa into submission, in total contradiction to the speeches of de Gaulle glorifying the right of self-determination of all peoples. It was a kind of organized political schizophrenia, allowing the French Republic to save face: preaching universal values, while at the same time, exploiting, with no qualms whatsoever, oppressed peoples. It is a masked dictatorship, betraying every single day the principles of *Liberté, Egalité, Fraternité*[15]. This slogan was not conceived for African children who, for generations, had to recite *Our Ancestors the Gauls*. Today, this lapse, hard to accept intellectually, demands the utmost discretion, since such shameful realities, if ever allowed to surface, could easily discredit France as it pursues its defense of democracy on the international scene.

The advent of a submissive African political class, hand-picked from institutions inculcated with the parameters of France's own survival and its narrow interests, helped the system to prosper. In presidential mansions across Françafrique, nothing is decided without a phone call or a trip to Paris. Most of the time, the personal safety of heads of state is entrusted to French police or military. Those who don't play by the rules pay dearly. Even today, the Elysée is a rite of passage, a must for any ambitious francophone African politician. Not being received at the Elysée is cause for extreme concern. The Elysian "papal" anointing is an essential ingredient for the making of African presidents and their opponents as well. Even the latter run to Paris to ensure the pontiff of the Republic that, if they come to power, they will not preach dissident heresy.

Since the Second World War, France remains one of the five powers making up the Security Council of the UN. Thus France still holds onto an important share of political power in the world. Under de Gaulle, small African countries aligned with France--a set of fourteen countries-- considered the "voice of Africa" at the UN and in the world...

The compass set to the Eiffel tower in Paris is the most significant and only technological innovation of the presidents in francophone Africa. In France and in Africa, a hundred years of Paris's absolute dominance has created in the subconscious of French officers, as well as in that of their African counterparts, a set of reflexes, customs, consensual relationships which they all adhere to.

In the collective memory of African leaders, there are still those hidden ghosts of those who refused France's dominance: Burkina Faso's

---

[15] Translator's note: This is the national motto of France since the French Revolution of 1789-1799.

23

Thomas Sankara was "dropped" by France, and then murdered in 1987 by Blaise Compaoré's men [this president was finally deposed by the people on October 31, 2014, after 27 years in power]. In former Zaïre, Patrice Lumumba, was killed in 1961. Sylvanus Olympio was assassinated in Togo. He had announced that, if elected president of the Republic in April, 1960, one of his primary objectives was for Togo to exit the CFA franc zone and to adopt Anglophone currency. The agreements which were to finalize the break between the Bank of France and that of Togo were to be signed on January 15, 1963. Is this sheer coincidence that Sylvanus Olympio was murdered by his successor, Gnassingbé Eyadema, two days before that signature, on January 13? Eyadema took power, created a one-party system and was re-elected five times until his death in 2005, all with the blessing of France. His son, Faure Gnassingbé, who succeeded him, is still in power in Lomé.

There is also the odd case in Françafrican history of the colorful Emperor Jean-Bedel Bokassa, president of the Central African Republic (CAR). He was overthrown by France, even after they had shown him favor. There is the killing of Félix Moumié, the separatist Cameroonian leader poisoned on November 3, 1960, in Geneva by William Bechtel, who posed as a journalist but was actually an agent of the French SDECE. Tried twenty years later, the French intelligence agent was acquitted by the French judicial system. Moumié was a Cameroonian dissident, and within his party, the UPC, an activist for immediate and complete independence. He was killed, among others, in the 1960s during a long and ruthless military offensive. Here's what he declared:

> "Under the leadership of the French army, Cameroonian troops razed the village of Yogandima, killing nearly 8,000 unarmed civilians. For ten years, the colonial administration had to deal with the 'Union populaire du Cameroun' (UPC). The French High Commissioner Pierre Messmer organized the murder of many leaders of the UPC and equally carried out punitive expeditions. On January 1, 1960, independence was declared and Jacques Foccart installed a puppet government headed by his friend Ahmadou Ahidjo. That very same day, the new state signed

a military agreement with France. Charles de Gaulle dispatched five battalions commanded by General Max Briand. Between February and March, 156 Bamiléké villages were burned and razed to the ground. Tens of thousands of people were massacred."

The French press, rendered dumb and blind by the crisis in Algeria, didn't even say a word, except for *L'Humanité* and *La Croix*. Finally, on October 2, [1960], the leader of the UPC, Félix Moumié, was assassinated in Geneva. The collective work entitled *Kamerun!*[16] presents different assessments of the number of deaths, depending on the sources, but it was not less than several tens of thousands.

We need to remember as well, Baré Maïnassara, the president of Niger, murdered by his own guards in 1999, right at the time he seemed to be moving away from his Western allies. The recent images of the ousting of Laurent Gbagbo, or those of Gaddafi's death would urge other African leaders to act cautiously. Jacques Foccart, the person in charge of the Françafrican edifice, who ordered numerous operations of destabilization even after the Gaullist period, never hid the fact that all the military coups perpetrated in Africa through his services were carried out in complicity with those sitting in the Elysée. General de Gaulle didn't want to know the details of how these things were carried out. It only took a phone call for the French army to intervene (or not intervene) in the name of the Cooperation and Defense Accords (CDA), to save a president threatened by rebellion, as was the case for Father Fulbert Youlou from Congo-Brazaville. This eccentric priest who ordered his liturgical robes from Dior, had broken ties with the Church, as well as his vows of chastity, was not well liked by de Gaulle. In 1964, when the army dissented, Paris "let him go" and he was overthrown[17]. After the 1947 insurrection in Madagascar, thousands of Malagasy were killed,

---

[16] Thomas Deltombe, Manuel Domergue, Jacob Tatsitsa, *Kamerun! Une guerre cachée aux origines de la Françafrique, 1948*-1971 (A Hidden War at the Origins of France-Afrique, 1948-1971), La Découverte, 2011.
[17] *Foccart, l'homme qui dirigeait l'Afrique* (Foccart, the Man Who Was Running Africa), a documentary produced by Cédric Tourbe, in 2010.

perhaps tens of thousands, in a relentless punitive war. After the bloody wars of independence in Indochina and Algeria, in the 50s, when the colonial empire began to collapse, Paris made plans to perpetuate its presence south of the Sahara, saving everything that could be saved, as far as France's resources and position were concerned.

Taking part in the civil war of Biafra, between 1967 and 1970, France provided weapons and ammunition to the breakaway province. The Nigerian state, obviously did not want to see this oil-rich region become independent and escape its grasp. Under the direction of the French SDECE, all of the barons of the then-Françafrique, from Houphouët-Boigny to Omar Bongo, participated in supporting the Biafran rebels. Airplanes from Air Gabon, flown by French pilots, smuggled weapons into Biafra throughout the entire war. De Gaulle expected that a Biafran victory would enable him to broaden France's oil base in the Gulf of Guinea, counting on Bifra's gratitude to the French who had covertly aided them. Forty years later, Pierre Messmer, de Gaulle's Minister of Defense admitted that mixed in with France's support for Biafra, there was also a desire for vengeance:

> *"I cannot forgive [Nigeria] for its attitude after our nuclear tests at Reggane. Our support of Biafra was our way of making them pay! Nigeria had been both provocative and ridiculous: provocative in its effort to turn African governments against the French nuclear tests, ridiculous in saying: 'We, Nigeria, we have the atomic bomb.' They were grotesque. I have not forgiven them[18]."*

Enormous budgets were put in place for a huge press campaign in Europe. Mark Press, based in Geneva, released more than 500 articles on the subject. They took advantage of the blockade put in place by Nigeria against Biafra and developed the by-line: genocide through starvation. Maurice Robert, who led the operation for French intelligence, later

---

[18] Jean Guisnel (dir.), Roger Faligot (dir.), *Histoire secrète de la 5ème République* (Secret History of the Vth Republic). Paris, La Découverte, 2007.

revealed that the term 'genocide' had been carefully chosen by the SDECE and made to figure on the front page of *Le Monde*. All other newspapers followed suit. In the end, there were nearly two million deaths in Biafra, and France quickly pulled out, leaving to their fate the defeated and the dying, among a mountain of corpses. To finish off the *French touch*--to help people forget the true responsibility of France in this sad history--*French doctors*, "Doctors without Borders" suddenly appeared, arriving from Paris to deliver medicines and care for survivors. The spotlight was turned on this image of humanitarian help, replacing the image they wanted to keep secret: the intervention of France, with disastrous results. So, French honor was preserved, but only on the surface. The remaining funds of this inglorious adventure were, we have been told, sent back to France by Omar Bongo, to finance the repression of the May '68 demonstrations in Paris.

These past sinister episodes of France in Black Africa are only a few among the hundreds of events--known or unknown, which paradoxically have forged a strong bond between France and its former colonies; it is the famous "common history," the dark pages which are not often revealed.

Due to their unspoken policy of assimilation on all levels (linguistic, cultural, and administrative) before 1960,--best seen in their willingness to join the battle to liberate France--Africans still felt divided between their two "homelands." It was only later they realized all this was all an illusion. In France, they were not at home, and in their African countries, they still felt part of France. It was too late. Sub-Saharan Africa had sent a great number of soldiers to Europe, and when they returned home, these men passed on their *francophile* fiber to their sons. Gbagbo comments:

My father was born in 1912, the year that the French entered our region for the first time. We were the only region which was not yet colonized. My grandfather died, we don't know exactly how, but there had been resistance fighting against the colonial army. My grandmother left when she was pregnant. She gave birth to my father, Paul Koudou, in a village that became the town of Gagnoa. In 1924, Catholic priests arrived. They founded a church.

27

My father went to their school. Because he was not the biological son of my grandmother's second husband, they sent him there. At the time, they didn't trust the White man's school.

My father became a Catholic. He was sent to Dabou, near Abidjan. And there, he met priests who later played important roles [in the Church of Ivory Coast]: Father Daniel, Father Noël, and Cardinal Yago. In 1932, at the age of twenty, my father started primary school. He was in second grade and he could read and write.

My father went to Tabou, near the border with Liberia and he worked on different ships, overseeing the accounts, the loading and unloading of the ships, as well as acting as bursar. Cargo boats were involved in coastal shipping. My father went all the way to Matadi, in the Congo. When he returned, he quit his job and volunteered for the navy, where he stayed two or three years. 'Real' military service was reserved for Europeans. Africans like my father could only be volunteers.

My father was incorporated into the 5th battalion of the Senegalese riflemen. He carried out part of his service in Ivory Coast, the other part in Dakar, Senegal. He worked in the radio broadcasting unit and he also worked as a second class sharpshooter. He completed his service in 1939.

Because he could read and write, my father was often promoted. He thus became a corporal and then a sergeant. When he was released, he went to live in the village of Babré [in central western Ivory Coast]. But he was recalled almost immediately to go to war in Normandy, France. He landed in France in January 1940, with the rank of sergeant. He was assigned to the 44th Colonial Infantry Regiment. In June, at Douarnenez, in Brittany, in the north-west of France, he was seriously wounded in his left arm. He was taken prisoner by the Germans but managed to escape. He was hospitalized for a time at Fréjus, then was demobilized and returned home. For years, he refused to eat meat because it reminded him of the smell of human flesh burning... And he wouldn't put up with any discussion about war. In May 2003, he received a medal from the French authorities, in recognition of services rendered, at the French military camp in Abidjan, located at the 43rd Bima, in the presence of our entire family. He was very touched. We were too. If I am named *Laurent*, it is a tribute my father wanted to pay to Captain *Laurent*, his chief officer, killed in 1940 before his own eyes.

On the 90th anniversary of the First World War, the contribution of Africans to the fight for the sovereignty of France was recognized by Jacques Chirac. President Chirac hailed the 72,000 recruits who were killed in combat, 7,000 out of 16,000 enlisted in the *Chemin des Dames* in 1917. Regarding the 179,000 Africans mobilized in 1940 [during WW II], 40,000 came to fight in France, 17,000 died. According to figures released by the French Ministry of the Defense, among these were 1,300 soldiers from the African continent, making up the total 1,800 of the 25th Rifle Regiment who fell in battle at Lyon on June 19, 1940. But for a long time, the commitment of these African combatants was only rewarded with cruel ingratitude: the retirement pensions of these veterans were "frozen" at the time of independence in 1960, a situation that was reversed only in 2006, when most of the beneficiaries had already died.

Then there is the famous and shameful episode that occurred in 1944: the massacre of 70 riflemen at Camp Thiaroye in Dakar, Senegal. These demobilized men made the mistake of demanding a little too loudly their allowances and pensions. Thirty years later, France's government still only sees what Africa can contribute economically to them, having somehow forgotten the sacrifice it imposed on its peoples. Thus, after the French military intervention in 1978 in Kolwezi, a southern city of the Democratic Republic of Congo, the following day, Valéry Giscard d'Estaing, then president of the French Republic said in a televised address:

> *"France acts in Africa on its own behalf. [...] Africa is a continent where traditionally a number of our resources and raw materials are obtained. A change in the situation in Africa, that is, insecurity or subversion [in the Democratic Republic of Congo] would have [serious] consequences for France and Europe."*

As France tried to fulfill its almost visceral need to take root in Africa, Giscard himself knew how to personally appreciate its charms. In 1974, having only just been elected president of the French Republic, his first official visit was not to Washington, nor to London, nor to Bonn nor to Moscow. He reserved the honor of his first official trip for Bangui, the capital of Central African Republic, where Jean-Bedel Bokassa, the future emperor, reigned, with his pretty empress Catherine at his side. As it is well known, following this first state visit, Giscard took many additional leisure trips to the country of his friend, Jean-Bedel, until a horrible story concerning diamonds published by the *Canard Enchaîné* interrupted his "honeymoon" with Africa. Gbagbo comments:

Democracy… In Africa, you can see what they make of it…

Thirty years later, the April 2012 report by the French Ministry of Defense entitled *Horizons stratégiques* (Strategic Horizons) seems to follow Giscard d'Estaing's early appraisal. Against the backdrop of an unbridled global economic competition based [in part] on African resources, France has cause for concern and reasserts the need to control this zone so close to France across the Straits of Gibraltar only 14.4 kilometers away. It is obvious that in the circles of French geopolitics, the mindset has not changed:

> *"[…] it is likely that nationalist or pan-African sentiments could grow, sometimes at the expense of Western interests."* Adrian Hart of Slate Africa, states: *"Everyone remembers the violent anti-French calls of some pro-Gbagbo political leaders during the post-electoral crisis in Ivory Coast. Does the African future hold in store the multiplication of clones of populist leaders such as Charles Blé Goudé or Julius Malema[19]? We hope not."*

---

[19] Translator's note: Blé Goudé is the former leader of the Ivorian patriotic youth. He is currently being held prisoner at the International Criminal Court in The Hague. Julius Malema is a South African Nationalist leader.

The report was cited in the Ivorian newspaper *Le Nouveau Courrier* of October 10, 2012, allowing Théophile Kouamouo, a political observer, to analyze the state of mind of the report's editors. He states

"Once one is convinced that the main threat feared by the official strategists of the Hexagon is the awakening of 'Dignified Africa,' France may even consider alliances with forces representing tribal feudalism [...] in their fight against African heads of sovereign states. Secessions and civil wars become [...] 'problems' [...] that legitimize a strategic military presence, presented in virtuous terms as the way to 'prevent massacres' and 'to save Africa from itself.'"

The use of such a dialectic of "candid honesty and white linen," to paraphrase Victor Hugo, in order to cover up institutionalized interference has enabled France to establish its position and entrench itself in Africa.

Chapter 4
"Do they want the death of Ivory Coast?"

This rhetorical question, which heads this chapter, comes from President Gbagbo as he reflects on the future of Ivory Coast. At issue is the immigration policy in a country where over 30% of the population is made up of foreigners. The case of immigrants from neighboring Burkina Faso is a special sore point, as many conflicts have arisen between indigenous peoples and these newcomers.

There has always been an 'open door' policy towards foreigners, but perhaps due to their growing numbers and various land conflicts, in 1998, Henri Konan Bédié, the Ivorian president at that time, passed the Land Act, stipulating a person must be an Ivoirian citizen to become a landowner. However, when the time came, Bédié's party, the PDCI, approved Ouattara's policy of selling off Ivorian nationality to Burkinabè immigrants. Some foreigners try to circumvent laws to become legal owners of land they occupy, even though this land has only been "lent" or rented to them, and still rightfully belongs to indigenous nationals. Truckloads full of Burkinabè arrive regularly from Burkina Faso, as part of what would appear to be Ouattara's "expropriation" tactic.

From his prison cell in The Hague, President Gbagbo opposes such policies. "Do they want the death of Ivory Coast?" he asks. There seems to be an outright attempt to transform the very fabric of the nation, with Ivory Coast simply dissolving into Burkina Faso.

The British used to say they were the ones who colonized Africa. "We just let the French rooster rub his spurs in the sands of the desert..." Indeed, between Mauritania, Morocco, Algeria, Chad, Mali, Niger, Burkina Faso, formerly Upper Volta, in this [francophone] part of the African continent, there is mostly only desert. The phenomenon will only get worse with global warming and the advance of the desert. This is without a doubt Ivory Coast's most crucial problem. Besides Ghana next-door, we are the only place offering a combination of forest and other riches.

From time immemorial, people from the Sahel have migrated down into Ivory Coast in search of better living conditions. Furthermore, French colonizers recruited their workforce from those regions, and Houphouët-Boigny intensified this trend. The road from the Sahel to Ivory Coast dates from long ago and is wide open. Houphouët used workers from the Sahel, and France has always encouraged such a practice, because the more immigrants who entered Ivory Coast, the less immigrants headed for France.

Indeed, Ivory Coast has absorbed huge numbers of immigrants from all over the sub-region, including Nigeria, Guinea, Togo, Burkina Faso, so that now the country's population is made up of over 30% foreigners. This is a record rate. Through the years, from an administrative viewpoint, a kind of laxity has reigned and this has given rise to all kind of land and electoral issues. Who owns the land in Ivory Coast?

Disputes are rife, feeding on conflicts between native indigenous communities, who rely on unwritten traditional laws, and newcomers having sometimes lived in the area for several generations, who lean on the written law. What happens is that once immigrants arrive and are in place, they have someone from the government come to attest and certify their occupancy and exploitation of a piece of land, and then they make their request for legal ownership. The land issue is extremely sensitive and it does not take much for this situation to blaze out of control, with inhabitants pitted one against the other. Since the early 2000s the rebels have continually thrown salt on the fire, using these tensions to legitimize their presence and justify their actions...

Even in the north, there were attempts to create a community of the "people of the North," but even if that is been done, certainly their rights would have not been sufficiently recognized. Laurent Gbagbo has a stand on the sensitive land issue, noting:

I have always refused to distinguish between Ivoirians. We are all sons of the same land. We all have the same dreams and aspirations and the same rights. For each one to be able to live the best life possible, whether he or she is from the North, South, East or West, whether Christian, Muslim or animist, rules must be respected. There are rules for land acquisition and there are rules for acquiring Ivorian nationality. If rules are followed, each individual has a certain status, certain rights and obligations. If rules are not respected, there is nothing but anarchy.

The Burkinabè have next to nothing in their country, except for a little gold. They hardly have anything to sell, except sheep. We used to charter trains and trucks to pick sheep up for the Tabaski Feast, the Eid al-Adha for our Ivorian Muslims...

Unlike Burkina Faso, in our country, without even mentioning mineral resources, we have farm land, about 150,000 km2 out of the 320,000km2, where we can grow coffee, rubber, cocoa. We can grow just about anything here in Ivory Coast.

Initially, our major wealth was our timber, especially our mahogany. Then it was coffee, then cocoa. We have to admit, Houphouët did well, anticipating the global market for cocoa. Then came rubber. The Burkinabè came and learned how to farm these commodities in Ivory Coast because they didn't exist in their country of origin.

Bédié's Land Act of 1998 stipulated that in order to be a landowner, you had to be Ivorian. Thus, a foreigner could not acquire property. Today, apparently 700,000 people, people without a country, so to speak, have been identified (I wonder how?) and are entitled to naturalization as Ivorian citizens, based simply on their request. They will become *ipso facto* owners of the land they occupy. Burkinabè immigrants are getting their reward ahead of time, in exchange for their votes in the next presidential election, scheduled for October, 2015. The problem of nationality and land ownership are one and the same.

In a country where the census is not an easy exercise and where civil registers and administrative records are often missing, the establishment of electoral lists of those entitled to participate in a democratic election poses a real problem. Laurent Gbagbo comments on this issue:

To be naturalized in accordance with the rules does not pose any problem; to become a land owner according to the rules does not pose any problem. But a serious problem arises when Ivorian nationality is "sold" in order to allow foreigners to acquire land which already belongs to native communities. This is not acceptable. It is taking away the rights of Ivorians, whatever their origin, whatever their religion. It means citizenship is nothing, being a legal landowner is nothing, and this denies the very existence of certain legal rights.

If the PDCI [party of Bédié] continues to endorse Ouattara's policy on this issue, it will be committing a grave error: changing the makeup of the Ivorian population, letting Ivory Coast dissolve into Burkina Faso. I am aware that in the western part of the country, truckloads of Burkinabè are dumped in that region, and the newcomers actually drive out the indigenous peoples living there, taking away their farms. Who cares about the suffering of our populations? Do they want the death of Ivory Coast, to allow Burkina Faso to live?

The other problem is France. That country never wanted to relinquish its grip on our nation. France holds on as long as it can. Even if France has been of some service [to our country], it is not its own home, and does not have the eright to offer blind support to a bunch of rebels and supply them with arms.

The problem of Mali--where you've seen how the crisis developed up until the French intervention--, didn't begin yesterday. I became aware of it through Edgar Pisani[20] who went there in 1992. This problem should have been resolved twenty years ago, all the more so because everyone knew that there was oil and uranium there. All these years, neither ECOWAS (the Economic Community of West African States), nor the African Union, nor France bothered to bring people together to find a real solution to a real problem. In Mali, the Tuareg, the Arabs, have long expressed their demands: when Pisani went there, they already wanted to create an independent state comprising northern Mali, northern Niger, eastern Mauritania, and a portion of southern Libya. In the countries of the region, as in Sudan and Mauritania, Arabs try to subject black people to their laws through force, and the Blacks therein are frustrated.

Today, the question of Mali may seem settled. But it will come back. And the same problems will reappear in Niger, Nigeria and Chad. The Western world seems unaware of the fact that with the death of Gaddafi, they have lost a great deal, since he was the one who provided stability to this region. He dealt often with the Tuareg. We cannot count on the Algerians to step in. They are concentrated on their own problems, and except for the [Western] Sahara, where they like to hassle Morocco and keep a little space between them and northern Mali and Niger, they don't get involved too much anymore in Africa. At times they create a little tension among their neighbors by supporting particular groups, Arab or

---

[20] Translator's note: Philosopher by training, Edgar Pisani, whose parents were of Maltese origin, was born in Tunisia, in the Magreb. Having served as a Minister of Agriculture in France, Pisani was quite aware of the land issues President Gbagbo reflects upon in this chapter.

Tuareg, but they only do this from afar. And then they call their neighboring countries and say, "Hey, something doesn't smell too good over there."

Suffice it to say the International Community, that is to say, France, Great Britain and the United States, intervene in crises in ways that do not solve any problems and they do not offer sustainable solutions to conflicts. In Syria, a conference should have been held much earlier, while the French government was already all set to intervene militarily! It should come as no surprise to the West that the Chinese and the Russians oppose their actions, even if the West is covered by the United Nations [Security Council's Resolutions], because they have seen how the West oversteps its boundaries and goes beyond the mandates it is given. The UN never asked the West to kill Gaddafi, nor to come and arrest me in my own home. In Ivory Coast, there was an electoral dispute, and it should have been treated as such, without weapons.

Jean-Marc Simon told me: "You know, *the UN is a mindset: in and of itself, it does not exist,*" which shows that the great powers have the freedom to act as they please within their mandates. De Gaulle had a similar perspective when referring to "this joke of a United Nations."[21]

---

[21] Translators note: the French reads this "machin des Nations Unies." The word could mean a 'thing,' 'a gadget...' This popular jargon shows that de Gaulle was scoffing at this organization.

Chapter 5
"In 2002 Villepin and Bourgi urged me to cough up money for Chirac's presidential campaign"

The heading of this chapter quotes President Gbagbo as he explains how he was forced to make a contribution to Chirac's political campaign in 2002. In 2001, he was approached by Dominique de Villepin, then advisor to President Chirac and Robert Bourgi, the secret African advisor to Chirac. Both men urged him "to cough up" money for Chirac's 2002 election. Laurent Gbagbo believed this was the price to pay to maintain peace in Françafrique. He thought that such a compromise would allow him to move towards the goals he had set for his presidency. But today, on reflection, Gbagbo admits he is not so proud of this episode in his presidency.

This chapter also offers François Mattei the opportunity to comment more on the problem of the CFA currency, still in use in francophone countries--more than half a century after independence. This issue is one of the three means that allows Françafrique to keep its grips on former French African countries-- countries that should have become sovereign long ago. He speaks of "a triple lock which is political, military, and financial [...] a currency issued in France since 1945, guaranteed by the reserves stored in the Bank of France. It is a real vice-like grip."

Another issue the French public is not aware of is the debt cancellation policy that France is supposed to apply to African states. The truth of the matter is that there is no such "cancellation." The debt is simply "privatized," meaning that monies will be paid to French companies to carry out various types of work in the country concerned. The choice of the construction sites and businesses getting contracts is, of course, made in France, not in Africa.

The control of the currency of African countries by the former colonial power shows that there is still a tight dependency of these countries on their former master. This economical control has kept these fourteen countries of the franc zone "on the leash." This unusual situation, linked to and dating back to French colonization, is at the heart of the political and social underdevelopment in Africa. This is not something people like to talk about in Paris. This CFA currency points the figure at us, we the French citizens, and makes us realize our responsibility, together with the African leaders who have been "persuaded" not to break free, but rather to accept this "hold" in exchange for a kind of benevolent protectionism. Some of the African leaders, perhaps put in place for that very purpose, are the first to defend the status quo, particularly as regards their monetary dependence. Alassane Ouattara is one of them.

The establishment of the CFA franc zone since 1945 has prevented those countries it is imposed upon from minting their own currency. The CFA banknotes are printed in Chamalières, in Puy-de-Dôme, in France, removing any hope that these African countries will one day achieve true sovereignty. Even before they came into existence, these new states were held captive and forced to remain immature, subjected to the whims of their financial overseers-- France being the first and foremost. The eventual "coming of age" in political consciousness, as well as access to true independence and dignity has obviously been late in coming. The financial childishness and irresponsibility into which these countries have been forced has produced a generation of people in constant need of assistance. Their heads of state have become beggars and thieves, on the one hand, who practice a policy of reverence and submission towards the foreign powers who "hold their pocketbooks" and protect them, and on the other, exploit and rob their own people. Without going into the technical details of a very complex system, it is clear that the amounts of money issued to each of the African countries in the franc zone is subject to a quota and, in the end, France can at any time cut down or stop altogether its delivery of CFA francs. It can also decide to devalue the currency, as it did in 1994, in agreement with the International Monetary Fund (IMF), and the United States, with all the subsequent brutal consequences for these states and peoples of Africa.

Moreover, to cover its interests and provide its own guarantees, France is authorized to store in Paris and manage 50% of the foreign currencies coming from exportations on operational accounts. Until 1973, the totality, that is to say, 100% of the revenues from these exports was out of reach of the beneficiary countries. As of 2005, the rate dropped to 65%. Thus, the majority of revenues earned from the worldwide sale of cocoa, coffee, rubber, oil, cotton, uranium, gold, diamonds, magnesium, and other rare metals, etc., are for the most part held by the Bank of France, not in the African countries generating

40

these exports. The French Treasury, watching the fluctuating rates of the dollar, the pound sterling, the yen, and the euro, puts products on the international market at will.

Nicolas Agbohou, an Ivorian professor of economics at the Sorbonne, estimates that a total of 17 billion euros from the CFA franc zone is being blocked in France instead of being held in and working in favor of the Central Bank of the States of West Africa (BCEAO) within the franc zone and the countries they serve. Along with many others, three African intellectuals have launched a desperate plea, creating a petition against this historic colonial anachronism which undermines the fourteen countries in the franc zone, prohibiting them from developing their own market or their own currency, given that the CFA franc of one country has no value in neighboring countries. There are indeed almost as many different CFA francs as countries using them and they are non-convertible between themselves. A Cameroonian cannot use his CFA francs in Senegal nor in Ivory Coast and vice versa...

It is clear that the goal of those who created this financial system was simply to "divide and conquer." Makhily Gassama, a literature professor, former Minister of Culture and former Ambassador of Senegal, Martial Ze Belinga, an economist and sociologist, and Bamba Sakho, PhD in science with a degree in economics, made a call for a "Free Franc Zone" which just shows a state of denial. It is a scandal that has been so much a part of the Franco-African landscape for so long that people no longer even see it as an issue. :

"In the name of an alleged 'guarantee of convertibility' of the currency used in 14 countries, more than 3,000 billion CFA francs [4.5 billion euros] belonging to the issuing zone of the BCEAO were deposited in the French Treasury by the end of 2011, nearly twice the wealth created in Togo in 2010, and more than four times the total wages and salaries paid by the Ivorian government in 2011! For the issuing zone of the BEAC[22], the reserves deposited in the operational

---

[22] Translator's note: BCEAO and BEAC are two Central Banks for the two CFA zones respectively serving eight and six former French colonial African countries. On the one hand in West Africa, they are Benin, Burkina Faso, Guinea-Bissau, Ivory Coast, Mali, Niger, Senegal and Togo. On the one hand in Central Africa, they are Cameroon, Central African Republic, Chad, Equatorial Guinea, Gabon, and the Republic of Congo. The Republic of Congo also known as Congo Republic or Congo-Brazzaville must be distinguished from the neighboring country which goes by a slightly different name: the Democratic Republic of Congo or DRC or Congo-Kinshasa. Actually, the CFA franc zone comprises two sub-zones which are totally independent from one another: the UEMOA or WAEMU zone and the CEMAC or CAEMC zone.

41

account of the Treasury of the former colonial power exceeded 6,100 billion CFA francs, roughly the equivalent of ten times the wages paid by the Cameroonian government to its civil servants!

"In 2011 the issuing zones of BCEAO and BEAC totaled nearly 14 billion CFA francs in foreign exchange reserves which were unavailable for the needs of African economies. For BCEAO these holdings represent, in terms of issuing currency, a coverage rate of 109% against a required coverage rate of 20% and 98.7% for BEAC. Note that these amounts exceed what is officially known as France's 'public assistance for development' in favor of the great African recipients, including Ivory Coast, Cameroon, Senegal, Congo, Mali and Burkina Faso put together! It is enough to raise several questions...

"To appreciate the exorbitant cost of the constraints linked to the CFA franc and illustrate this massive destruction of riches in terms of funding for infrastructures, an absolutely urgent question we need to keep in mind, for example, is the estimated 40 billion needed for the road project which is needed to open up the Sahel region, as well as the 300 billion CFA francs required for the urban clean-up and stabilizing operation in the capital city of Benin: Cotonou which is threatened by incoming waters, or the nearly 50 billion needed to build the bridge to link Kinshasa and Brazzaville [the capital cities of the two central African countries of the Congos separated by the second largest river in the world by discharge].

"Indeed the confiscation of African reserves destined to fund development and local economic activities is nothing less than an economic crime. [...] It is important to point out that few African elected leaders or even their opponents have bothered to ask specifically about these exchange reserves, or more generally about the outrageous way monetary issues have been managed in the franc zone. It only reveals the lack of concern that these African leaders and elite have for the well-being of their own people. If the mechanisms at work in the franc zone have a clear neocolonial bent, the excess reserves with respect to the required ratios are largely due to incomprehensible decisions made in Africa itself, decisions which do not even seem to consider the challenges of economic and social development. [...]

"The franc zone and its central banks today, which number around fifty, are truly a historical and economic anachronism. The CFA monetary zone was born as a colonial variant of the French franc zone.

It has out-survived the French franc which itself has "melted" into the euro [...] It runs counter to all emerging countries who have complete sovereignty as far as their currency is concerned: China with its yuan, South Africa with its rand, Brazil with the real, South Korea with the won, and India with its Rupee. What inconsistency! How much misery has this all generated?

Another confiscation which hugely benefits France is the deposit of Africa's gold in the coffers of France. This confiscated gold ensures France's currency and allows France to have a respectable worldwide ranking due to its reserves of 2,435 tons. Such a figure puts France into the ranks of other Western countries with the highest gold reserves, with France only coming after the United States (8,400 tons), Germany (3,400 tons), the IMF (3,200 tons), and before Italy (2,400 tons)... In times of crisis, France certainly has an advantage. Its position enables this former colonial power to reassure rating agencies and the financial markets from whom it borrows, as it tries to balance its budget. Finally, the CFA franc is, above all else, a political lever that allows direct interference in a country's internal affairs. What is Laurent Gbagbo's opinion on this particular issue?

France has its representatives on the Board of Directors of the CFA franc, and the Bank of France holds the funds. Each one of the operational accounts is linked to one of the African central banks which are nothing but subsidiaries of the Bank of France. These operational accounts cash in currencies earned through African exports and all the profit goes to the Bank of France. When France helps one of our deficit countries, always the same ones, of course, the poorest countries, it is with the surpluses and profits generated in the other countries of the CFA franc zone. Thus, France appears to be a very generous country, when in reality, it is taking the money coming from Africans to lend to other Africans! Obviously, due to its high economic volume, Ivory Coast is the essential stumbling block of the CFA structure in West Africa. This is the reason why France needed a head of state in Ivory Coast who would never call anything into question.

All credit transactions negotiated with indebted countries generate interest, always gained on the African countries own money, but with the benefit going only to the lender, namely the Bank of France, at rates set unilaterally by the Bank of France. These credit transactions put the poor countries even further into debt, letting them sink further into

underdevelopment. For France, the gains are considerable, and contribute to your [France's] budget. But, these funds blocked in Paris would be better used in investments for the development of Africa. And it is the Bank of France which has the plates for printing CFA, and they only print in proportion to the credit that we commit to, with our own export surpluses.

In the CFA franc zone, there are the countries like us [Ivory Coast] in West Africa, as well as others such as Gabon, Chad, Central African Republic, Cameroon, and Equatorial Guinea [in Central Africa]. On the Board of Directors overseeing the CFA franc, there are, I repeat, French representatives. During the post-election crisis in Ivory Coast, these French representatives were able to block the BCEAO from allowing me to access revenues of my own country. Is that what being 'independent' means? This direct control of eight countries in West Africa, those belonging to WAEMU, the West Africa Economic and Monetary Union, including Ivory Coast, Burkina Faso, Mali, Togo, Senegal, Guinea-Bissau, Benin, and Niger, always amazed Anglophone heads of state in Africa. They used to tell me:

"Why does France still have its hands on all your business? Even the British changed after American independence. It is only in India where they were surprised in 1947 and were overwhelmed by 'the Gandhi phenomenon.' Otherwise, they were able to truly de-colonize their colonies."

Moreover, their former colonies in Africa, such as Ghana, Kenya, Nigeria, as well as India and Pakistan, in Asia, they have each their own national currencies. Even Algeria, Tunisia, and Morocco, which were also former French colonies, are different from us in sub-Saharan Africa: they're not dependent on the Bank of France. They said in substance: *"We prefer trade to domination."* That too is my credo. But it is not France's credo, as it has continued to "milk its African cow," instead of moving towards some collaboration, worthy of our time and certainly more profitable for everyone.

A strong card needed to be played. I am not, nor have I ever been anti-French. Am I to blame if France did not want to leave the colonial pact behind and turn towards a future based on a different kind of relationship?

We were ready for it. I was ready for it. They simply did not want it. And that is the crux of the issue.

The problem has never been our relationship with French enterprises or companies, nor with the French people, but only with the French government, that is, with the Elysée. It was easy for Sarkozy, in 2007, to say in his speech in Dakar, Senegal: *"Africans have not really entered into history."* Without going back to the slave trade and the colonization that is all past history, he pretended to not know about the role that French "guardianship" has played, how it has blocked our emancipation, how it has blocked the building of our nations. But is it really ignorance? It is rather incompetence. With some Christian compassion, let's just say it's a lack of sincerity.

Jean Boissonnat, an economic journalist and member of the Monetary Committee at the Bank of France, described in 1960 other significant advantages of this CFA currency:

> *"...The franc zone has enabled France to get a hold of significant amounts of raw material without paying cash. This has saved the French government* [in 1960] *up to $250 million per year in foreign exchange... It is estimated that 500,000 citizens from Metropolitan France made their livings from such dealings with the CFA franc zone."*

One can only imagine what must be the present value of these savings, since the CFA franc has been pegged to the euro. The figures for the CFA franc zone are a "state secret" and they do not appear, for example, in the balance sheets published by the Bank of France.

In a book by economics professor Nicolas Agbohou, *The CFA Franc and the Euro against Africa*[23], these financial mechanisms, perverse and even deadly for African development, are fully analyzed. The terrible comments of François Mitterrand on what he considered the scam of the century are quoted in Nicolas Agbohou's work. The following arguments are taken from the book of interviews by Laure Adler, *The Year of Farewells*[24]:

---

[23] Nicolas Agbohou, *Le franc CFA et l'euro contre l'Afrique, Pour une monnaie africaine et la coopération sud-sud* (The CFA *Franc and the Euro against Africa, for an African Currency and South-South Cooperation)*, Solidarité Mondiale, 2000.

[24] Laure Adler, *L'Année des adieux* (*The Year of Farewells*), Flammarion, 1995.

"It is in fact a huge deception to have French people believe [...] that De Gaulle permitted the decolonization of Africa. When I hear the Gaullist anthem of decolonization, I can't believe it. The Brazzaville conference did not represent the emancipation of Black Africa. De Gaulle had failed in Dakar. So he needed to seduce a certain number of Africans. He never carried out the abolition of forced labor which he talked about in his Brazzaville speech. In fact, he removed any chance that Africans might be able to rule their own countries. And yet at the same time, the British accepted the complete emancipation of their colonies, including those judged important, such as Hindustan, Pakistan, etc. From 1941, the Dutch also accelerated the independence of Indonesia. All these countries became free and sovereign [...] De Gaulle never thought about self-government; he had no vision for Africa [...] De Gaulle wanted submission. For him, the price to be admitted into the [Franco-African] Community was to give up sovereignty.

Laurent Gbagbo comments on both left wing and right wing French presidents under the Vth French Republic (October 1958 to present):
François Mitterrand, who himself didn't act any differently when he came to power, was shocked to hear some saying that De Gaulle had decolonized Africa.

The mysteries of the dichotomy between thought and action are the quintessence of politics: during the fourteen years Mitterrand spent in the palace at the Elysée, he maintained the Gaullist system to the point of appointing his son Jean-Christophe as the head of the very opaque African Bureau of the Elysée. Mitterrand was undoubtedly a humanist and third world advocate, but maybe only until they explained to him that the loss of Africa would trigger a deep hole in the coffers of France.

In his own way, Jacques Chirac has been truthful. After he had retired from office, in *Africaphonie*, a 2008 documentary authored by Michael Gosselin, the former French president unveiled what had really been happening with the tinge of false sincerity he is known for:

"[...] a proportion, not all, but much of the money that is in our wallet comes from the centuries-long exploitation of Africa. So we need a little common sense, I am not talking about generosity or justice, just common sense, in order to be able to give back to Africans what we

46

took from them. This is necessary if we want to avoid the worst convulsions and difficulties, with all the political consequences that would entail."

Speaking of the French's "wallet," the former French president forgot to talk about the wallets of the various political parties, including his own and the wallet of other French politicians. Robert Bourgi, one of Chirac's secret African advisers, who later served Nicolas Sarkozy, told *The Sunday Journal* on September 11, 2011, how suitcases filled with banknotes used to circulate between African capitals and Jacques Chirac's Elysée. These monies were meant to pay for political campaigns, particularly for the election held in 2002. This lawyer boasted:

"It was through me that five African heads of state, Abdoulaye Wade (Senegal), Blaise Compaoré (Burkina Faso), Laurent Gbagbo (Ivory Coast) Denis Sassou-Nguesso (Congo-Brazzaville), and, of course, Omar Bongo (Gabon), paid about $10 million for the 2002 campaign."

Over a period of several days, Bourgi, in interviews, claimed to have seen *"Chirac and Villepin counting the banknotes."*

The book, *The Republic of the Briefcases*[25], authored by Pierre Péan and published around the same time, made similar revelations. Laurent Gbagbo admitted that the practices denounced by Pierre Péan were common place. He told me he had been approached by Villepin and Bourgi in 2001 and was strongly encouraged to finance the election campaign of Jacques Chirac during his run for president in 2002. Gbagbo knew that the protagonists of the "Black Mercedes" coup[26] were hiding in Burkina Faso and were ready to try again if

---

[25] Pierre Péan, *La République des mallettes* (The Republic of the Briefcases), Fayard, 2011. Translator's note: in French the word 'mallette' refers to a small suitcase, somewhat larger than a briefcase.

[26] Translator's note: Following a coup which overthrew President Henri Konan Bédié on Christmas's Eve 1999, General Robert Guéi ran the country during a ten-month military junta. Former body guard of Alassane Dramane Ouattara, Ibrahim Coulibaly nicknamed IB who was part of the coup against Bédié hatched his own coup against Guéi on September 19, 2000. This coup was dubbed the "White Horse" coup (the pet animal of General Guéi). In January 2001, IB tried another coup againt President Laurent Gbagbo ("Black Mercedes" coup) dubbed after the vehicle used to perform this umpteenth coup. After Gbagbo was ousted, as soon as Alassane Dramane Ouattara took power, IB was executed by the rebel forces who hailed Ouattara as their strong man.

they felt sufficiently backed by these powerful interests. It is especially not easy to say 'no' to the representatives of French authorities, when they are the military bosses on the ground, as they were in Ivory Coast. When there is such an imbalance between the powerful and the weak, what room does the weak have to manoeuver? This is what the proponents of Françafrique count on.

Laurent Gbagbo couldn't agree more:

> **It was in 2001, I believe. Villepin and Robert Bourgi asked me to "cough up" some money for the 2002 election in France. We were at the Voltaire, a restaurant on the *quai* with the same name, near the *Documentation française* building. It was the price to pay to have peace in Françafrique. I also had a meeting with Chirac, and everything went fine. He walked me out, he was very friendly, and on the steps of the Elysée, after giving me a little tap on the shoulder, he said, *"I won't be ungrateful."* I am not proud of this episode in my presidency, but I thought it would leave some room to manoeuver, allowing us to move towards our goals. Of course, I was criticized for this, accused of "double talk," of leaning on neocolonialism and at the same time criticizing it. But you need cunning and diplomacy to be able to deal with such powerful partners. From the beginning, they put me in a state of crisis and constant urgency... At least, Bourgi and Villepin never came back. They knew I wouldn't be accepting any more deals. And of course, this didn't do anything to improve our relationship.**

> **Later, Chirac said that I had "failed" him, but I have never understood why he said that. He claimed I had let some information leak out...**

> More than a bonus for our economy [in France], more than a state secret, the wealth of Africa is [in France] our nest egg, the family secret de Gaulle passed on to his successors for forty years. This is not excluding the fact that we [the French] were the cause of the debts in these countries under our control. And these debts regularly are transformed into juicy profits for our [French] big corporations. [French] public opinion turns negative each time another cancellation of debt in a given African country is announced. Another gift! ...So we think! In fact, the debt of the African state to the French state is never canceled but "privatized." The debt will ultimately be paid, in full, to French companies, who will carry out works "for the common good" in the country concerned. The choice of construction sites and businesses is made, not in Africa, but in France... As they say, every part of the pig can be put to good use. And in Africa, it is all about money, even when we are talking debt.

The secret to French policy on the African continent is this: Africa may cause a few worries here and there, but it's still a good deal. And what's more, at the international level, France's position in Africa is an invaluable commodity, which makes us [the French] a valuable and influential partner. Once France re-integrated into the high circles of NATO leadership, the United States was suddenly able to slip into the continent and make some headway--a continent they knew very little about, but where, for once, they did not need to openly engage their military troops.

Anyone in French political circles, or in Africa, who dared to attack this "state within a state," that is to say, Francafrique, never made it. If you moved the smallest piece of wood, the whole house would fall on your head...

Jean-Pierre Cot, François Mitterrand's short-lived Minister of Cooperation, resigned in 1982, the day his personal ethics clashed with the reality of France's neo-colonial attitude toward Africa. Later, under Nicolas Sarkozy, Jean-Marie Bockel, one of the successors of Cot at the same Ministry, also had the unfortunate idea to make a public appeal for an end to Françafrique. This led to his swift departure under the pressure of two political heavyweights he had indisposed, and who feared for their revenues: Denis Sassou-Nguesso [Congo-Brazzaville] and Omar Bongo [Gabon]. The latter phoned Robert Bourgi, the official "tam-tam" between African presidents and the Elysée, with the message "Get rid of Bockel!" These orders were followed. Jean-Marie Bockel's appointment was changed to Secretary of State for Defense and Veterans Affairs in the Fillon government. Today, he works for the French government on a project with a view to reorganizing relations between France and Africa...

Admittedly, Bockel's ideas have been better received by the François Hollande administration. But will they signal the end of Françafrique? The Obama-Hollande communique of February 10, 2014, before the official visit of the French president to the United States, opens a new perspective:

"Africa is the most visible theater of the new partnership between France and the United States..."

A song Obama and Hollande sang in chorus in articles published that day by *Le Monde* and *The Washington Post*. France has always made its military expertise and its knowledge of Africa available to the Americans, who till the 70's have let France manage things there. However, in the 80's, greed for African resources, including oil and strategic security issues convinced the

United States they needed to be more directly involved on the continent. And they began to take on their share. In 2006-2008, they created *Africom*, the military command for Africa. Based in Stuttgart, Germany and in Djibouti, the Bureau includes various African departments formerly working out of Washington. The Bureau oversees the strategic, security, and economic interests of Uncle Sam in Africa. But on the ground, you still see French soldiers running all over the place: in Ivory Coast, Mali, Central African Republic, with American diplomatic and sometimes logistic support. Is it goodbye "Françafrique" and long live "Atlanticafrique"?

Ever since Nicolas Sarkozy pushed for France to rejoin NATO's top posts in 2009, France's army defends far more than France's national interests. *"You have become the Senegalese riflemen of the West,"* African comedians say with irony. A well-known French commentator well-acquainted with Africa resumes the situation this way: "From now on, *it's the Americans doing the cooking; the French are doing the dishes."*

This commentator referred to the first U.S.-Africa Summit, which took place in Washington DC, August 5 & 6, 2014, to which Barack Obama invited 47 African heads of state. According to the White House, the goal was to strengthen ties between the two continents. For the first time, they by-passed the usual channel, France, their normal intermediary. On the menu of this important event was *"Trade and Investment in Africa"* and *"Security and Democratic Development."* Promising young talents were also invited to the mega summit. People in Paris were wondering, *"For whom is the bell tolling?"* This vast Americafrique meal took the place of the numerous "village feasts," those summits held so often between France and its old colonies. America struck a heavy blow and puts a definitive stop to the exclusive one-on-one talks France had with its former colonial countries. Will African leaders get the idea and change the balance of power with France, thanks to their new mentor?

And what if the Washington summit really was the "beginning of the end" of Françafrique, a 'death' which has been announced so many times over? Could this be a reversal within the global alliance, with France being kicked out of its own backyard by its American friend? Indeed, hasn't the recent crisis in Ivory Coast accelerated this process by causing a fatal blow to the "family" relationship between France and its former colonies? In May, 2014, *Africom* organized a training symposium in Germany for press agents and journalists from Francophone Africa. The second EU-Africa summit held in Brussels on April 2 & 3, 2014, was certainly, among other things, a way to counterbalance the rise of American influence on the continent.

France plays it both ways, but in the end has its rear-end caught between two chairs, a real challenge for the current French government which has to make up for the errors of the past. Other players are besieging the prized citadel of the ex-French feudalism, investing as they see fit. There is Morocco's Mohammed VI, already dubbed the new king of Africa, who has been multiplying his trips to sub-Saharan Africa to establish cooperation agreements with Mali, Gabon, and Ivory Coast. He offers an original partnership, attractive because it is not "imported," and what's more, not imposed by former colonial powers. He explains:

"Africa is a truly great continent due to its vitality, its resources, and its huge potential. But Africa must take responsibility for itself. Africa is no longer a colonized continent. This is why Africa needs to trust Africa. It needs less help now. What it really needs is human and social development projects. Africa should not be held hostage to its past, nor to its current political, economic and social problems[27]..."

In July, 2014, the head of the Ivorian Treasury instructed the Foreign Trade branch of the Bank of Morocco to raise a loan of $500 million on Euronext[28].

In various meetings around the world involving conflict resolution, unusual go-betweens have emerged. For example, the MNLA Tuareg separatists--Azawad National Movement of Liberation--went to Moscow in the second week of March 2014 for consultations with Boubacar Keita, the president of Mali, elected in 2013. Even if there have been historical ties between Mali and Russia, it is clear that Paris is no longer the only destination for such encounters. And what about South Africa, who aligns itself with Brazil, Russia, India and China in the BRICS emerging countries? South Africa's networks and high technology make it another serious competitor for France and Europe. Like Morocco, as a country in Africa, it has the advantage of not appearing to be an invader.

As for the Chinese giant, it comes into the game through its Ministry of Commerce and Ministry of Foreign Affairs, as well as through the China

---

[27] Abidjan.net, February 24, 2014.
[28] Translator's note: According to Wikipedia, *Euronext* is a pan-European exchange based in Amsterdam, Brussels, London, Lisbon and Paris. In addition to cash and derivative markets, it provides market data, market solutions, etc.

Development Bank and China Eximbank. According to *La Lettre de l'Expansion*, China

> *"is now the largest lender to the black continent. Its loans easily add up to more than 2.5 million euros [...]. China is already responsible for 92% of the financial investments in African infrastructures."* The 'diplomacy of the *checkbook*' gave birth to 'Chinafrica,' *and for the first time, in 2013, the Sino-African trade exceeded the symbolic threshold of $200 billion."*

Jealous of its neighboring rival, in 2013, Japan allocated 7.7 billion euros over five years to finance infrastructures in Africa.

Chapter 6
"Inside the cage where they keep us, we only look like we're free"

The forced dependency which France imposes on African nations makes them feel trapped. While there is an apppearnce of freedom and democracy, Gbagbo says these countries "only look like they're free."

In this chapter Laurent Gbagbo talks in more detail about the three major obstacles to real independence in Ivory Coast. These obstacles block the way to true sovereignty and sustainable development. They include:

the presence of the French army
the French control of the currency
the French control over who ascends to power

Gbagbo especially had hopes of gaining economic independence for his country, and for him the answer was to get out of the CFA franc zone, a system imposed on the francophone countries since "independence," actually since 1945. While president, he had been looking for a coalition of countries, to make a similar move, perhaps within the context of the West African Economic and Monetary Union (WAEMU). But not every president or country is looking to break its bonds from France. Gbagbo notes that many Francophone African presidents are afraid to "step out," for fear of losing their own personal perks and benefits. Indeed, many who have even thought about "stepping out" have been stopped in their tracks.

From the exploitation of mineral riches in the soil to the establishment of high quality medical facilities, Laurent Gbagbo has a vision for a modern and self-sufficient Africa, where the riches and human resources of the continent would be put at the service of that continent. But for there to be real progress, the three "holds" on francophone Africa must be dealt with. This is the only way for Africa to escape from the "cage where they keep us."

We can't just move from one dependency to another. The only way to move forwards is through partnership and independence.

A group of West African ECOWAS experts (the Economic Community of West African States) met in Yamoussoukro, the political capital of Ivory Coast, in early 2014 to discuss the issue of creating a single currency. Those who already have their own currency, such as Cape Verde (escudo), Nigeria (naira), Ghana (cedi) and Guinea-Conakry (Guinea franc) would like to see a merger with those using the CFA franc towards a single currency. But there is not enough political will, and thus no progress on this front... On October 12, 2012, while visiting Dakar, François Hollande dared to mention the issue. With what seemed distinctly new thoughts, the president of the French Republic said: "... I am convinced that the countries of the franc zone will be able to actively manage their currencies and mobilize more reserves for growth and employment." But Laurent Gbagbo has his doubts:

For the time being, these are just words. Clearly as long as the pillars of Françafrique still stand, that it, the presence of the French army, the CFA franc, and the choice of African presidents, the sovereignty of [French-speaking] African countries is but an illusion, and Françafrique remains the only reality. This dependency is an anachronism. It constitutes such a huge scandal that large-scale lies had to be put in place to hide it...

Let's get serious. It is high time French people understand why their leaders, whether from the right or the left, have been, for decades, so closely linked to Africa! They need to understand why their leaders maintain garrisons there, and carry out such costly military expeditions, while they say they don't have a penny. They even convince others that it is we Africans who are costing them so much money...

I was right about things, but right too early. Now it's time for others in Africa to take up the fight against Françafrique. It's worth it, not only for Africa, but for France. The end of this system will open an era of shared progress, which can be carried out in dignity. We need you [the French], because we are under-developed, and you need us [Africans], because we have what you need, because you yourselves are in a crisis situation.

We need the sovereignty that we are entitled to. To not allow us to obtain that sovereignty can only lead to continuing frustration among new generations. It can only lead to more trouble. Without that sovereignty, how can you ask us to build our democracies? Gaddafi said to me once:

"Lawrence, why are you tiring yourself out with the North [of Ivory Coast]? Cut the country in two. Keep the South and let them have the North, and you will have peace."

Gaddafi was like a loud-speaker: he repeated what he had heard, or what was suggested to him to tell me. I thought the division of Ivory Coast was a prefabricated plan. And I just smiled, since I have always defended the unity and integrity of the Ivorian nation, and I have never accepted that it be infringed upon. That is an idea from outside, an idea which emerged in the 1990s, when Ouattara was Houphouët's Prime Minister. At that time, there was talk of the "Charter of the North," a document which was circulated all over the place and which advocated the dismemberment of the country. Houphouët himself was offended by the idea.

African leaders must take responsibility and take their own destiny in hand. When you see these big international conferences in Africa, those dealing with the Ivorian crisis are the glaring example, be it at the African Union or at the ECOWAS meetings, there are more Westerners, more Whites, more fund raisers, and more representatives of outside powers than there are African themselves, all there with the goal of putting pressure on Africans. This is why I do not pass judgment on my colleagues, even when they fail me.

There is one among them that you all take for a staunch Françafricanist, because he doesn't make a lot of noise. But he is not for Françafrique, and his name is Paul Biya of Cameroon. One day at the UN in New York, after my speech at the UN podium, he threw his arms around me and said: *"You are our pride."* After the problems in Syria, he himself went to Russia to discuss defense agreements with the Russian authorities. As for his own country, he just said, *"Well, Cameroon is Cameroon."*

It is not easy to make things happen. It's not easy to oppose dictatorial ideas. What happened to me is a good illustration of that. Inside the cage where they keep us, we only appear to be free. Our finances and our economy are under tutelage, we have no real weight at the international level. We are in danger of being fined if we do not obey. It is unbearable. One day, together we will break our chains and walk free from our cage.

Ivory Coast had the chance to free itself from its dependency in the franc zone even it meant going it alone. I was about to carry this out, and this is why they wanted to stop me. **Without Ivory Coast and without what we represent economically, the CFA franc would just collapse, and with it, all the Françafrican structure. And what a bad example for our neighboring countries! When you realize that we are in fact part of the euro zone, it is easier to understand how France was able to drag the European Community and the United States into the Ivoirian crisis. Nobody had any interest in seeing Ivory Coast exit the CFA zone. I understand: a president coming from the IMF who understood *their* interests was preferable to Laurent Koudou Gbagbo!**

France has painted its postcolonial relationship with Africa with the hypocritical colors of a long-standing friendship, stemming from its pompous "common history" with Africa. Even if we cannot deny the individual emotional ties created during the colonial period, we still have to admit that today France defends what it considers its historic acquisitions. Without these, France would be like Spain or Italy, restricted to its borders and economically dependent on its own resources. As De Gaulle used to say "*A state has no friends, only interes*ts."

The defense agreements signed with France's former colonies, which ensure these countries of French military intervention in case of external attack, are, along with the currency issue, another keystone in the Françafrique "cathedral." The hidden economic clauses these defense agreements contain, providing France with compensation for its protection, give it privileged access to natural resources in the subsoil of its former colonies. These agreements not only justify intervention on demand, but also justify the presence of French troops on the continent. They are a guarantee of security for the military under-equipped African governments. For Paris, these defense agreements are yet another means of subliminal pressure. It was a kind of an institutionalized interference that Laurent Gbagbo could no longer put up with. This is what caused his demise. An Ivorian army officer confided in me, in 2005 in Abidjan:

> "*Put your foot anywhere. There is not a tiny square meter that does not belong to France.*"

This "property deed" was, according to him, a simple consequence of the French military presence, the third pillar of Françafrique. The Ivoirian soil is so rich it can produce almost anything, but the subsoil is full of resources of incredible value, without even mentioning oil. Indeed, Africa has often been described as a "geological scandal." Gbagbo notes:

In the 1960s, a French company called Mokta was working manganese mines in Grand Lahou, in southwest Ivory Coast. One day the company just upped and left, no one knew why. It left tons of ore in the port of Abidjan. In 2001, some Chinese bought all that was left on the docks. They did a little more research and discovered reserves hitherto ignored. There was gas, bauxite, gold, and diamonds. The French geologists had mapped the Ivorian subsoil and had known for a long time about the rich natural resources there.

In 2002, after France refused to help us fight against the rebel attacks, I didn't want anything more to do with these defense agreements that had proved not only their uselessness, but their harmfulness as well. So since these agreements also give away all our strategic raw materials to France in exchange for a non-existent military aid, I decided to stop this fool's bargain. I made my intention clear to end this agreement. This was expected to occur after the 2010 elections. We had plans to restructure and strengthen our own army. Sarkozy knew it and must have not been happy about it. In 2009, to appease me, a French delegation was sent to renegotiate these agreements, but without success.

Félix Houphouët-Boigny had a great fear of military coups. A number of his colleagues had been overthrown in the neighboring countries. The Ivorian president was therefore not in a hurry to invest in a national army. He relied entirely on France for Ivorian security. The perfect illustration or even the caricature of his Françafrican mindset can be seen in the construction of his private residence, his "bunker." It is located a few meters away from the residence of the French Ambassador in Abidjan, and the two buildings were connected by a tunnel to allow the "father of the nation" to run to safety [into French territory] in case of a coup. The whole mentality of Françafrique, fueled by collusion, submission and protection, is symbolized by this tunnel. The Françafrique mentality is also revealed through the defense agreements, signed in 1961, which could be better described as agreements of dependency. Mamadou Koulibaly notes:

"We should call them agreements of administrative, commercial and monetary protection of our countries by France." They are protectionist agreements."

These agreements were renegotiated and signed in Paris on January 26, 2012, by Alassane Ouattara and Nicolas Sarkozy. What does Laurent Gbagbo think of this latest development?

I had taken a firm decision to get out of the CFA franc zone. We had the contacts for the purchase of paper and printing machines. But you do not make such fundamental reforms, it is almost a revolution, during troubled times. Maintaining the state was the priority.

And as far as I was concerned, I wanted this to be done within the framework of the West African Monetary Union [WAEMU], the 8 francophone countries: Ivory Coast, Burkina Faso, Mali, Guinea-Bissau, Senegal, Togo, Benin and Niger. And to do this, you need courage; each head of state has to stand up to his mentor and guardian: France. We needed to turn, together, towards the Central Bank of West Africa, instead of towards the Bank of France.

Or else, Ivory Coast would have to go it alone: Cape Verde had done it and has a currency that is holding its own. In Ivory Coast, we represent 40% of the GDP of the West African Economic and Monetary Union, UEMOA, and 62% of its exports.

But you cannot make such fundamental reform in a turbulent period of war. Again, we needed to maintain stability in the country. That is a major obligation everywhere, especially in Africa, where so much remains to be done...

Unlike Asia and South America, Africa has not found its way. It is time to get started. We should by now be able to get adequate medical treatment in Dakar, Abidjan, Lomé, etc. Formerly, this was the case. You could also go to Kinshasa. But today, we go to Europe, or to Cape Town, South Africa: that's what I mean by the failure of Black Africa...

In the heyday of Françafrique, special advisers were named to serve in the offices of African heads of state. "Secret agent" ambassadors like Robert Maurice and Maurice Delauney *("Policy prevails over morality in the exercise of my official mission,"* he said one day), and mercenaries were dropped into hot spots, watchdogs like Bob Denard. The entire state apparatus of Francophone countries was in the hands of civil servants and French agents. They kept presidents in power, like the case of Léon Mba of Gabon, who was "put back on his throne" through a French military intervention after a coup deposed him. Then, at his death, he was replaced by Albert-Bernard Bongo, by means of the creation of the post of vice-president, a post hand-tailored for him.

These are some of the known examples, not to mention the other dirty tricks: rigged elections, and assassinations....

Behind all these actions, there is one name: Jacques Foccart. After the president of the [French] Republic, he was the most powerful man in France, not appearing to be anyone special, living on his private export business. Foccart had no official position and refused to be paid by the French government. What a shame, when you consider that, as the one in charge of African and Malagasy Affairs, he overlooked an incredible money-making machine, through networks that to this day bear his name. No one objected to the covert nature, and even mafia-like character, of his operating procedures. All this was part of the war against Communism during the Cold War.

Ideology often hides the most materialistic of motivations or makes the best of it. Foccart's African Bureau installed at *2 rue de l'Elysée*, with more than a hundred personnel, made all the major decisions concerning Africa, and this, in the greatest secrecy. This was all done without any democratic input, far from parliamentary debates and the eyes of the media. It was a 'shadow' cabinet, put in place to secretly run the empire. Foccart was answerable to no one except the French president. During De Gaulle's two terms, he was the only man allowed to see the French president each day, usually in late afternoon. He had unlimited resources in cash, due to the slush fund of ELF[29], an oil company created and run by Pierre Guillaumat which exploited oil in Gabon. He even had control of special services such as SDECE and was able to recruit men from the Gaullist secret service, BCRA, an intelligence agency created during the war. Through these men, for a period of thirty years, Jacques Foccart was able to carry out, under several French presidents of the Vth Republic, the mission assigned to him by De Gaulle, namely to "keep Africa" for France. It reads like a sordid police thriller. After his departure from office, General de Gaulle never again saw his regular evening visitor, Foccart, the one with whom he had never missed a single appointment. Columnists still talk about this strange attitude of denial shown by men who carried out a great deal of "dirty work." From SAC to Françafrique, the two creations of Foccart were modeled on two principles: (1) necessity determines the law and (2) the end justifies the means. You can have real dreams of grandeur, but sometimes to govern, you have to hold your nose, to block the smell.

---

[29] Translator's note: ELF, whose full name is Elf Aquitaine, is a French oil company which, in 2003, merged with another French oil company called TotalFina. The new name of the two merged companies is TotalFinaElf.

At that time, Paris was accustomed to seeing African politics as a simple extension of French politics. Ivory Coast was treated as an exterior dependent territory of France, and the leaders of its former colonies as debtors who "owe" France. Most of these African leaders have so well understood what is at stake they fall over themselves to cooperate, more out of personal interest than out of any conviction. They sometimes become the best advocates of a system of alienation that Gbagbo has always criticized. It only stands to reason that the French right wing presidents from 1995 to 2012 could only consider Gbagbo as an enemy. First, he is a socialist by family history, his father had joined the SFIO in 1947, and for a time Gbagbo was vice-president of the international Socialist group. But along with this, what has always bothered those in Paris, whether from the right or the left, is that, besides his membership in the Socialist party, Gbagbo has never been a "yes-man." He belongs to no clique or underground network; he is not a freemason. So it is hard to figure out who he is, to understand or co-opt him, it is even hard to know how to put pressure on him. His fellow francophone African heads of state are head over heels to participate in secret masonic initiation rites and ceremonies, and all the other paraphernalia that open the door, they think--to the world of the powerful, i.e., the world of the Whites.

But Allassane Dramane Ouattara is not like Gbagbo. Through his contacts with international finance stemming from his former position at the IMF, and with the incredible network of his wife Dominique, both in the media and in other domains, he does not need to rely on his "brothers of light" to get what he wants. But he just might need them to restore his image, after the picture painted of him in *The Economist* in 2013: a president surrounded by militia leaders and criminals, of whom he himself is prisoner. In December 31, 2012, an article in the *Huffington Post* is even more radical. Penned by Philip N. Howard, professor at Princeton University, Alassane Ouattara enters the list of the top sixteen aging dictators, whose eventual deaths portend troubles and "surprises" in countries where they now rule. This ranking, coming out of America, unfortunately occurred after this man was "chosen" by the International Community to become the commander in chief of Ivory Coast.

Chapter 7
"Let's focus on the facts"

This quote comes from a long quote from Laurent Gbagbo who describes in detail what happened in his country in the aftermath of the failed coup of September19, 2002. He describes France's refusal to respect the defense agreements signed in 1961 to military assist him against the invasion of the Ivorian territory. He tells how armed rebels, coming from neighboring Burkina Faso, entered from the North, with the complicity of France and ended up occupying 60% of Ivorian territory. Laurent Gbagbo tries to "focus on the facts" so that the real truth about the war in Ivory Coast could be known.

Ironically, while in the aftermath of the attempted coup of September 2002, Michèle Aliot-Marie, then French Minister of Defense declared the defense agreements obsolete, in his speeches during state visits to Dakar and Kinshasa in October 2012, President François Hollande spoke of "rebel attacks from outside and the support of France for attacked states."

"Why do you French prefer Alassane Ouattara?" I once asked a famous Parisian journalist. He looked at me and said: "Because he is like us!"

Gbagbo often tells this story because it makes him laugh and seems to him to put in a nutshell what is at the bottom of his problems. Henri Emmanuelli, former president of the French National Assembly, a friend and "twin brother" of Gbagbo[30], summarizes this antagonism:

"From the beginning, Laurent Gbagbo has cared about only one thing: making Ivory Coast an independent country. They simply cannot forgive him for this."

---

[30] They were born the same day in the same year: May 31, 1945.

Emmanuelli recounts the first attempt to overthrow Gbagbo. It occurred at the beginning of his presidency:

> *"In 2002, the Ivorian president had warned France that there was an uprising in progress. But the French authorities told him they knew nothing about it.*

Evoking the massive military attack which came from neighboring Burkina Faso, which led to the rebels occupying half of the country, removing his control over most of the Ivorian territory, Gbagbo remembers that answer coming from the French authorities: **Of course they didn't warn me. They were in on the coup.**

Michèle Alliot-Marie was the then-Minister of Defense in Chirac's government. When she was asked about the French passivity in light of these events, to give an official explanation of why France did not comply with the defense agreements--signed in 1961 between the two countries--stipulating France was to provide military aid to the legal government of Ivory Coast in case of external aggression, Alliot-Marie responded, in the most hypocritical fashion possible:

> *"This is an Ivorio-Ivorian affair. Of course, it was out of the question for France to interfere in Ivory Coast's internal affairs..."*

For Alliot-Marie, these agreements were obsolete. That's what she dared to say to me when I asked her to intervene based on these defense agreements. She is the kind of person who speaks first and then tries to justify herself later. Sometimes it is just grotesque.

Laurent Gbagbo, who survived the attempted coup d'etat of 2002, who survived the subsequent refusal of military aid from the "historical ally" and then for twelve long years, who endured the occupation of 60% of Ivorian territory, made the following comments:

In 2000, when I was elected, there was a huge smear campaign against me in France, all because my election was not accepted. Again in 2010, they refused to accept the fact that I was elected. That is the substance of the debate; the post-election crisis in 2010 is simple: who won the election? They did not want this debate. They dismissed this debate and tried to delegitimize me once again. Instead of recounting the votes and reviewing the records at the polling stations, they preferred allowing the

rebels to launch violent attacks against the forces of law and order and then turn around and accuse me of starting the violence. No one wanted to know the facts. But when you deny facts, when you try to ignore them, you are a hypocrite. You are a liar. I'll tell the facts, whatever the circumstances, not because I am looking to convince anyone. I just want people to verify the facts. That's the way to get to the truth.

But thanks to the proceedings at the International Court, the truth they tried to hide is beginning to emerge. My Defense team showed how the charges against me were politically motivated. The accusation that I had a peaceful demonstration suppressed on December 16, 2010, doesn't hold for even a second, since the purported peaceful demonstration was in fact an attack carried out by groups of well-armed professional mercenaries, well-equipped and well-trained, carrying out a strategy put in place by Ouattara and his warlords with the precise aim of seizing power by force. All the evidence is there, including film of what happened at rebel headquarters. Nobody wanted to see the evidence because the idea was to use this alleged suppression of a supposedly peaceful march to convince the International Community of the moral illegitimacy of my presence in power.

What about the accusation that I ordered troops to fire on a women's march in March 2011? It doesn't hold water either, as my Defense team demonstrated in February 2013. My lawyers have shown that one of the favorite modus operandi of the Ouattara camp, seemingly on the advice of the French, was to organize fake "peaceful marches," putting women and children at the front and concealing armed combatants, with not only war weapons like Kalashnikovs but also heavier weapons such as RPGs [Rocket-Propelled Grenades], amidst protesters that they used as human shields. Again, the facts didn't really matter: all they needed were the accusations, taken up by French media, with no investigation, of course. What did all this accomplish? It put an end to attempts at mediation that we had initiated.

What about the accusation that government forces bombed a neighborhood of Abidjan in March, 2011? My lawyers have challenged such a bogus charge. They tore apart the foundations of this allegation: vague testimonies, inconsistent and contradictory stories, many of them obtained by hearsay. Again, the French media have become open allies of the Ouattara camp.

What was the purpose of these accusations? A few days later, France was trying to force the adoption by the UN Security Council of a resolution allowing the use of force against us. French journalists were already comparing the bombing of Abobo market to the Sarajevo market bombing. The purpose of all this was to appeal to the conscience of the West, to convince them to let the French launch a military offensive [against Ivory Coast]. As soon as Resolution 1975 was voted, the French army launched rebel groups from the north of the country towards the south, groups which they had organized and provided with necessary logistics. As they made their way down to attack the civilian populations in Abidjan, heinous crimes were committed.

As in 2000 and 2002, in 2010 we were the ones assaulted, and if there were deaths, so many deaths, it is because a war was declared from abroad, translated into an invasion by mercenaries recruited from surrounding countries, supported by French forces. The aim was to bring down the government of a sovereign country and seize its institutions.

Does anybody want to make a list of the victims of the attacks perpetrated by the rebels in 2000, 2001, 2002, 2010 and 2011? I am not afraid of the truth. I've always asked that the truth be revealed. There is truth in the documents exchanged before the International Court, particularly in the syntheses my lawyers made in response to the Prosecutor's accusations. Those sitting across from me, my opponents, flee the truth. They always reject any method that might reveal the truth. They pushed for a confrontation between Ivorians and they alone know why. They tried to make me responsible for the war they waged. They went even further, claiming that the abuses were carried out by Ivorian government forces. But as I told you, these charges do not stand up to scrutiny.

Whoever the accuser is, even if it is the Prosecutor of the International Court, they will never succeed in imputing a large number of the victims to the Ivorian FDS[31]. And yet there were scores of victims during the post-election crisis in 2010 and 2011. Who is really responsible for the killings? It is the armed rebel groups that infiltrated Abidjan before the elections. Also responsible is the "Invisible Commando" who attacked and killed Ivorians in the heart of Abidjan. French forces conducted numerous attacks against my government forces and caused much

---

[31] FDS reads in French *Forces de défense et de sécurité en Côte d'Ivoire* which translates as *Defense and Security Forces in Ivory Coast.*

collateral damage. Rebel forces invaded the south in March 2011, leaving behind them a trail of blood and horror. How many innocent victims were there? These victims seem to interest no one. Yet, thousands of civilians were killed.

After the attack on the country in September 2002, and the subsequent invasion and occupation of our territory by rebels from Burkina Faso, [the then-Senegalese president] Wade and Chirac [the then-French president] asked me to grant the rebels amnesty for all their crimes. There were over three hundred dead in 24 hours in Abidjan. They were officers in our army, along with my Minister of the Interior, a friend since my youth, Emile Boga Doudou, all of them were assassinated. And there was also General Robert Guéi, whose murder was ascribed to men in my camp. I granted a general amnesty to ensure that links were not cut with those who attacked us, even if they were wrong, even if they had led the country into a bloodbath, into fire and destruction. I wanted to give a chance for future peace. And today they hold me accountable? All my supporters who answered by my call for appeasement and reconciliation are today persecuted, hunted down, and imprisoned by the new Ivorian authorities. They are said to be criminals to somehow justify in the world's eyes their ill-treatment. But the evidence is out there, as obvious as it can be, but this does not prevent the ongoing suppression of rights and confiscation of property. How many have been imprisoned for no reason? How many have been driven from their homes? Their houses were stolen, confiscated, and occupied by the rebels and foreigners who invaded our territory to seek their own fortunes.

When François Hollande went to Dakar and Kinshasa in October 2012, I listened to his speeches about northern Mali and about the northern Kivu state in Congo. I listened to him talk about rebel attacks coming from the outside and France's support of these countries under attack. These remarks deeply affected me. I didn't hear any such talk when I was attacked in 2002. Those who should have reacted, France and the International Community, did nothing. Why? Because they were in on the coup! From that time onwards, I had to react, to see who could help me, since those who were supposed to help were against me.

When they claim that I have a double standard, because I, who had criticized French's military presence on our territory, called for French military aid, they are cheating. I was born in a country under French domination. I became president in a country where, before my term in office, a decision was taken to not build an army, since defense agreements existed. This was not my choice. I had to make with the system in place. In politics, you can't overestimate your own capacities, you have to deal realistically with what you have and evolve from there.

Barely three months after my election in October 22, 2000, in January 2001, there was a first attempted coup led against me by the Ouattara's camp. This was called "the coup of the black Mercedes", named after the car droven by IB[32], the former body guard of Ouattara and head of the rebellion. Those who carried out this operation remain close to Alassane Ouattara to this day.

In September 2002, I was on a state visit in Italy when there was another coup d'état. This one ended up dividing the country in two and began the politico-military crisis that lasted ten years.

I remember that we had just passed the law on national health insurance and the attack took place shortly after that. I see a link between this new law and the attack. They wanted to undermine this particular project. If we could have set up two health insurance systems, one for farmers and another for all other workers, the life of all Ivorians would have been transformed. The project for the farmers was easy to finance, with cocoa, coffee, and rubber revenues. For all the other workers, it was more difficult, but we had planned to finance it, by raises taxes on the mining industry, namely gold, diamonds, etc. We had already purchased the building that would have housed the offices of this health insurance scheme.

We had started the process of decentralization, with the creation of city councils that still exist to this day. High schools, clinics and roads have already been built by these councils. But they didn't let us do what we planned to do. With the creation of ten major regions and departments, we were going to raise money for development in each of these regions. As for free schooling, both at primary and secondary levels, we implemented this program immediately. And if the entire country was not able to benefit from these programs, it was because of the war and the country being divided in two.

These kinds of policies scared people in Paris. They realized that Ivory Coast had the means to carry all this out by itself. During the ten

_____

[32] Translator's note: IB is the nickname of Ibrahim Coulibaly. He was killed by the men of Ouattara after the latter took power.

years of my administration, we provided electricity to more villages than had been done in the past forty years. We did not have time to move ahead with what we had planned for solar energy. Our plans for development were cut off before they could really take off.

We were self-sufficient, and we continued to be so after the 2002 attack, even though we only had control of 40% of the country. The salaries of all the state employees were paid, and only twice did we have problems to pay back our debts. Once we owed 100 million to the African Development Bank, and once we had trouble covering our debt to the World Bank. But we made it.

Economically, despite the huge debts left by the previous Bedié's government, we were always self-sufficient, and finally through very careful management, we met the criteria of the HIPC--a program intended for the Heavily Indebted Poor Countries. We were ready to request the annulation of the Ivorian debt, and had already begun the necessary procedures. You have to understand what it means to "cancel a debt." Many French do not have a clue about this and believe it is a "gift" made to Africans. But nobody makes a gift to anyone in this world. The state debts that are announced as "canceled" are, in fact, privatized. This means that the amounts due are ultimately paid to private companies of the creditors' countries to carry out work in the borrowers' countries. This is a golden bonanza for Western business, in particular for French companies. It's clear: the poverty of some makes others rich. That's the system.

On September 18 & 19, 2002, I was on an official visit to Rome. As I arrived, guess who I bumped into at the hotel? Robert Bourgi. Of course, I found this quite an unusual coincidence. And frankly, it could not have been one…We had dinner together.

I met with the president of the Republic of Italy. Then I met with Silvio Berlusconi, who was at that time, the president of the Italian Council. We talked politics and projects. He talked brilliantly about "e-government" and offered his country's assistance in the digitalization of our administrative offices. He told me he had lost a lot of money in France. He walked me to my car, holding my arm, and when we were alone, and he was certain no one could hear, he said to me:

"I really like you. If I can give you some advice, let me say this: beware of Chirac. He is very nice, but he can stab you in the back."

After that, I saw the mayor of Rome, and I was to see the Pope the next day. I returned to my hotel. Around 3 or 4 in the morning, it was 2 AM in Abidjan, I was informed by phone call of a massive military attack launched across the country. I decided to return immediately to Ivory Coast. It's at this moment Robert Bourgi suddenly appears and says with insistence:

"Go first to Paris to see your big brother," meaning Chirac.

Right then, I thought of all the heads of state in Africa who had gone on trips and were never able to return to their countries. I did not go to see the Pope. I did not go to Paris to see Chirac. I headed for Abidjan.

There was a problem with my flight schedule. The pilots had not been informed quickly enough, so I was not able to leave Rome that same day. I returned home September 20, 2002. The Minister of Defense and the Prime Minister were waiting for me at the airport. They were the ones who told me about the death of Emile Boga Doudou, the Minister of the Interior who was assassinated while he was trying to flee from his home, alone and unarmed.

I made a televised address to the nation the very day of my arrival. I called for people to remain unified against the attempted coup. I spoke of our objectives for development. I pointed out that from the time I took office on October 26, 2000, our country had passed from a negative growth rate of -2.3% to -0.9% by the end of 2001. According to the experts, we were on our way to reaching a 5 to 6% growth rate. Our place among international institutions had been restored. I said it was out of the question that someone could come and steal the fruit of our labor. I would not stand for people to threaten the future of the country for the sole benefit of a few. Obviously I condemned the putsches.

Chirac telephoned me and told me off, saying my remarks were too harsh:

"You called them terrorists!"

But I told him, "Wait a minute, *If you wake up in the morning and are told rebels have attacked the capital, what would you say?"*

He told me: *"You must negotiate with them."*

I suspected that the rebels had been trained at the military camp at Po, in Burkina Faso. Rumors had been circulating to this effect. But the day that I had talked about it to Villepin (the then-French Minister of Foreign Affairs) some time before the coup, he replied:

"*Blaise* (Compaoré, then president of Burkina Faso) *would never do that!*"

The coup failed, leaving hundreds of dead. But the rebels were able to occupy more than half of the country. France sent a peacekeeping force which established a "zone of confidence." I decreed a general amnesty law. It was a message of peace.

Chapter 8
"It was a coup d'etat in white gloves"

The stage had been set. Heavily armed rebels invaded the country from the North, killing untold thousands as they moved south to occupy almost two-thirds of the country. Shortly thereafter, in January 2003, a round table was organized by the French at the now famous Marcoussis, headed by Dominique de Villepin, then Minister of Foreign Affairs under Jacques Chirac. Rebel representatives were invited to the table, but Laurent Gbagbo was not. He first thought it was a French strategy to stamp out the rebellion. He was wrong. In fact, the plan of Villepin was to reduce Gbagbo's presidency to a ceremonial position and to put in power leaders who would be more favorable to French interests... Faced with the travesty of these supposed "peace talks," Mamadou Koulibaly, president of the Ivorian National Assembly walked out of the talks. Looking back on the scene, Laurent Gbagbo describes it as "a coup by gentlemen in white gloves."

This chapter reveals some of the incredible pressure put on Gbagbo by the French government and the behind the scenes manipulations carried out to get rid of him. This was not unusual: France has been intervening, to not say "calling the shots" in African politics for decades. Benedikt Erforth and George Deffner note: "France has a long history of military interventions in sub-Saharan Africa, which traditionally have served the safeguarding or installation of governments friendly to France, the protection of French economic interests, or boosted France's role in the world. In the period from 1960 to 2005, there have reportedly been 46 French military operations in Francophone Africa. France, thanks heavily to Africa, has been able to maintain its status as an important player on the international scene. And although the old neo-colonial Françafrique system may be dead or dying, French foreign policy remains very much alive when it comes to Africa."

Footnote at note: *http://thinkafricapress.com/mali/old-wine-new-bottles-justifying-france-military-intervention, March 18, 2013.*

Dominique Galouzeau, better known as Dominique de Villepin, Minister of Foreign Affairs of the Chirac government, put in place the France Linas-Marcoussis Round Table of January 2003. This conference was presented to the world as a French initiative whose goal was to re-establish peace in Ivory Coast, to carry out disarmament, and to set up a collation government with the rebels. I was not invited! Understand me well: the head of State of Ivory Coast was not invited to participate in talks on the future of that country! I was only summoned to the meetings at Avenue Kleber, which were to follow those at Marcoussis and where agreements of the round table were to be signed. I did not participate at the round table, I was not allowed to utter one word there, but I was asked to come to sign the agreements... These meetings were the great undertaking of Villepin, a man who always seemed so sure of himself! Around the table of negotiations were all the Ivorian political parties, some of which emerged from the rebel forces. Thus the rebels were acknowledged by the French authorities as valid participants, at the same level as parliamentary and democratic parties of the country. At first, I thought France just wanted to use this forum to stamp out the rebellion. I was wrong.

I have always been a person of dialogue, talking to everyone... In order to find a way out of the crisis, talks were held in Lomé, Togo, in Accra, Ghana, in Pretoria, South Africa on three occasions, in Marcoussis, France, then in Ouagadougou, Burkina Faso... This is without mentioning all the meetings held in Abidjan: the Reconciliation Forum in 2001, the local elections I organized despite all the obstacles, and all the informal contacts made trying to negotiate and find a peaceful resolution to the crisis.

I am a historian. And I can tell you I have never seen one case in history of a "dictator" negotiating with his enemies, and even making so many concessions.

Even within my own camp, some have never quite understood why, after the war that was waged against us in 2002, I pushed so much for dialogue... Is that the mark of a dictator?

Well, in Linas-Marcoussis, France "presents" me with the armed opposition, an opposition which they themselves put in place, and they ask me to govern with them. Then Dominique de Villepin and Pierre Mazeaud even tried to name rebels as Ministers of the Interior and Defense! It didn't seem to matter that the rebellion had just carried out a military putsch against an elected president and killed hundreds of Ivorians! In fact, they had not even won the war, but France was trying to put them in the driver's seat, at the same level as the legitimate powers... Villepin called this *"diplomacy of movement."* Me, I saw it rather as a coup d'etat carried out by gentlemen wearing white gloves.

This leveling of responsibilities in the Ivorian conflict at the 2003 Linas-Marcoussis Round Table, putting the aggressors and the aggressed on equal footing, along with keeping Laurent Gbagbo, the president in office, away from the talks was the beginning of France's official method of handling the situation. As Mamadou Koulibaly stated in his book, *The War France waged against Ivory Coast*[33]:

> *"After the coup (of September 2002) failed, and the coup was transformed into a rebellion organized and supported by France, it became clear that everyone needed to admit there could be no military solutions. Having itself failed, France would not allow the Ivorian state to counter-attack the coup. It rather obligated Ivory Coast to negotiate with the rebels... [...] I still remember the scene, where [Pierre] Mazeaud, from his high perch, with his arms open in a rallying gesture, proclaimed loud and clear that there were no rebels in Ivory Coast and neither were there any rebels around the table at Marcoussis. From that moment on, anything was possible since no one had been aggressed; there were no victims and therefore no guilty parties..."*

Mamadou Koulibaly, the then-president of the Ivorian National Assembly, was so shocked at what he saw—the future of the country being taken hostage, the sovereignty of his country being denied--, that he got up and slammed the door in their faces and returned to Ivory Coast.

But the historical 'turn about' was already well underway. When those behind the coup d'état realized its "military software" wasn't working any more, they decided to shift into "political mode." They moved the cursor to the same place Gbagbo had his: organizing a presidential election. It was a convergence of minds, operating at very high risk.

The round table at Marcoussis thus took place without me. They brought together a majority of opposition parties and rebellion groups (they were seven) and a minority (only two) representing the government,

---

[33] Mamadou Koulibaly, *La guerre de la France contre la Côte d'Ivoire* (The War France Wagged against Ivory Coast). Paris, L'Harmattan, 2003.

with my Prime Minister, Pascal Affi N'Guessan for the FPI. I hesitated before deciding to go to the meetings at Avenue Kleber. People around me argued a lot about it. Some were in favor, telling me I shouldn't leave my 'seat empty,' while others wanted me to refuse to go, saying it would mean entering a long tunnel with no exit. It was true that it looked like a trap. But finally, I decided to go to the meeting at Avenue Kleber, just to be able to see, to listen and to keep a hand on things. I could not let the situation evolve out of control. Very quickly, I realized that it would not be easy. I arrived [there in Paris] on January 23, 2003 by a regular commercial Air France flight, because I was afraid my presidential carrier might be shot down. At that point anything was possible. I was to see Chirac the next day at 4 PM at the Elysée.

The morning of this famous encounter, a Friday, I found, slipped under the door of my room at the Meurice Hotel, the text of the Marcoussis Agreements. Bongo [the then-president of Gabon] was staying at the same hotel, obviously there to try to convince me to accept their proposal. Bongo was a friend of Ouattara and since the death of Houphouët, France's most faithful friend. At 11 AM, I left for the Elysée. In the car taking me there was a copy of that day's Le Monde, and on page 2, I read the name of the new Ivorian Prime Minister, Henriette Diabaté, a close ally of Ouattara and a member of his party, the RDR.

At the Elysée, as the three of us met together, Chirac, Galouzeau, and myself, Chirac told me he wanted Henriette Diabaté to become Prime Minister…Well, thanks, I had already read that in the morning newspaper…This is exactly what Françafrique is all about. I refused to sign. Chirac asked me why. I explained that for Ivorians, this would be perceived as a reward to the rebels. It was well known Ouattara was the author and organizer of the September 2002 attack against Ivory Coast. Chirac admitted this.

So I asked them to find another name. I also proposed several names. Chirac asked Villepin to take into account the proposals that I would be making in the follow-up meeting. Galouzeau told me we would get together again at 7 PM at the Quai d'Orsay [office of the French Prime Minister]. He told me: *You will be received at the main entrance and will be welcomed with all the honor due to your rank."*

At 7 PM, when I entered the meeting room, Ouattara and Bédié were already there, seated. Soro wasn't there. Villepin called him on the phone. When he finally arrived, he came through the main entrance escorted by ushers, like the other two before me. Thus Villepin made it very clear how little respect he had for me and for my role as president of my country.

Villepin, Soro and Ouattara joined in together the singing the same song, They wanted Henriette Diabaté [as Prime Minister]. They were like a choir which had rehearsed its piece. I said to Villepin: *"You don't even listen to your own president?"* Villepin seemed to think he was Jacques Foccart or even Jacques Chirac, and I wondered whether or not he considered himself superior to both of them—this important Dominique de Villepin. He was also looking for revenge for the tumultuous welcome he had received while visiting Abidjan a few weeks earlier. A few hundred Ivorians tried to stop him from reaching the French Ambassador's residence, adjacent to the Ivorian presidential mansion, where I had just welcomed him. His overt friendliness towards the rebels, his handshake with Guillaume Soro, their leader on his visit to Bouaké in rebels' territory on January 4, 2003, enraged Ivorians in Abidjan, still traumatized by the previous attempted coup of September 19, 2002.

France has never been a simple arbitrator in Africa. It has always found all kinds of reasons to remain an actor with a strong directing role in the internal lives of the countries it controls. Guy Labertit writes[34]:

"...France, officially supportive of the rule of law, actually legitimized an armed rebellion supported by neighboring countries, and humiliated an elected president, Laurent Gbagbo, for whom the city of Bouaké and half of his country became forbidden territory."

Villepin told me if I did not accept Henriette Diabaté [as Prime Minister] he would give the Ministeries of the Interior and Defense to the rebels. I refused everything he proposed and deeply angered, I left the Quai d'Orsay.

In exiting this extremely difficult meeting where the alliance of Ouattara, Villepin, Bédié and the three rebel groups stared him in the face, Gbagbo remembers having shouted to his friend Guy Labertit: *"The headquarters of the rebellion is the Quai d'Orsay!"*

---

[34] Guy Labertit, *Adieu, Abidjan-sur-Seine! Les coulisses du conflit ivoirien* (France's Farewell to Abidjan-on-the-Seine River: the behind the scenes negotiations of the Ivorian conflict), Autres Temps Editions, 2008.

We had a formal meeting on Saturday, January 25, at the Conference Center on Avenue Kleber, and before the meeting, I was granted a meeting with a restricted committee made up of President Omar Bongo, the UN Secretary [General], Kofi Annan, Villepin and myself. We talked about the problem of Prime Minister which was still an outstanding issue. We agreed on the choice of Seydou Diarra, the former Prime Minister under Robert Guéi, who along with Pierre Mazeau was the master of ceremonies at the Marcoussis Round Table. Villepin was very insistent. I know he was talking about me when he said: *"You've got to twist his arm."*

Then we went about dividing up the Ministeries with a goal to forming a government of coalition.

It was that night, Saturday night, that Guillaume Soro set fire to the whole city of Abidjan by declaring on French public radio that the rebels had obtained the Ministries of the Interior and Defense. Soro was just trying to make people forget that he had not succeeded in obtaining what he wanted. It was his way of crying "victory" and at the same time stirring up trouble, because he knew that without a doubt, Ivorians would not stand for the French favoring the rebels in this way. The idea was that these troubles in the streets would be ascribed to me, or against me, by those who would think I had betrayed them.

In fact, this solution was not presented at Marcoussis. All they wanted, in fact, was to turn me into the "Queen of England," so that I would no longer play any real political role in Ivory Coast. They wanted to undermine the Ivorian Constitution and my status; that was what Chirac was really looking for; and that was my main criticism of him. I would not acknowledge his right to weaken the Ivorian state. As for Villepin, he simply wanted me out of the way.

During the same year of 2003, Jacques Chirac paid little attention to problems of "orthodoxy" in the realm of democracy in neighboring countries [in Africa]. He congratulated General Eyadema even before his umpteenth re-election was made public. Needless to say the regularity of his re-election was shrouded in doubt. Eyedema had, in fact, come to power in 1967 through two successive coups d'etat: the first against Sylvanus Olympio, whom he and his accomplices eventually assassinated in January, 1963, and then against his friend Nicolas Grunitzky, whom he overthrew in June 1967. By 2003, Eyadema had held on to his dictatorial powers for a full thirty-six years, all due to the massive support of France for whom he played the role of "policeman" throughout the region. When he died in 2005, Jacques Chirac was filled with compassion and spoke of having *"lost of a personal friend."*

Chapter 9
"These people have no shame"

This is Gbagbo's reaction to the media campaign against him, which is epitomized in Jean-Christophe Notin's book, The Crocodile and the Scorpion. The author who admits to very little knowledge of and minimal interest in the Ivorian crisis, turns the bombing of the presidential residence and the brutal capture of Gbagbo, his wife Simone, and his son Michel into a veritable soap, complete with an inventory of what was purportedly found on the scene. It is a vulgar attempt to belittle a modest-living intellectual family: Gbagbo himself, a historian and university professor, his wife a strong Christian believer and politican in her own right (she was a representative in the Ivorian National Assembly till the fall of the Gbagbo government). As Gbagbo comments here, "these people know no shame." Throughout this chapter, Mattei gives us a view into different parts of Notin's "unofficial" book, which is essentially filled with lies.

Footnote to a note: In 2007, Simone Ehivet Gbagbo published a 511-page book, *Paroles d'Honneur* (Words of Honor), in which she gives her own account of her country's history, from the time she was a teenager until the time she became First Lady.

Jean-Christophe Notin, author of *The Crocodile and the Scorpion*[35] and an "unofficial official" of Sarkosy's military campaign in Cocody, claims that Dominique de Villepin boasted about his achievements:

> "I really pulled off a good one, a real stroke of genius: giving the Ministry of Defense and the Ministry of the Interior to the rebels. They will be obliged to disarm themselves."

---

[35] Jean-Christophe Notin, *Le Crocodile et Scorpion: La France et la Côte d'Ivoire--1999-2013. (The Crocodile and the Scorpion : France and Ivory Coast--1999-2013)*, Editions du Rocher, 2013.

Isn't this a show of pure contempt for Ivorian institutions? Isn't it, in fact, a complete refusal to acknowledge the existence of a government elected by the people of Ivory Coast? Notin sees Villepin's "coup" as a sign of progress. But in claiming that Villepin's maneuverings were acceptable, due to his good intentions, forcing the rebels to disarm, Notin seems to be rewriting history. In fact, it boils down to *a posteriori* justification of France's unjustified manoeuverings towards a president of a sovereign nation. Known as a historian of military affairs, Notin suddenly becomes the Elysée's specialist on the Ivorian crisis. He was encouraged to look into the Ivorian dossier, when, according to his own admission, he had no knowledge and no particular interest in the Ivorian conflict. Yet, his book provides an answer on every issue. He was provided with dossiers from high up, dossiers concocted by government and French military authorities of that time. In this regard, his acknowledgements in his book are enlightening. There they all are, like so many ghost co-signators, all Nicolas Sarkozy's top advisers: from Claude Guéant to Jean-David Levitte, his diplomatic adviser, to André Parant, the adviser for African Affairs. There is also General Benoît Puga, the chief of staff to the president of the Republic and all the members of the Quai d'Orsay, of the Public Treasury, of the Army, etc. (all those who participated in the anti-Gbagbo offensive). Signed with the tip of a sword, there is an "'S' for Sarkozy" appearing behind the name of the author. The French state was totally mobilized, as it was for the "Great War." In the throes of this epic story, a Licorne officer even dares to compare the courage of his soldiers at the moment of the assault on Gbagbo's residence to the courage of the French soldiers in 1914! This is an incongruous allusion, and an insult to the million and half French men and women who died during the First World War, celebrated one hundred years later in 2014.

In 2010, all the French heroes returned safe and sound from their assault on Abidjan. At the end of the operation, one of the officers boasts: "[We had] zero deaths." Well calculated, with details worked out down to the millimeter, this saga of the Ivorian crisis was clearly conceived in high places, with the perspective of a presidential victory for Nicolas Sarkozy in the election of 2012. This was, again, an *a posteriori* justification of the French intervention, especially the military intervention. The close relationships woven by French civil and military personnel with the new owners of Abidjan were brought to the forefront, with all put in place to protect them from eventual judicial accusations. But it was especially the first real attempt to build up a global narrative intended to set the scene for the accusations to be leveled against

President Gbagbo in The Hague. *The Crocodile and the Scorpion*, the book authored by Jean-Christophe Notin, is all these things put together.

In the past, Abidjan deserved the nickname, "Little Paris." The city spread from Mitterrand Boulevard to Charles-de-Gaulle Bridge, from Boulevard Valery-Giscard-d'Estaing to Boulevard Angoulvant[36], arriving at suburb of Port-Bouët (the Commander Bouët-Villaumez was sent by the king of France in 1837 to negotiate agreements with the local authorities). The topology of the capital is loaded with French names. They are everywhere, particularly in *Zone 4*. It is understandable that a French person feels at home in that city. During his ten years as president, Laurent Gbagbo never renamed a single street, locality or bridge. He put no African name in place of a French one, as so many have done since the years of Independence. Mentioning that fact in his book would have softened the anti-French attitude Notin chooses purposely to lend to Gbagbo, where he stigmatizes him and sets him up to be the object of hate.

On the other hand, Notin's book is filled with huge "revelations." Concerning Mamadou Koulibaly, Notin says that at Marcoussis, he tried to bribe various participants. Those who know and appreciate the former president of the Ivorian National Assembly, even along with those who hate him, including some in the entourage of Laurent Gbagbo, just burst out laughing when they hear this. If there is a flaw that the former number two of Gbagbo's government cannot be accused of, it would be any propensity for mafia-style *combinazione*. Koulibaly has no taste whatsoever for that. The Mamadou Koulibaly that François Mattei [and everyone else] knows avoids compromise; he is unwilling to run the risk of committing any moral fault. Koulibaly's intransigence in regard to the fundamental values of the Republic, considered by some of his opponents as not very politically savvy, has often been criticized.

The Prosecutor at The Hague, Fatou Bensouda, will certainly have not missed reading Notin's book. In its pages, she can even see herself in wild highs and lows of the Ivorian tragedy. Jean-Christophe Notin does everything he can to make Gbagbo look like a dictator, but he is just grasping at straws. The truth is he interviewed no one who could have given a different version of the facts than the one conveyed by French officials and their media. Since Gbagbo's arrest, research has shown that Notin's version of the facts simply doesn't hold up, especially in the testimony brought to light by the Ivorian

---

[36] Translator's footnote: Gabriel Louis Angoulvant was a French colonial administrator who was instrumental in the 1908-1910 pacification of Ivory Coast who already had become a French colony as of March 10, 1893.

president's Defense, headed by the international lawyer Emmanuel Altit before the International Criminal Court in The Hague. To make his point of view credible, Notin spares no detail, evoking secret political meetings, declarations by French officials and even details of troop deployments. All of his rhetoric is based on huge amounts of detail regarding various events which took place from 1993 to 2011 in Ivory Coast. How can anyone doubt a text full of precise details: names and surnames of the lowest officer involved in various operations, detailed topographic descriptions, the precise identification of equipment used and the timetable, down to the minute and hour when the various events occurred? This multitude of information is cleverly scattered throughout the book in an attempt to legitimize French activity on the ground, to respond point by point to all possible objections, and first and foremost, to discredit Laurent Gbagbo once and for all.

Painting his own picture of Gbagbo, Notin throws aside his keyboard and picks up a spray gun:

> "Like Charlie Chaplin, in the film The Dictator, sitting and playing with a globe, the Ivorian president manipulates his so called patriotic "galaxies": bunches of unemployed young people... His anti-colonialist rhetoric makes them forget their misery."

But sometimes Notin's own rhetoric reveals tiny cracks which allows the truth to suddenly appear, as when he quotes France's ambassador in Abidjan, Renaud Vignal, who served in 2001-2002, as saying in a written report:

> "In Gbagbo, we have one of the best heads of state this country could possibly have."

Try and figure that one out! As for Laurent Gbagbo, he remembers well the day that French Ambassador "turned his coat" [--as they say in French].

In 2000, once the socialist presidential candidate Lionel Jospin lost the election, and Chirac won, followed by his transferring the Ivorian dossier to Dominique de Villepin, everything changed. Renaud Vignal never again had the same attitude towards me.

As if writing for People magazine, Notin makes spicy disclosures. After the arrest of President Gbagbo, he writes:

82

"[...] some French people went to scavage among the ruins of Gbagbo's home. They of course discovered the classic marks of all despots: cigars, great wines, hundreds of pairs of shoes and suits, but also a large stock of viagara for 'Monsieur' along with brown heroin for 'Madame.'"

Simone Gbagbo has been so discredited by the French media that there is, to this day, no limit of decorum, even if Notin has the decency to put in a footnote that he does not know if the heroin was "for her personal use or that of her entourage." Simone Gbagbo, who was at times described as a religious fanatic, and at other times as a witch leading *"death squads,"* is now presented as a drug addict, or even better, a dealer. Anyone who has ever been around Simone Gbagbo, friend or foe, knows that these facts are simply ridiculous. If the facts about the drugs were true, how is possible that all the people watching her every move for the past ten years could have missed this? —especially since the Gbagbo circle was infiltrated from all sides.

As far as the head of state's wine cellar is concerned, it contained no more and no less wine and cigars than any of his fellow heads of state keep for various receptions and ceremonies. Gbagbo comments with a smile:

I stopped smoking a very long time ago. Yes, there was wine, champagne and cigars for our receptions. Certainly there was a hundred times less, maybe even a thousand times less than there is right now at the Elysée. As for the cigars, most of the time, they were gifts from visitors. And so I would offer them to other visitors who were fond of cigars. As far as I'm concerned, I know what this attack is about. But for alcohol, go see Ouattara who is fond of scotch. Go see Bédié who prefers cognac... As for the Viagra and heroin, this comes right from the top French political circles during Nicolas Sarkozy's term... Do these people have no shame? To see them in action in Africa only shows what they are capable of... It's when they are in our countries, that they show their true selves. What they should have said, what is really the truth concerning my possessions, is that I probably had the best private library in all of Africa, filled with French classics. They destroyed it all with their bombs.

Notin sets out to demonstrate the legitimacy and the efficiency of the military campaign of France's supreme chief Nicolas Sarkozy, but it also reveals that a French DGSE[37] officer was made available to Alassane Ouattara as a speech writer during the crisis. These speeches were broadcast by satellite TV installed and paid for entirely by Paris. The bill at the Golf Hotel, where Ouattara, Soro, their government, and a few hundred armed men were housed for more than five months was paid by France as well--board and room and transport provided by French and UN helicopters. Jean-Christophe Notin, so exact and covering so fully all these events perhaps even knows the sum total of the military's bill. In this period of financial crisis in France, the budgetary aspect of this expedition would be of interest to many French nationals and would reveal what price Nicolas Sarkozy was willing to pay for the victory of his friend Alassane Ouattara in Ivory Coast. It surely cost a lot more than a simple recount of votes would have cost. This detail is nowhere to be found in the huge 441 page volume by Jean-Christophe Notin. But we know that Jean-Michel Fourgous, then Defense budget "rapporteur" at the French National Assembly, gave the official figure of 65 million euros as the cost of the French military intervention in Ivory Coast. The annual cost of the French military presence in Ivory Coast, in 2010, was estimated by some[38] at 150 million euros and by others at 200 million euros. Unfortunately, Jean-Christophe Notin remains discrete on the amount and the details of the bill of the intervention of the French military special services.

Finally, Notin's narrative of a phone conversation from the Elysée office of Claude Guéant [Sarkozy's General Secretary] between Laurent Gbagbo and Robert Bourgi is simply baffling. The lawyer and Franco-African go-between, Robert Bourgi, has since confirmed that this phone conversation did indeed take place. But contrary to what Notin reports, Bourgi did not say that Laurent Gbagbo had used a menacing tone or had made threatening remarks. Perhaps, to make credible his un-nuanced portrait of Laurent Gbagbo, Notin attributes these words to him:

> *"Tell Sarkozy that I will be his Mugabe! I will never let Ivory Coast into the hands of Ouattara. I would rather see it* [the country] *covered in blood!"*

So after the liquor and the drugs, Notin's narrative moves on to the *"bloodbaths."* I met Robert Bourgi, the influential intermediary between France

---

[37] Translator's note: This DGSE which spells out as *Direction générale de la sécurité extérieure* is the French "General Directorate for Security Abroad."

[38] *Le Monde diplomatique*, April 15, 2011.

and "its" Africa. He received me in his Parisian office on *Rue Pierre-1ᵉʳ-de-Serbie* on November 29, 2012. Amidst Napoleonic relics that make his office look like an imperial museum, and surrounded by framed pictures of Omar Bongo, de Gaulle, and a photograph of himself with a white shirted Gbagbo, and with drawings of his daughter Clarence, god-daughter of Laurent Gbagbo, Bourgi told me about this famous phone conversation.

In early December 2010, at the request of Nicolas Sarkozy, Bourgi called Laurent Gbagbo. Like a perfect actor, Bourgi reproduced the dialogue he had for few seconds with Gbagbo, which was on loud speaker at the Elysée while he was with the president of the French Republic and his General Secretary, Claude Guéant.

> "*Laurent, I beg you, give up your* [presidential] *seat. Five years can go by very quickly. You can run again and you will easily win. Meanwhile, you can enjoy the status of a chief of state and you can have a professorial chair. You can travel between Paris and Abidjan and around the world, anywhere you want. Listen to me. You know, we're the same age!*"

Laurent Gbagbo replied with a laugh '*No, you're one month older than I am.*'

Bourgi says: I argued the best I could, I pleaded. But he [Gbagbo] old me he would not budge. In the end, he hung up on me and I broke down and wept. President Sarkozy walked me to the stairs and I told him, '*Nicolas, you cannot do this, you cannot.*' '*If Bongo were still alive, you wouldn't dare do this!*' I added with a tone filled with meaning. Nicolas looked at me and said as I left, '*It's over, Robert, and I will not change any part of what is already happening.*"

According to this testimony of Bourgi, Nicolas Sarkozy had already made up his mind about the Ivorian dossier, and he had probably already decided on the military intervention at the beginning of December 2010. This is the same analysis of an Ivorian politician from Abidjan, who often came to Paris, who chose to remain anonymous:

> "*My friends at the Quai d'Orsay clearly told me at the end of November 2010, that the goals of the Elysée were to chase Gbagbo from power. The elections were only a pretext. The army chief of staff*

and the whole French machine were already preparing the demise of Laurent Gbagbo."

I told Laurent Gbagbo what Robert Bourgi had said to me. He shrugged his shoulders and said: **When I am now asked if I know Bourgi, I always say I only know one: Albert.** This Albert, a political science professor is the brother of Robert Bourgi. Albert Bourgi has always unselfishly supported Laurent Gbagbo. Obviously, Robert, the other Bourgi, no longer inspires much confidence in Gbagbo who looked sulky when I mentioned Robert Bourgi's name. He then waved his hand in the air, as if to say, "let us just forget the whole thing."

The version of Jean-Christophe Notin makes no sense. Laurent Gbagbo, at the most difficult times in his life, even as they bombed his home, even in prison, has never threatened anyone. Indeed, he has not even been impolite. Robert Bourgi knows better than anyone that his brother Albert, a university professor in Reims, would never have maintained a thirty-year friendship, as close as brothers, if this weren't the case.

Concluding this set of lies which hit like mortar fire is Mr. Notin's account of the death of Désiré Tagro, which leaves its mark. The author has given new meaning to the expression "flail a dead horse." Laurent Gbagbo's former Minister of the Interior was assassinated, his jaw blown to bits at point blank range, while carrying a white flag, trying to give himself up to the rebels. Losing blood, he was taken to the Golf Hotel where he was pronounced dead. For Notin this event is like an incident occurring at a neighborhood police station: *"Having been beat up, he [Tagro] died the next day from his wounds."* What a delicate euphemism! Tagro had, in fact, received assurances from the French Special Forces [of fair treatment], the same forces that besieged and bombed the presidential residence. This man was shot down as French soldiers looked on.

Two things let us know Notin is not completely insensitive. I asked him if he saw the picture of Simone Gbagbo at the time of her arrest, kneeling before her captors, held down like an animal, as soldiers pose for a photo, as hunters pose with their prey. He told me that he saw those pictures, and others as well, that were shown to him, which were worse and that prove that Simone Gbagbo, along with many others, underwent unspeakable violence at the hands of the rebels. The cameras of the French army filmed everything that happened before, during, and after the attack on the residence of President Gbagbo. Did Notin see the photos of Tagro's dead body? Did he see the pictures of all those who were captured in the Ivorian president's residence and who were assassinated in the hours that followed? To be honest, we must add in passing, some civilians who were going to be executed were saved by French soldiers.

Chapter 10
"The fault was on the French side, not on ours"

In 2004, French-Ivorian relations took a terrible turn for the worse. While the national reconciliation was underway, the rebels were still in control of 60% of the territory and through extortion and other forms of brutality rendered the life of the people in the north unbearable. Meanwhile French forces were everywhere on the ground, refusing to help the government forces and, we now know, secretly helping the rebels. Gbagbo had a plan to attack the rebels from the air and put an end to suffering of the peoples in the north. Though--or perhaps because--he kept the French authorities aware of his plan, the plan backfired. On November 6, 2004, it was reported that nine French soldiers and one American in Bouaké had been killed. The French immediately riposted by destroying Ivory Coast's entire air fleet.

Gbagbo's analysis that "the error was on the side of the French" is perhaps too kind. The French forces helped the Eastern European pilots flee across the border, and when the Togolese finally captured them, the French government turned down their offer to extradite them. Mystery still surrounds this incident though the French families of the young soldiers who died that day are taking the French government to court to try to uncover the facts.

After the attempted coup of 2001, I asked the Ambassador of France, Francis Lott, to send us some French technicians, because we had problems maintaining our military equipment. The Ivorian army was small. We only had a few soldiers and we were not very well equipped. There was no need to have a large army since the French were supposed to come to our aid, as needed. For example, we only had a few airplanes. And they could barely take off: their engines always getting jammed. Two officers of the French Air Force arrived at our Bouaké air base. They inspected our aircraft and started laughing. Every engine had frozen up. So we tried to order parts, but to my great surprise, the French suppliers--we had French planes--refused to sell us these parts. It was clear: the goal of the French authorities was to render our police force and our army inoperable, with no arms to fight the rebels who had surfaced several times already and certainly, would attack again. Not only did the French authorities refuse to honor their defense agreements which were to protect Ivory Coast from the repeated rebel attacks, as they regrouped and rearmed in Burkina Faso, they did everything they could to prevent the Ivorian officials of law and order from carrying out their duty: protecting the Ivorian population from criminals.

I couldn't leave the country at the mercy of highway bandits. You have to understand, these first rebel groups were like those large associations that devastated Europe in the sixteenth century. Later on, particularly in 2010, mercenaries were recruited in mass and trained in Burkina Faso by foreign advisers using high tech equipment, and these troops moved down into northern Ivory Coast. In 2011, these mercenary troops were let loose, invading the south, with the French helping and even directing.

To come back to the beginning of the rebellion, when the Ivorian Minister of Defense was offered some equipment from Eastern Europe and he accepted it, to prevent Ivory Coast from being completely unarmed, needless to say, the French turned this the wrong way.

But by 2004, the situation had changed. The reconciliation process was underway. The central government was acknowledged as legitimate by all parties including some former rebels. In the north of the country, still occupied by the rebels, the population was facing more and more hardship. They were victims of racketing, extortion, and illegal detentions. Time and time again, they asked for help from the Ivorian government.

We thought it was high time to put an end to these crimes and in the process, try to reunify the country. Thus our Army Chief of Staff prepared a targeted military operation. Getting wind of this, the rebels fled back to Burkina Faso. The goal of this military operation was to destroy the arms that the rebels had amassed in Bouaké, in the central part of the country. I repeat, I had done my part by integrating the former rebels into my government, while they never abided by their commitment, which was to disarm. On the contrary, these rebels got rich through arms trafficking, and they were totally unwilling to give up this activity. If only the rebels had kept their promise, the country would have been reunified and all the armed groups would have dissolved. So our plan of action was justified on two counts. On the one hand, we needed to re-establish order throughout the country and, on the other, we needed to prevent illegal armed groups from carrying out criminal acts.

On November 6, 2004, I was informed that nine French soldiers were killed in Bouaké, supposedly by a bombing carried out by our two aircraft. We were stupefied. We later figured out that this was part of a plot to overthrow the legitimate government and to oust me from power. For a very long time, no one wanted to believe our version of the story. Today, the truth is starting to come out, thanks to some of the families of those killed and also thanks to some French officers who have spoken out.

It is important for everyone to know what happened. Since 2010, I haven't spoken about this incident. I lived through this terrible situation, all the while knowing that I did not have access to all the details. I was on good terms with Gildas Le Lidec, the then-Ambassador of France in Abidjan and he too was taken aback by the turn of events.

Contrary to all that has been said or written, including quotes of things I never said, I can tell you today that I was not opposed to a military operation which was to destroy the rebels' infrastructures in Bouaké. This would have led to the reunification and pacification of the country. A few times prior to this, I had to stop some officers from launching an offensive on Bouaké without clearance from their chain of command. The soldiers had arrived near Bouaké, a town located roughly in the center of the country on the median line between the north and the south, and they wanted to attack the rebels. I immediately got into a helicopter and went to talk to these soldiers, to tell them that no decision to attack had been made, and they should retreat. Their attempt showed how much the Ivorian army and the Ivorian population wanted the rebel atrocities to stop.

I was aware that my Chief of Staff, Mathias Doué, was very close to the French military, in particular to French General Poncet. Doué had been trained at the French military school of Saint-Cyr, near Paris. I was aware that Doué was reluctant to go along with the planned military operation in Bouaké. He never told me this, but I heard that this is what he was telling other people. But with me, he was not very forthcoming, and I didn't know what he had in mind.

I called the French Ambassador and told him that the situation in the northern part of Ivory Coast was unbearable for the populations there. The atrocities of the rebels had intensified. They acted like the country was theirs; they would not obey the laws or respect their written agreements. I made the Ambassador understand that we had no choice but to launch a targeted military operation. The Ambassador and I trusted each other and were close enough for me to assume that he was not opposed to such a preventive military action.

Two days later, it was on Tuesday, November 2, I believe, that I received him and General Poncet in my office. Poncet told me not to go ahead with the operation, warning me against launching the attack. While Poncet was speaking, the Ambassador turned his head, smoking his cigarette, seemingly distracted. I listened to what the general had to say, but I ended up replying:

> *"I did not ask you to come here to ask your opinion but to inform you about what I have decided to do. France is a friendly country that has troops in the field. The goal of this operation is to destroy the rebel military infrastructures in Bouaké."*

On Wednesday November 3, my phone rang. It was Chirac yelling at me:

- *"Seydou Diarra* (The Prime Minister I appointed following Marcoussis to head up the government of national union which included some rebels) *was not informed! This is incredible!"*
- I responded:
- *"Seydou Diarra was never even elected as a municipal council member. I am the head of a republican state which functions according to the laws of the Republic and the laws of the Constitution. The laws of the Republic must be enforced and the rebels must stop their atrocities. Remember, they had promised to disarm."*

On Thursday November 4, we launched the operation which was supposed to last two days. At the end of the first day, the ONUCI announced officially that the intervention had been carried out in a very professional way, and that there was no collateral damage. We had of course meticulously identified all the installations of the rebels. There was no margin for error and more than anything, I wanted this operation to be a success.

Our targeted objectives were reached, and I told people I would be making a televised statement to inform Ivorians that the combats had come to an end, that our soldiers were in Bouaké where they would reach out to our enemies, to negotiate an end to all the hostilities and envisage projects for the future. This was the political "translation" of the military operation.

On Saturday November 6, while I was in my office drafting the text of my public statement, Doué came to see me and said:

"Our aircraft dropped bombs on some French soldiers. There is one dead."

I asked him to bring me back a full report on what happened. I never got that report.

Barely one hour later, I was informed that our two Sukhoi aircraft in Yamossoukro had been destroyed by the French forces. At the same time in Abidjan, French soldiers took axes and began destroying all our helicopters and small aircraft on the tarmac at the Ivorian international airport. At the end of the day we had no engine that could fly.

The Ambassadors of France and the U.S. came to see me. They informed me that there were nine deaths among French soldiers and one American. The U.S. Ambassador did not say one word to me except for "hello" and "good bye." Le Lidec was the one who informed me about what happened and I was devastated. I immediately asked our Minister of Defense to suspend the army chief of staff so an investigation could be carried out. I summoned some ministers and the military prosecutor and asked them to do all they could to shed light on these tragic events. I insisted that the military prosecutor carry out his investigation in the field at Bouaké. But the French General Henri Poncet prevented the Ivorian military magistrate to access the French barracks at Camp Descartes in Bouaké where the bombing took place. He opposed our investigation. As far as I know, till today, there has never been any investigation by the French.

As for the Americans, I heard almost nothing from them about this incident. A woman came to see my Minister of Finance, but the Americans didn't even bother to send me a memo concerning their citizen who was killed. For the first time in the history of Ivory Coast, we were not able to honor French soldiers killed on our land before their caskets were transported to France.

Having hardly been informed of these distressing events, I was told that a column of French armored tanks had left the center of the country and was nearing Abidjan. In the middle of the night, this group of tanks surrounded the presidential residence, where I was. The rumor was circulating that Doué was inside of one of the vehicles in the French armored column. Afterward, Doué disappeared to only reappear after my ousting, when Ouattara acceded to the post of president. We were expecting the worst. We called the Elysée to sound out what their intentions were and to warn them against any ill-considered attack. We also informed the various other foreign diplomatic missions in Abidjan. Maybe this is what saved us. After a while the French troops retreated from the presidential residence, just a few hundred meters away to Hotel Ivoire. Explaining later their presence at the presidential residence, the French said *"They had taken the wrong road."*

For anyone who knows the layout of the city of Abidjan, it is impossible to believe their version. They obviously were coming to either run me out or have me killed, so they could replace me. Their plan was to put Doué in my place "en interim," but Doué backed out. For that one reason their plan failed.

The destruction of our entire air fleet and the threat of attack against the residence of the president caused the Ivorians to take to the streets in anger[39]. They protested against the presence of the French military, the Licorne force. There were a lot of reactions, and even looting against French property. There are always thieves and looters ready to make the most of such situations. It was equally true that the tension and frustration were at their zenith. The French army fired on the crowds crossing the Charles-de-Gaulle Bridge as they headed on foot towards the French barracks of the 43rd BIMA to demand their departure. French soldiers fired on the crowd from their helicopters, causing dozens of deaths, hundreds of injured, with many handicapped for life.

Around Hotel Ivoire, tension was rising. After a while, French troops were given the order to break through the line of people surrounding the hotel. The French military convoy made its way through the crowd, leaving a bloody path of dozens, maybe hundreds of dead and

---

[39] Translator's note: The destruction of the entire Ivorian air fleet provoked very strong anti-French feelings. Violence targeting French homes, businesses and individuals, broke out all over the city of Abidjan, leading to the largest exodus of French residents in the history of Ivory Coast. Despite the deplorable acts perpetrated by some Ivorians which led to destruction of assets of many French businesses and individuals, the great majority of the Ivorians concur with President Gbagbo to believe, *"The problem has never been our relationship with French enterprises or companies, nor with the French people, but only with the French government, that is, with the Elysée."*

wounded. All of these were civilians. Then French soldiers fired again at the crowd who was demonstrating around this hotel which the Licorne troops had established as their headquarters. They killed and seriously injured many unarmed civilians[40], because they were afraid of the crowd.

On Sunday, the day after the death of the nine French soldiers, Ambassador Le Lidec told me that French intelligence had located and captured the pilots responsible for the bombing. They were the Bielorussian nationals who were in charge of the maintenance of our two aircraft. The French knew exactly who they were. They knew they were members of the maintenance team of our two airplanes, and they knew what these Bielorussians were doing, minute by minute. Day and night, the French military security never let them out of their sight. They knew how many bottles of beer they drank. They knew when they went out, where they went, what time they came back and which girls they brought back with them. French soldiers were around them all the time, in night clubs and "maquis"[41] in Abidjan. The French military had actually filmed and photographed the two Bielorussian pilots when they came back from their mission. Now that they were arrested, we sincerely thought the truth would come out.

No words can describe my surprise when I learned that the two Bielorussians and all their maintenance team had been escorted by the French to the Ghanaian border, and from there, they made it to Togo. When we asked the French authorities what happened, they told us they had not interrogated them and that there was no public record concerning the case.

The Togolese Minister of the Interior, François Boko, had them arrested. He kept them for ten days. He called the Ambassador of France,

---

[40] Translator's note: In an interview on ivoirebusiness TV (February 24, 2014) with Nicoletta Fagiolo, Gildas Le Lidec, former French ambassador to Abidjan (2002-2005), justified General Poncet's order to fire on unarmed Ivoirans crossing the Charles-de-Gaulle Bridge. He argued that if the order had not been given, the crowd would have gotten the upper hand on the French army. Then, according to him, the situation would become similar to what happened at the Battle of Dien Bien Phu which, in May 1954, culminated in a comprehensive French defeat, leading to the Geneva negotiations on the future of Indochina. The moral of all this boiled down to fire on unarmed Ivorian civilians to have France's honour satisfied. Is it that the French republican values?
[41] In Ivoirian French, a 'maquis' is an open air restaurant, known for its African cooking, especially barbecued fish and chicken.

the Ministry of Foreign Affairs in Paris, and the Ministry of Justice and told them: "We are keeping them here at your disposition."

President Eyadema, who was always very servile towards France, because he needed France's and Europe's aid, would do anything to please Chirac. Well! France didn't want anything to do with these Bielorussian pilots. This shows beyond a shadow of a doubt, the fault was on the French side, not on ours.

My take on the situation was that there was a parallel command, working above the head of the French Ambassador and even General Henri Poncet.

A French journalist from the *Parisien* newspaper told me one day that, according to him, it was the French secret service that had employed the Bielorussian pilots and that there was some kind of accident that led to the death of the nine French soldiers.

From a distance, I followed the legal suit which the families of the French soldiers instigated. I have also read what was written on the obstruction of justice committed by the French authorities with respect to the successive judges handling the case. I do know that the lawyer of the victims' families is convinced that I am completely innocent, as are all those in the inner circles of French power who know anything about this case.

On November 11, 2004, that is, the day after these events, our Ambassador in Paris and our military Attaché, General Camille Lohoues, were warmly welcomed by Chirac and their military counterparts at the WWI commemoration ceremonies. Had the French authorities been convinced of our guilt, they obviously would not have invited us. In France, there are people who know exactly what happened… That is why they always found better things to do than conduct an investigation about this incident.

Thus we were deprived of our military superiority over the rebels, which our air fleet gave us, and so we were unable to win the war and unify the country. If that was their goal, to prevent us from unifying the country, they succeeded.

No autopsies were carried out. There was no investigation. The bodies were picked up off the ground, still in their bloody fatigues, covered with dust and rocks, as if the French wanted the whole incident to disappear into thin air. Following two families' insistence to see their son's body one last time, and their success in obtaining the order to exhume the body, it was even discovered that two bodies had been mixed up. As they were found, one had been buried under the name of the other. As for those directly involved in the Bouaké raid, namely the Bielorussian pilots, Yuri Sushkin and Barys Smahin, they vanished into thin air. According to some people they were killed. There was opposition to any investigation by the French justice system. Their disappearance remains a mystery. Jean Balan, the lawyer of the families of the French soldiers who were either killed or wounded (there were thirty-eight in all) called this *"an affair of State."* In preparation for an eventual trial (and this has been going on now for nearly ten years), despite the obstacles he has faced, and due to the courage of a few judges, such as Brigitte Raynaud, who complained about people trying to stop her investigation or Sabine Kheris, currently in charge of the case, Jean Balan was able to reveal the inconsistencies in the explanations of Michèle Alliot-Marie, the then-Minister of Defense. However, Jean Balan was unsuccessful in having her formally accused; his request was denied in 2013.

The attitude of the French authorities with regard to the Bielorussian pilots, responsible for the bombing was very suspicious indeed. They not only helped them flee before they could be interrogated, but they also refused to extradite them when they were arrested in Togo. France's Minister of Defense's ambiguous remarks seemed to be hiding facts and trying to gain time, all of which turned into brazen lies. Speaking before the judge responsible for the case, Alliot-Marie claimed that no legal framework would allow the French judicial system to arrest these individuals suspected of murder. Such a statement is far from the truth, since one year before the events in Bouaké, on April 14, 2003, the Pelchat law, which allowed the French judicial system to pursue, arrest, and try those who had committed such crimes, was voted into law under Jacques Chirac. How is it that the French Minister of Defense did not know about this law?

Dominique de Villepin, first Minister of Foreign Affairs, then Minister of the Interior, and then Prime Minister, was as close as anyone could be to the Ivorian dossier. He had practically monopolized the case. Today, he explains he knew nothing about this incident and that he played no role whatsoever in what happened in Bouaké. Yet it is common knowledge that he was already taking over from Chirac, who was totally worn out, just prior to his stroke. Villepin was the one intervening at all levels of consultation and decision-making. On December 20, 2005, after the cerebral hemorrhage of President Chirac, Villepin confided to Bruno Le Maire:

"You know, the president is struggling for his life, and that is the only thing he is struggling for. All the rest: power, government, elections, our political party, none of this interests him any more."

How can anyone possibly believe that in 2004 this Minister would not have been let in on the details during such an acute crisis?

Today, what is clear, after the judicial proceedings of October 16 & 22, 2013 where several French military authorities were auditioned, is that the Elysée is not telling the whole story. On October 31, 2013, Philippe Brou of *Jeune Afrique* disclosed the testimonies of three high-ranking military officers who were very knowledgeable about the events:

"Thus, when questioned by Judge Kheris, General Malaussène, second in command after General Henri Poncet at the time of the events, obviously in on all the secrets, declared Gbagbo innocent. He accused rather the French authorities, and cited Alassane Ouattara as well."

Having now had access to the same information, here is exactly what General Malaussène said on the topic in front of the judge at the hearing:

"I think there was a political plot, whose goal was to put Ouattara in place [as head of state] *and to remove Gbagbo from power. Gbagbo is in fact an intelligent, cultivated person who has gone through many crises and who is sincerely fond of France." "I am convinced that Gbagbo had no desire to kill French soldiers and that someone from his entourage took the decision without telling him ..." "I believe that the Gbagbo camp fell into a trap."*

Gbagbo notes:

I was always persuaded that this was a plot hatched by two or three people in Paris in some small committee, a plan which was then infiltrated into my army.

Contrary to what is stipulated as constitutional law, General Bentégeat, the then-French chief of staff, revealed that he never participated in any higher level defense meeting at the Elysée, before or during the operation of the Franco-Ivorian "quasi-war" sparked off in the month of November 2004. This is another important element that supports the theory that a plot was put together [at very high levels] against Gbagbo.

As for the participation of General Mathias Doué, on the basis of this new evidence, it seems possible that this might have been an attempted coup d'état, as suggested by General Destremau. This General had explained that at the time of the events, the presence of the French tanks in front of the residence of the Ivorian president was a GPS error. But before Judge Kheris, he gives a different explanation. In *Jeune Afrique*, we read:

> "[he] evoked *a mysterious 'guide' who was to lead them towards the Hotel Ivoire (while Michèle Alliot-Marie speaks herself of the residence of the Ambassador of France) while he was flying overhead in a helicopter. This 'guide' committed 'a professional error' because he was afraid and incompetent."*

When the patrons of the French army decide to speak out, a pretty rare event, politicians are perplexed as what to say. And in such circumstances, military authorities might be willing to save face, especially when they feel that they are being manipulated and when some of their own are among the dead. Involved in the Ivorian military operation nicknamed 'Dignity' from beginning to end, and in the management of the consequences of this operation in Abidjan, Mamadou Koulibaly recently told me with the forthrightness that is so characteristic of him:

> *"One day tongues will loosen; people will begin to talk."*

And he was not wrong. Maybe one day all the efforts to cover up what really happened and to protect those responsible for these tragic events will come to naught. Jean Balan remembers that in 2005, the very day when this bombing incident was headlined in *Le Monde*, another story--that of Firmin Mahé--diverted all the French media. Firmin Mahé was a highway bandit arrested by the soldiers of General Henri Poncet on patrol in Ivory Coast. While in French custody, Mahé died of suffocation, a plastic bag over his head, as he was being transported in their armed vehicle. General Henri Poncet was acquitted. One of the soldiers responsible for his death was given a four-year sentence, which was suspended. His accomplice got a one-year suspended sentence. According to Jean Balan, this case constitutes

> *"a smoke screen launched by Michèle Alliot-Marie who personally intervened to ensure that the story about the bombing in Bouaké would*

be squashed and be superceeded in the French media by this second story."

Laurent Gbagbo was also very surprised to see the way in which the Firmin Mahé story became suddenly so important. He noted:

Please, don't get me wrong. I am never unaffected when a human being dies. But when an unfortunate event is blown out of proportion, such as the Kieffer or Mahé cases, I say to myself there must be some hidden reasons for doing it. In Ivory Coast, people who think they have something important to say care nothing for the thousands of citizens who have been assassinated or who have died in the wake of the rebel's violence. Then they exploit the death of others when they need to. And at the same time, one is careful to avoid anything my government has ever done: [for instance], the investigations launched to bring to light the truth behind these tragic events, as well as the willingness of the Ivorian authorities to help whenever possible.

For instance, in 2006, I instructed the Minister of Defense to ask the Ivorian police to arrest Youssouf Fofana, the head of the gang known as the Barbarians, who had abducted and tortured to death Ilan Halimi in Paris. We went beyond what the French judicial authorities requested. The investigating judge, Madam Goetzmann, only asked for information about Youssouf Fofana, an Ivorian, who had escaped French police and was hiding in Abidjan. We put out a search warrant for him and arrested him on February 23. We rapidly went to the judge and signed his extradition decree so he could stand before the French authorities. On March 5, he left the country under escort. The Ivorian police, the judicial system and the Ivorian president were just doing their duty, but they did it well. Yet I do not remember any one on that side thanking us for our faithful collaboration.

You don't need to be a graduate from a top military academy to know that something was not right about the official version concerning the tragic events of Bouaké. I remember that in the newsroom of *France-Soir* where I was working at the time (and I had not yet ever set foot in Ivory Coast), after a quick investigation, we decided to headline the story "How France veered off course." It appeared on the front page of the November 8, 2004 issue. Despite the fact that we didn't have access to all the information we needed, it still seemed to us suspect: there were too many pieces in the puzzle that just didn't fit. It seemed like people were happy to see those pieces quickly scattered, as if they were hoping no one could put them back together. Since then, all kinds of speculations have abounded, but this had not led to evidence coming before the courts, even if the factual reconstruction of Jean Balan and the statements of the various protagonists before the various judges are convincing. What is missing is a tiny spark which would start the explosion, blowing away the lead armor covering those who lied about the incident in which nine young French soldiers lost their lives.

By the end of April, 2014, Sabine Kheris went to Scheveningen to hear Laurent Gbagbo's testimony from inside his prison. She was accompanied by Jean Balan, the lawyer of the families of the French soldiers killed in Bouaké. Gbagbo comments:

After the Bouaké incident, here's what Le Lidec [the French Ambassador] said to me:

"After this, you're going to stay in place for twenty years!"

He was referring to the many victims the French army had caused. According to him, this incident would stop the French from carrying out any new violent acts in an attempt to destabilize me. The French Ambassador was wrong.

Chapter 11
"I am a politician, not a businessman"

In this chapter, François Mattei humorously recounts the odyssey of four French lawmakers of Sarkozy's UMP party who had decided to go to Abidjan "to see for themselves." Mattei was invited to come along, but waited in vain for the four to arrive at the Paris airport. Someone had pulled the plug on their mission.

But there were other French politicians, like Jacques Lang, former Minister of Culture and Jean-Marie Le Guen, Vice-president of the French National Assembly, who made it to Abidjan, and supposedly tried to provide some support to the Ivorian president under siege by rebels. But even his comrade-in-arms, socialist Jacques Lang, who had been 100% behind Gbagbo, later calls for him to step down.

Details recounted here will surprise some readers. Mattei speaks openly of the money-filled "envelopes" which were being prepared for the four French visitors who never arrived. Though shocking to many in the West, this was and remains standard practice in Francafrique. Important people are paid to influence their governments to "lean" this way or that. They are paid to spin the right story.

As for Gbagbo, he says, "I never paid any of them...." I am a politician, not a businessman."

On January 4, 2011, during the presentation of his New Year wishes at the military airbase in Saint-Dizier, Nicolas Sarkozy reaffirmed France's intentions to work for peace. He added that the goal of the French army present in Ivory Coast *"is not to meddle in the domestic affairs"* of the country.

These words had nothing to do with the reality on the ground. They certainly were said to throw his enemies off guard. What really was happening in 2011 was that the Licorne force made up of 900 soldiers, present in the territory since 2004, and supposedly the arbitrator between the warring parties, doubled its effectives. Four UMP lawmakers[42] who were invited to Abidjan to meet with Laurent Gbagbo maybe thought they could do a little negotiating behind their boss's back. They would be the ones to calm down the situation created through Nicolas Sarkozy's impetuousness. But on February 4, as they were packing their bags, before heading to Terminal 2E at Roissy airport to board their 11.30PM flight, they were called back. Details concerning their secret mission had been leaked to the media, and Sarkozy himself called Jean-François Mancel, forbidding him to make the trip.

Approached by a softspoken organizer of this "Gbagbo Tour," a Senegalese newcomer to the world of communication, I accepted to join the small group of those chosen, hoping to be able to observe them in action. What in the world could motivate four representatives of the presidential majority to defy the wrath of the Castle? I asked myself. At the outset, those on the trip only intended to exchange with President Gbagbo, not with the other president, meaning, Ouattara. On February 4, 2011, I showed up in the departure hall at Roissy airport and was waiting for the bold "Musketeers" to arrive. It is under these circumstances that I almost had the chance to meet Jean-François Mancel, Cécile Dumoulin, Yves Censi, and Jean-Michel Fourgous… But in the end I only met with Emmanuel Caullier, a lawyer and university professor. I was looking around trying to recognize anyone who looked like these lawmakers, and I finally went up to Caullier, who was himself pacing up and down in the terminal, almost empty at such a late hour.

We shared the last sandwich and the two last cans of soft drink from the little kiosk facing the departure desk. Around midnight, I got a call from the Senegalese guy who was there in Abidjan waiting for the delegation to arrive. He was calling to tell me he had been informed that the UMP operation had been called off. And the lawyer and I turned around and went home…

Intrigued by all that had happened, a situation that could have caused Nicolas Sarkozy to lose face, I kept an eye out for developments. The footage of French lawmakers playing hooky in Africa might lead to something big. Those who were presented in the French media as being behind this adventure, namely Mamadou Koulibaly, the president of the Ivorian National Assembly, and the lawyer Marcel Ceccaldi, had certainly nothing to do with this affair.

Thus there were, before the presidential election and in the last weeks of the Ivorian crisis, some sincere, and maybe some not so sincere, visitors

---

[42] Translators note: France is a republic and has 'deputies' elected to Parliament. These officials are roughly equivalent to US senators and representatives. The UMP is the *Union pour un movement populaire*, the party of the former president Nicolas Sarkozy.

making their way from Paris to Abidjan. Probably Laurent Gbagbo, in those difficult times, needed these visits to believe and to show the world that he still had many friends and supporters.

Already in March 2010, when the climate seemed a little more serene, Laurent Gbagbo had launched his own media tom-tom. Together with the former French Minister of Culture, Jack Lang and Jean-Marie Le Guen, Vice-president of the French National Assembly, we had seen Laurent Gbagbo dance at the Queens, football star Didier Drogba's nightclub, one of the most popular along *Rue Princesse*, Abidjan's hot spot. While Lang, straight-faced, said he was on a *"mission to re-establish the link between the French Socialists, President Gbagbo, and Ivory Coast[43],"* our eternal Minister of Culture, exhilarated by the African nightlife, waxed lyrical with Dali-like[44] praise for his host:

> *"Gbagbo is a solid man of the left...He knows the real meaning of the word 'solidarity.' ... I am in perfect harmony with the president--in complete complicity, in sync, with him. I love people like him who are both patriotic and have a sense of the importance of the State."*

Fast forward to December 30, 2010, just nine months later, when speaking live on RTL[45]: *"Laurent, you must step down."* Citing the results of the elections, which were contested by both the "winners" of Abidjan, Lang simply abandoned ship. Laurent Gbagbo commented:

You have to understand him: at that time, Jack needed a job.
In late 2010 and during the first weeks of 2011, many others stepped in. In Africa, it is customary that a guest never leave without a gift. The Senegalese organizer of the "Gbagbo Tour" had prepared "envelopes" of 30,000 and 50,000 euros each for the French UMP lawmakers. During this last dance in Abidjan, the "orchestra of egos" kept on playing even as the ship was sinking, just like the violins on the deck of the Titanic. But the musicians were never paid. Gbagbo remarks:

I never paid anyone. Even for the opinion polls before the elections, I paid nothing. All such things were paid by supporters richer than I am.

---

[43] *Fraternité Matin*, March 29, 2010.
[44] Translator's note: Salvador Dali was a Spanish surrealist painter (1904-1989) who was known for his flamboyant and exaggerated life style and language.
[45] RTL, formerly known as RTL plus or just RTL is a cable and satellite German commercial television station.

There never was any crossover between the State budget and political expenditures. I never gave a single euro to Fouks, to RSCG[46]. I always agree when there is no cost for me involved. Same thing for my guests. Those who wanted to do something for me gave them a little "something." I never wanted to know about it. I am a polictician, not a businessman.

---

[46] Stephane Fouks was the political adviser of Havas Worldwide.

Chapter 12
"I was arrested as bombs were falling"

In this moving chapter, Gbagbo reveals some of the detail of his capture. Having lived through numerous attempted coups d'etat and other rebel attacks, Gbagbo does not escape the final attack, as the French army "accompanies" the rebels to the door of his residence. There was not just some shooting, as Gbagbo explains "I was arrested with bombs falling on my head."

Here we hear Gbagbo explaining to Bensouda, the prosecutor of the International Criminal Court not only how he was captured, but more importantly, what he feels is at issue in the hearing she is directing. Bensouda declared that it doesn't matter who won the elections in Ivory Coast—what she cares about are the crimes committed against humanity. But Gbagbo takes the time to explain to her that the question of who won the elections is at the heart of the whole matter. If there had been a recount...and if in fact, Gbagbo did win the elections, then a sitting, democratically elected president was illegally arrested by rebels clearly backed by the French and many in the International Community.

The U.S. position openly expressed by Hilary Clinton, the Secretary of State at the time shows how incredibily naïve and uninformed American foreign policy makers can be. She states:

> *"The arrest of Laurent Gbagbo sends a clear signal to dictators around the world that they cannot ignore the results of free and equitable elections. There will be serious consequences if they cling to power."*

Had the U.S. merely bought into the incredible media campaign launched world-wide against Gbagbo or had strong French pressure convinced them that Ouattara would be more favorable to their interests? As Gbagbo points out to the Prosecutor, the real question is who won the elections, and were these elections--to quote Clinton--truly "free and equitable?"

During all these years, I was like a fish people try to kill by constantly taking it out of the water. But I always was able to dive back in,

catch my breath once again, and carry out the difficult job the Ivorians elected me to do. In the end, it was Sarkozy who took the biggest hit.

Laurent Gbagbo wasn't overthrown--neither in 2002 nor in 2004. And even if he was ousted in 2011, he did not die under the rubble left by the real bombs that fell on his head, nor was he wiped out by the treachery of some of his close aids, by the condemnation of the Elysée, the UN, the European Community, the Organization of the African Union, the International Court, and the French and international media.

On December 5, 2011, during his first appearance before the International Court, he arrived before his judges like a swimmer out of breath, but one who still had enough energy and willpower to declare:

"I was arrested with French bombs falling on my head... It was France that did the job..."

On February 28, 2013, he again appeared before the International Court, this grand edifice with its Nordic design, white wood, combinations of concrete and glass, modern and sober, its interior dotted with computers and computer screens. President Gbagbo stands up to speak. It is the last step of the fifteen days of hearings to confirm the charges against him. The judges have to decide whether a trial is warranted. To do this, they have to weigh the Prosecutor's charges, in other words, they have to determine if the allegations of the Prosecutor are consistent and credible enough for Gbagbo to stand trial.

During the first days, the Prosecutor deployed all her rhetorical prowess, trying to convince the judges. They say that, never, in the Court's history had a prosecutor prepared a hearing with such care. But in the following days, things changed.

President Gbagbo's Defense team took the floor. This well-prepared team knew the content of the case like the back of their hand. Led by Emmanuel Altit, one of the best specialists in the domain of international penal justice, the Defense team patiently, meticulously and inexorably destroyed bit by bit each piece of evidence the Prosecutor brought forward. And Emmanuel Altit demonstrated that, contrary to what the Prosecutor was affirming, it was not President Gbagbo who plotted to remain in power regardless of the election results. It was rather the rebels, covertly supported by French authorities, who had put together a plot conceived a long time before, to seize power. The question was to find out who had conceived the plot to destabilize the country. After fifteen days of hearings, the answer was crystal clear: the French authorities. But the Prosecutor seemed to obstinately want to "forget" their involvement…

Thus it is a president, serene and confident, who rises to speak, even though he was still suffering from the inhumane treatment received during his eight months of imprisonment in Côte d'Ivoire. Known as an experienced public speaker, Gbagbo stands up, and ignoring his surroundings, he speaks out freely. In very few words, he puts forward his own vision of the post-electoral crisis, as seen in the following excerpt:

> *"Madam the President, Ladies and Gentlemen, Honorable Judges,*
> *I have closely followed all the debate. I have heard a lot of things. At times I found myself in Ivory Coast, but at other times, I found myself very far away from the country I know. This is because the questions that were asked were so far from the experiences we lived through [...]*
> *"I would like to simply say that Madam the Prosecutor pronounced one sentence which somewhat shocked me…*
>
> *"She said that we are not here to speak about who won the elections or who did not. But we cannot speak about the post-electoral crisis in Ivory Coast; we cannot debate about what happened, without knowing what actually took place during the elections.*
>
> *"We need to know who won the elections. Because it is the candidate who did not win the election, who brought about thepost-electoral troubles. I believe that this is the logical way to handle the issue. So the question is: who won the elections? When I asked for a recount of the votes, it was not empty rhetoric. You have yourself seen the documents that are available to the Prosecutor's team. The votes are tallied up on these documents. In just one city, Bouaké, you can see 100,000 votes were added to my opponent's score.*
>
> *"This is the heart of the question [...]"*

It was the culmination of fifteen days of hearings which will be remembered. Up till then, all the observers considered Gbagbo the loser and had anticipated that he would inevitably be convicted. They were all heading in the same direction they thought the wind was blowing. But having heard Emmanuel Altit, his colleagues and Laurent Gbagbo himself, and especially having listened to their claims and having analyzed what they presented, the majority of observers now were persuaded that a trial under such circumstances would be disastrous for the International Court. They believed that Gbagbo would, in fact, be freed.

But if this happened, hundreds of millions of euros spent to delegitimize an elected president, to organize slander campaigns against him, to put in place an army of rebels, to impose all this on the International Community, to convince the media, to persuade the International Community, and the Security Council, all this would have been wasted. At the end of that hearing, it still looked like Gbagbo might win.

The violence perpetrated by Alassane Ouattara's supporters, the countless crimes they committed and for which they were guilty, even began to be a problem for those closest to Ouattara. [An Ivorian president was captured by French commandos and Burkinabe and Nigerian mercenaries in the rubble of his residence, after repeated attacks that caused dozens of dead, many civilians, who had taken refuge there]. Gbagbo's wife, Simone exhibited like captured prey, on her knees after being arrested, surrounded by *Dozos*[47] covered in gri-gri[48], holding her by her hair. Pictures of Gbagbo's son, Michel, show him stripped to the waist and arriving in a bloodied state at the headquarters of the purported "winner." He narrowly escaped death at the hands of the Ouattara supporters. And the cadavers of the innocent were strewn everywhere in Abidjan, and scattered, as well, all over the south of Ivory Coast.

Born in Lyon, France, Michel Gbagbo is a Franco-Ivorian. He is the son of President Gbagbo's first marriage with Jacqueline Chamois, a French teacher who still supports Gbagbo today. The only wrong this professor of psychology at the Faculty of Criminology at the University of Abidjan committed was to have taken shelter at his father's residence with his wife Viviane. Michel Gbagbo has never held a political office. Having been imprisoned for two years in incredible conditions, he was released August 5, 2013 on probation along with thirteen other supporters of Laurent Gbagbo. But again on February 14, 2014, he was arrested once again as he made his way to the Abidjan airport. He was about to fly to Paris to respond to the summons of Judge Sabine Kheris, who wanted to hear his deposition in his case against Guillaume Soro and the rebels for *"abduction, confinement and degrading inhuman treatment."* He was

---

[47] Translator's note: Dozos are a corporation of traditional hunters who live in the area spanning northern Ivory Coast, South-eastern Mali and Burkina Faso. Today, due to rebel movement, "Dozos" are also spread all over southern Ivory Coast.

[48] Gri-gri is a popular name for fetishes, usually bracelets, armbands, etc., worn to protect those wearing them from harm. These marks of witchcraft are openly worn by the Dozos who make up part of the Ivorian rebel forces.

released three days later, but told he is not allowed to leave the Ivorian territory. Nobody, whether in Abidjan or Paris, wants to open this Pandora's box. Gbagbo comments:

The treatment of my son Michel raises a lot of important questions. He was kept hostage. Today, he is denied the right to have his day in court after all he was subjected to. It is France who should be helping him to make good on his rights as a French citizen. Otherwise, how can this obstruction of justice be understood?

There is no room for sentimentality when the goal is to show the world what bastards who defy Western democracies must face. The more violent their downfall, the clearer the message. The arrest of Saddam Hussein, as he was pulled out of a hole where he was hiding, the furtive images of his hanging in some dark corner after his trial, the lynching of Gaddafi in the middle of a street, beaten, bleeding, finished off and exposed on the floor of a hangar, all these images prepared the way in the public mind for the ill-treatment suffered by Gbagbo and his supporters... The former president of Ivory Coast is classed along with all the other tyrants. All is a function of how the images are interpreted. Lumping everybody together, that's what works the best. You have to do what you have to do. A society driven by the Western media takes away the sanctity of the image, like those primitive tribes who believe that you can't take a picture without capturing the soul. How much easier when it involves an African head of state, with negative prejudices building up around him day after day, and he himself having no media "machine" comparable to the ones used by his detractors. Simple-minded comparisons are used to reach one's goals.

The then-U.S. Secretary of State Hillary Clinton does not wear kid gloves when she declares:

"The arrest of Laurent Gbagbo sends a clear signal to dictators around the world that they cannot ignore the results of free and equitable elections. There will be serious consequences if they cling to power."

The message from Capitol Hill was that lovers of power should take notice and be forewarned.

During the first weeks of May 2011, people believed the proof against Laurent Gbagbo was conclusive. In newsrooms in Paris, people went around saying *Ite missa est*, "Mass is over." Before justice could rule, Gbagbo is already judged and condemned. All is set in place as soon as Ouattara proclaims

111

himself president in December 2010. Henri Emmanuelli and François Loncle, in a joint communique, note:

> *"The majority of the French media, supported by a number of political leaders, [...] all of whom are eager to give advice [...] have launched a one-way campaign to raise suspicion and to denigrate Ivorian authorities."*

The sophisticated diplomatic "machine" put together by Jean-David Levitte, adviser to Nicolas Sarkozy, working alongside General Puga, and described by Jean-Christophe Notin in *The crocodile and the Scorpion*, functioned perfectly. It diverted attention and permitted that France not be accused of neo-colonialism. The same scenario was reproduced in Libya, where it was necessary to give an appearance of respectability to military intervention coming from the outside. You have to build an alibi beforehand and then sell it to the International Community. This is no problem at all for France, member of the UN Security Council, where its "expertise" in African affairs makes it credible and convincing. Notin, trying to justify France's military intervention in Ivory Coast, writes in his book:

> *"Anyway, Gbagbo would not have remained in power for longer than six months after he lost the elections, or at least after having been rejected by Paris."*... ([isn't it] a Freudian slip?) *"Thanks to their network, in Abidjan with Ambassador Simon and General Palasset, with the representative of France in New York, Gérard Araud, and within all the French and international administrative officials involved, the Levitte-Puga duo contributed to the creation of a new model of crisis management which was also implemented in Libya [...] and in Mali in January 2013. First, a legal or a legitimate government in a given country must call for assistance. Then a regional organization makes a promise to help. Then there is a UN mandate. And then and only then, France intervenes diplomatically, economically, and militarily"* Jean-David Levitte specifies: *"Each one of these four steps is essential."*

Contrary to all that has been reported, here is the admission of a cold and calculated plan to carry out France's plan of operation in Abidjan. How far from the humanitarian pretexts invoked at the time, justifying the French attack on Laurent Gbagbo's residence. *"I concurred with what you did,"* Nicolas Sarkozy said to Levitte and Puga, using the same tone Emperor Napoleon used when he congratulated his troops at Austerlitz: *"Soldiers, I am proud of you."*

The only thing needed after that was to get the seal of approval of the International Community. This seal of international justice, dipped in indelible ink and prepared so long in advance was to be stamped with the finest wax. It is interesting to note that the Prosecutor of the International Court never found it necessary to bring to justice the rebels guilty of crimes against humanity and other war crimes in Ivory Coast in 2002 and 2003, even though these cases were brought before her. Rather, as quickly as possible, she accused President Gbagbo. And, it is a little hard to ignore the fact that the Prosecutor of the International Court seems to have been in constant contact with the Ouattara camp since the run-off election of November 2010. Yet the same Prosecutor had never bothered to contact the representatives of the Ivorian government. Repeatedly, the bias of the Prosecutor appeared, as when in an interview given to the Kenyan Channel K24 at the beginning of 2011, she threatened President Gbagbo with a "bad ending." Who is worse than the blind person who refuses to see? The indictment of the Prosecutor indicates that:

> *"Laurent Gbagbo is accused of being individually and legally responsible as an indirect co-author on four counts of crimes against humanity: a) murder, b) rape and other sexual violence, c) acts of persecution and d) other inhuman acts which would have been perpetrated in the context of post-electoral violence which occurred in Ivory Coast between December 16, 2010 and April 12, 2011."*

This is the final blow, one which Gbagbo's opponents believe will lead to his permanent withdrawal from the political scene, and which will be paralleled by the triumph of Alassane Ouattara. Until February 19, 2013, most believed that Gbagbo's trial at the International Court was already over, a "done deal," and that his condemnation, by the saintly system of justice, would be the last step in ostracizing Laurent Gbagbo from the annals of history. His universal condemnation would be but a formality. But on February 19, 2013, when Laurent Gbagbo stood up at the tribune where he was supposedly going to be burned at the stake, who was afraid of him? At that moment in time, no one was.

Chapter 13
Too bad for those who voted

Unlike most of the titles in this book which are quotes from Gbagbo, this title comes from François Mattei, referring to the 2,475 Ivorian electors throughout France who stood in the cold to cast their votes, to only later learn that these were declared nul and void by Bamba Yacouba, spokesperson of the Independent Electoral Commission (IEC).

It had been widely predicted that Gbagbo would have easily won that presidential contest against the candidate Ouatara, obtaining at the very least 57% of the vote. By invalidating these votes, the pro-Ouattara camp was able to convince the world that the Ivorian diaspora was in favor of the French-backed candidate, as announced by 'Le Monde' of December 2, 2010: 'victory abroad for Ouattara.'

Mattei wonders out loud how it is that Jeb Bush had the right to do a recount for his brother and how Sarkozy's UMP was allowed to do a recount for the banal election of their party president. Why is it that no one was listening or wanted to hear when Gbagbo begged for a recount in Ivory Coast?

Between late November, 2010 and early April, 2011, Ivory Coast was regularly in the news on French channels--often the lead story. On the 8 PM news on France2, Marie Drucker spoke in the same tone as her colleagues, who continually referred to Laurent Gbagbo as the *"self-proclaimed president."* Who can blame her? The official version was continually sent out by the most powerful protagonists. France, the UN, and the U.S., all co-authors of the drama, were considered the legitimate sources of media information. What's more, within the French opposition, except for Labertit and Emmanuelli, who for some time have been pushed aside, the Socialist Party as a whole endorsed the Elysée's rhetoric. Only Jean-Luc Mélanchon and Marine Le Pen refused to "run with the pack." Even though these two are implacable opponents, both ideologically and politically, they both mistrusted the International Community's alliance against one single man, and they denounced the about-face of the UN mandate, the UN who as supposed to be protecting civilians, and not overthrowing and arresting a head of state.

Antoine Glazer, former chief editor of *La Lettre du Continent,* invited in his capacity as an "Expert on Africa" by the French television stations to comment on the results of the Ivorian elections, did not question the results. But today, he admits he was not certain that the vote was transparent and the count valid. In a phone conversation on July 3, 2013, he confided in me:

> *"At the time, I didn't carry out any investigation. And since no recount took place, we will never really know who won."*

Indeed, who can claim to have investigated the election in Ivory Coast, verifying the actual voting conditions, the tally of the votes, the analysis of the figures, and the violence and fraud that occurred during the vote? Indeed, such careful control was never carried out in France, where the polling stations were down at the neighborhood street corner.

But the fact is, the Ivorian diaspora in France went to the polling stations in Lille, Toulouse, Strasbourg, Lyon, Bordeaux, as well as in Nice, Amiens, Arras and Valenciennes, and they cast their votes in relative calm, even exhibiting an almost peaceful "co-habitation" of supporters of both candidates. The necessary materials for the election were sent from Abidjan by the electoral commission (run by the friends of Ouattara), but they only arrived in Marseille the day after the first round of voting. And then, the voting apparatus for Toulouse was strangely sent to the Ivorian Embassy, located at Avenue Poincaré in Paris. Fortunately the Toulouse officials made a quick *aller-retour* train trip to Paris and recuperated what was needed in time.

But in Paris, for the supporters of Gbagbo things were not smooth: voters were intimidated, threatened and physically aggressed. The acts of violence that occurred that day can be still seen today on videos on the Internet and police registers still show the logs about these events.

Out of the twenty-eight polling stations which were put in place in the *Ile de France,* eight were closed down because of raids by gang type "loubards" who came in and started destroying tables and ballot boxes. They stole lists, voting bulletins, print, ink, and stamps, and they beat up pro-Gbagbo voters.

As a precautionary measure, some ballot boxes were transported under police escort to the headquarters of the IEC (Independent Electoral Commission) in one of the secondary venues of the Ivorian Embassy in Paris located at Boulevard Suchet. Even in that venue, there were bands of gangs opposed to Gbagbo. They sat in waiting and ended up damaging the gate of the building.

The representative of the opposition party, faithful to his candidate, Alassane Ouattara, arrived one hour late, at 10 AM instead of 9 AM. Since the voting procedure had started without him, he started opposing the vote, refusing for it to take place. As a result, only eighteen ballots processed before the arrival of this man were tallied. This man's sense of right and wrong obviously was applied to others, not to himself.

Too bad for all those Ivorians who got up early and who froze, standing all day in line in the streets of Paris, hoping in vain to be able to carry out their civil duty.

Too bad for the twenty Parisian polling stations where everything went along fine, without a single incident. Too bad for Marseille where the vote could not take place. Too bad for the 2,475 electors in Reims, Amiens, Bordeaux, Nice, Toulouse, Lille, Arras, Valenciennes, Lens, and Lyon, who cast their votes with no problem, in true transparency.

Why too bad? Because all those who succeeded in voting would have to hear the spokesperson of the IEC unabashedly declare on November 29, 2010, the day after the run-off: *"Almost no one voted in France."*

And because of this, all the results of the votes of Ivorians living in France would be declared null and void.

Is it presumptuous to think that there is perhaps a correlation between the composition of the IEC, made up, for the most part, of the parties opposed to the incumbent Ivorian president and the fact that the victory of Gbagbo in France (57.58% versus 42.61% for Ouattara) was allowed to disappear into thin air?

These facts and figures are available and can be checked. They were validated by the representatives of both parties, both the FPI and the RDR. All this happened in the biggest cities in France. Who was aware of this or was even concerned? No one, even if the 2,475 votes of this partial electorate, representing valid votes, which should have been counted, is superior to the Ivorian electorate in three countries combined: Belgium with 709 voters, Germany with 279 voters, and Burkina Faso with 1,400 voters. Even if, in terms of the number of registered voters, the electorate in the most important cities in France comes in third position behind the U.S. (3,184) and Italy (2, 611). Even if the electorate in these most important French cities has a strong symbolic value, due to its specific resonance in Ivory Coast and around the world, and because it is linked to France...

In its December 2, 2010 issue, *Le Monde* preferred to declare the *"victory abroad of Ouattara with nearly 60% of the recorded votes against 40% for Gbagbo,"* with no details of the voting. Yet, the Ivorian diaspora around the world was made up of 15,000 electors. Had the 2,475 votes cast in France been included, the outcome would have obviously been very different. What happened in Paris and Marseille gives us a hint of what might have happened in the savannah in northern Ivory Coast where polling stations, surrounded by rebel Kalashnikovs, were generally controlled by the political friends of candidate Ouattara.

Of course, it is not only in Ivory Coast that such incidents affect the voting process and where dubious scores have disturbed elections. Jean-Pierre Raffarin himself pointed out similar problems during the UMP crisis. In the U.S., one still remembers the 2000 election which opposed George W. Bush and Al Gore and the absurd recounting of "little holes" on computer-generated voting cards. That operation lasted several weeks with, at the end, a result that, if unclear, was accepted by both candidates. Doubts remain, however, concerning the possibility of computer manipulations and on the decisive role of the state of Florida in the overall national elections, with Jeb Bush, acting governor of the state giving the victory to his brother, George W. Bush.

But in August 2009, Western democracies are not so concerned with the transparency and fairness of elections in places like Afghanistan. Hamid Karzai, the West's favorite, ran for a second term against Abdullah Abdullah, the former Minister of Foreign Affairs from the northern alliance. During the first round, one third of the votes for Kazai were invalidated due to massive fraud, as he was said to be ahead of his challenger. The run-off scheduled for November 7, 2009 never took place because of Abdullah's withdrawal from the race. Nevertheless, on November 2 of the same year, Kazai was declared winner and he officially took the oath of the office on November 19. When the International Community wants something… they usually get it.

In Haiti, in the fall of 2010, at the same time the Ivorian situation was developing, the OAS (Organization of the American States), gave in to pressure from protests in the street and opted for a recount for that presidential election. Even though the Provisory Electoral Commission had already publicized the results of the first round, news of fraud abounded. The protests risked degenerating into serious clashes in the streets. Demonstrators demanded a recount and finally succeeded in convincing the somewhat apathetic members of the European Union and the UN. The OAS, of which Haiti is a member, finally declared there should be a recount. After a new evaluation carried out from the outside, the candidate in the third position, the singer Minchel Martelly, who had been eliminated in the first round, was requalified for the run-off. And Maretelly finally won with nearly 68% of the vote. Eliminated from the first round, he was finally elected president of the Republic of Haiti.

In France, in late 2011, within the ranks of the UMP, a kind of Ivorian-style scenario occurred. The resemblances are disquieting. There is kind of "irony of history" or "pay back" here, since it involves the political party of Nicolas Sarkozy. Jean François Copé and François Fillon both claimed to be winner of the primary for the presidential bid of their political party. There were insults, threats, accusations of stuffing the ballot box and even suspicion of mafia involvement. It was a pathetic soap opera bringing to the light the ambitions and hatred typical of the relations existing among the leading figures of the UMP in France. A commission for a recount was set up, but François Fillon, in advance, refused their decision, while he went about…temporally trying to create his own party…

It is important to note that Copé was the president of the UMP until his downfall in 2014, when he was forced to resign after the existence of forged bills was disclosed. He was the one to organize this disastrous election, and so of course, he was the one calling the shots. François Fillon did not trust him. But in France, it is well known that after hot rivalries, everyone ends up "singing the same song." The two roosters met, talked and ended up reconciled in time for the group photo… Yes, in France, people can vote to see if they should vote and vote again to see who is really the president of the party! Even in Africa, people broke out laughing when they saw what happened in France. To what extent people would go, with such care and good manners, to sort out a dispute which only concerned a single political party, involving just several thousand French voters! When Jean-Jacques Bourdin reminded him that a new vote would "cost money," Henri Guaino, a former advisor at the Elysée, speaking on RMC radio on February 12, 2013, remarked:

> *"Well, sometimes democracy costs a little but when it is well done, it brings in a lot."*

I heard Guiano's statement on the radio, while in a taxi, riding along the banks of the Seine River. My taxi driver, by sheer chance, was an Ivorian living in Paris, listening for sports news on that RMC channel. As we drove right by the Radio station, he burst out laughing and said: *"You got it right, Henri."*

These words of the wise, Henri Guiano forgot to whisper them into the ears of those who needed to hear them when, a few months earlier, the fate of a country of 20 million inhabitants and the life and death of tens of thousands of Ivorians hung in the balance. Couldn't there have been a simpler scenario in Ivory Coast: a recount of the votes, a few negotiations, or a new vote? Nicholas Sarkozy's speech writer, who wrote his famous Dakar speech, wasn't thinking about Guiano's words during the Ivorian post-electoral crisis. Sarkozy (or his speechwriter?) didn't hear Gbagbo's request for a recount, because the African *"who has not yet taken his place in history"* is not "worth it" (like it says in the advertisement for l'Oreal, "you're worth it.") We might add that according to AFP, quoted in its issue of November 27, 2012 issue of *Le Nouveau Courrier*, during his lunch with François Fillon, Nicolas Sarkozy had advised, in relation to the UMP, a new vote *"to prevent the conflict from getting any worse."* It was Jean-François Copé, always rigid in his attitudes, who declared:

> *"For us, the National Appeal Commission is like the Constitutional Council. Who could possibly imagine an appeal after the Constitutional Council has taken a decision?"*

Unfortunately for Ivorians these French principles don't travel well. It's like trying to bring camembert cheese to the tropics. It's like saying these people [these Africans] aren't capable of appreciating principles of democracy. In Paris and in Port-au-Prince, they can count and recount, but in Abidjan, they sent out the tanks and the helicopters.

Let's get back to Africa, where France is omnipresent: its loves, its hates, its maneuvering (a little here, a little there) of its famous principles. The most recent case comes from a long line of "chosen" heads of state: Ali Bongo. His father, Omar Bongo, was put at the helm of Gabon, France's private oil producing emirate, and stayed there for more than forty years. Michel de Bonnecorse, former adviser on Africa for Jacques Chirac, is categorical: Ali Bongo never won the elections in 2009. He even lost them by a big margin. In Patrick Benquet and Antoine Glaser's documentary *Françafrique, 50 years under the seal of secrecy,* Bonnercorse confirms that the figures of 42% and 37% actually obtained by André Mba Obame and Ali Bongo were simply reversed, to the detriment of the first candidate and the triumph of the second. Jacques Salles, former boss of French intelligence in Gabon, says in the same documentary "Even the local AFP knew about it, *but nobody said anything* [...] *I was disgusted."* So that is how Ali took over from his father Omar, renewing the French "lease," nourishing well-known French interests. No one was allowed to rummage through the tons of evidence and more than forty years of Franco-Gabonese corruption, smelling strongly of oil. Within an hour of the announcement, Nicolas Sarkozy hastened to congratulate President Ali Bongo for his victory, in this clearly rigged election.

French tolerance guided by self-interest also allowed the very docile Eyadema Gnassingbé to rule over Togo for thirty-six years. Coming to power through a coup d'etat, he was maintained in power through several rigged elections. His son, Faure Gnassingbé, ignored by Sarkozy, welcomed by Hollande, took over from his father with the support of the army. The Franco-Togolese Kofi Yamgnane, a Socialist *député* representing the region Finistère, and who was State Secretary for Social Integration in the Mitterrand administration, knows exactly what this is all about, since he repeatedly tried to run in the Togolese presidential election, first in 2005 and then in 2010. He knows that in the twenty-first century, banana republics still exist in francophone Africa.

Chapter 14
A trap prepared well in advance

The trap referred to here had many components. While elections should have been held in 2005, the country was no where ready to face them. France tried to lull Gbagbo to sleep, sending him friendly "allies" assuring him he would win the election. International pressure, instigated by the French, weighed heavily down on him, as he waited for the rebels to disarm. This was of course the outstanding condition needed for fair and free elections to take place.

While a UN report, predicting serious consequences should the election be held without this condition being met, lay dormant (or hidden?), international pressure became almost unbearable. Gbagbo opponents had been saying for years that Gbagbo was a dictator, afraid of holding the elections because he might lose. As time went by, the rebels persisted in refusing to disarm and neither the French, the UN, nor the rest of the International Community showed signs of lifting a finger to help. Finally, Gbagbo gave in.

But the trap was even more complicated: France, through then Prime Minister Charles Banny, imposed its own choice of companies to oversee the practical aspects of the elections--down to the ballot boxes and the ballots themselves. Non-Ivorians were also arriving in Ivory Coast by the busload to fill up the pro-Ouattara electoral lists. Gbagbo, in his usual attempts at reconciliation, had accepted that the Electoral Commission be made up of a majority of his opponents. The trap was set. The deck was stacked. There was virtually no way the election could be fair and free...

The UN mission in Ivory Coast had clearly indicated that Laurent Gbagbo was the "most respected figure" in this West African country of Ivory Coast. In this chapter, Laurent Gbagbo is on record as saying that he was aware that the endgame of Compaoré and Ouattara was to have Ivory Coast melted into a larger entity which would include Burkina Faso and which would be run by both of them.

Already in November 2006, the French weekly magazine L'Express revealed the existence of a secret survey carried out by the ONUCI between

July 14 & 24, of that year. Laurent Gbagbo was at that time the "most respected figure" in Ivory Coast. With 39.3% of the favorable opinion, he was far ahead of Alassane Ouattara (9.4%), and Henri Konan Bédié (4.7%). As for Charles Konan Banny, the then-Prime Minister in the coalition government, presented in this weekly magazine as the "darling" of the International Community, he only got 7% of the favorable opinion. But the dice were already thrown…even if the roulette wheel would spin around for a fairly long time before stopping at a name…

In October 2010, Claude Guéant paid me a visit in Abidjan. He told me that the Elysée had no candidate. I politely listened to him. That very morning, I had been informed by a note of the DGSE that Ouattara had been designated as Sarkozy's candidate. The trap had been set for a long time. They constantly urged me to organize these elections. The international pressure was very strong, even though one of the first conditions to ensure a peaceful election was the disarmament of the rebels, a condition that was never met. In all the agreements, the disarmament of the rebels was a *sine qua non* condition for any possible settlement. In all the UN resolutions, there were eighteen all together, disarmament was included. Yet, they kept urging us to carry out these elections, because they wanted a quick and definitive conclusion. I made contact with people around me, specifically the socialist lawmaker François Loncle and told him I knew fraud and rigging were in the offing.

Nobody wanted to slow down the process leading straight to war, to the violence which would inevitably be the consequence. The real facts come out [postmortem] in an article on the website of *Slate Afrique* on May 28, 2011, which discloses a covert UN report. The website revealed the existence of a report dating back from before the presidential elections, stating that the conditions for holding the presidential elections in Ivory Coast were not met. Yet, this report was hidden from the world for months until the elections were held and the publication of the report would no longer have any impact. This means that at the UN headquarters in New York, people knew beforehand that these elections would have dramatic and dire consequences. In Ivory Coast, the foreseeable disaster was well underway and the UN authorities knowingly covered it up.

> *"For seven months a UN report that threw new light on the crisis which just took place in Ivory Coast was lying dormant…. […] Had it been published before the presidential election, it would have led to the*

postponement of the November 28, 2010 election or at least it would have downplayed optimistic forecasts concerning its outcome.

"On September 17, 2010, five experts designated to investigate the potential violations of the arms embargos and trafficking of raw materials sent a first letter to Maria Luiza Ribeiro Viotti, Chairperson of the Committee for UN sanctions put in place in Ivory Coast in 2004 by Security Council Resolution 1572. This letter preceded their report which was to be published a few weeks later. It was finally published seven months later, along with a letter dated April 20, 2011 with the signature of Maria Luiza Ribeiro Viotti, addressed to the UN Security Council Chairperson."

This report was published on April 20, 2011, one week after Laurent Gbagbo's ousting. The date chosen for this publication raises a question which probably answers itself. The proof brought by the report shows that there had been re-armament of both sides and that there was a strong likelihood of war[49], surrounding the upcoming presidential election. Consequently, the UN failed its mission, or did someone rather prevent the UN from stopping the plan to help Ouattara and his French backers seize power.

For me, all the activities leading up to the Ivorian elections, for example, the census, the establishment of elector cards and the implementation of all the electoral procedures should have been entrusted, as it had been up till then, to the NIS, the National Institute of Statistics. Yet, without my knowing it, the French authorities took hold of all the electoral process through Sagem, a company of the Safran group. I was never briefed and I never authorized a contract with this company. Charles Konan Banny, who had just become Prime Minister of the "national union" government did this behind my back. When I became aware of it, it was too late, because Konan Banny had already started paying the bill. What should I have done in such circumstances? Had I started a fight, they would have said: Gbagbo is afraid of facing the elections…

The Ivorian branch of Sagem was headed by Sidi Kagnassi, a Swiss-Malian. He was the one who set up the dark plot. He and his people travelled back and forth to Paris all the time. As a reward, after their victory, he received a market worth more than 100 billion franc CFA (152 million euros). As for the Electoral Commission which was made up of a

---

[49] Translator's note: the French author speaks of 'the fatality of war.'

majority of anti-Gbagbo members, it was caught in the very act of doctoring electoral lists. There were more than 450,000 names of bogus electors added to these lists.

As a matter of fact, Sidi Kagnassi's career literally "took off" and he went straight to the top of the Ivorian business sector, including BTP[50], a sector in which he had no competencies. As reported in *La Lettre du Continent*[51], this was due to some juicy state contracts:

> *"The businessman Mohamed Sidi Kagnassi is presently negotiating with the Ivorian Minister of National Education, Kandia Kamissoko Camara, for the construction of 10,000 classrooms throughout the country, and he is the only one vying for the market. Since Alassane Ouattara took power in 2011, contracts with BTP for the former boss of the Aiglon group (which no longer exists) and the ex-head rep of Sagem, just keep multiplying. Mohamed Sidi Kagnassi won a 160 billion CFA contract for the renovation and refurbishment of the Ivorian universities. Since that time, he has created the SMDCI (Company for the modernization and development of infrastructures in Ivory Coast)."*

It is important here to note that the Ivoiran rebels, along with the troops of both Licorne force and the ONUCI, reeked of incredible destruction during the events of 2011. Professor Jérôme Balou Bi Toto, General Secretary of the University of Cocody, arrested on April 19, tortured and then imprisoned in Bouna, gives the following testimony[52]:

> *"Missiles fell during the bombings. [...] The university was attacked with heavy weaponry. They destroyed students' lodging. They killed students and they went after the injured ones who sought help at the CHU (University Hospital Center). They killed them off in their hospital rooms. I saw convoys of ONUCI and Licorne soldiers on campus. They participated in the atrocities. I understand the reason why they needed*

---

[50] Translator's note: BTP is the French acronym for *Bâtiment et travaux publics*. It is an economic activity that includes the conception and construction of public and private buildings.

[51] N° 677, February 26, 2014.

[52] In an interview broadcast in August 27 2013, on the blog of René Kimbassa.

126

to refurbish the university so quickly. They spread paint over the bodies. There should be an investigation."

One day, will Sidi Kagnassi be called to speak in front of Prosecutor Fatou Bensouda, who was quoted in *Jeune Afrique*[53] in late February of 2013 as saying:

"Our desire is that all those who committed crimes in Ivory Coast, regardless of their political camp, be prosecuted"?

As time goes by, even if, from the beginning nobody really believed it, this seems less and less likely to happen. Contrary to what Madam Bensouda affirms, the International Court was never concerned with impartiality or remaining neutral. During the post-electoral crisis, which led to so much trouble, there was not one attempt by Luis Moreno Ocampo, the one then in charge, to contact Laurent Gbagbo or anyone in his government. Therefore, from the outset, it would seem that the Prosecutor of the International Court had *a priori* taken position for the Ouattara camp. Before any investigation was undertaken, it had already been decided which side was good, the one chosen by the great powers of this world, with France at the helm, and which side was bad, the one of "narrow" nationalism. Therefore, it is only logical that no investigation would ever be carried out.

I was surrounded by compromise, treachery, financial alliances, and duplicity. Of course, they had infiltrated my entourage...

It was easy for them, some of those around me were hoping all at once for my downfall and my survival...

This deplorable state of affairs was fueled by the fact that rebels were now part of the coalition government. For the sake of national reconciliation, I had accepted to include rebels in the government, and I even named the rebel leader, Guillaume Soro at its head [as Prime Minister]. I had hoped such a compromise would lead to real peace in the country. But the truth was that I was stuck. I couldn't turn my head right or left, without the risk of being beheaded. Therefore, I looked straight ahead toward the elections, hoping for the light at the end of the tunnel.

I purposely chose not to provoke a clash. What was needed was some political move, some discussion, to be able to make as much headway in the most peaceful way as possible, to end the crisis. It is part of my

---

[53] *Jeune Afrique*, N° 2720, February 2013.

personality to always try to come up with a negotiated compromise and it was in the interest of the country to reach a democratic solution. This is what I was yearning for and what I tried to put in place during many years, but this was always stopped by the rebels, backed by their French 'godfathers.' They refused to disarm and to stop their relentless atrocities against the populations in the north of the country.

Because he is "hooked" on politics, Laurent Gbagbo enjoys close and challenging contests, where he feels more comfortable than when dealing with the everyday routine. His past experience as a political opponent[54], and the electoral crisis which started as soon as he took office, has prepared and trained him well. Gbagbo comments:

In a geographically divided country where the northern part had fallen under the control of a bunch of gang leaders, and having to deal with various groups or political parties whose leaders enjoyed adding fuel to the fire and turning Ivorians one against the other, it was really important that every move be well thought out. This was the only way to put out the fires those rabble-rousers tried to start: we needed dialogue and negotiations; we needed to listen to each other and be ready to compromise. In the most difficult situations, it is important for a head of state to be someone everyone can believe in, like a father with all his children, showing no preference, letting each one who wants to talk, talk, and listening to all those who want to talk. This is why it was so important to me to protect civil rights and civil liberties. That is the essential condition for any peaceful debate. In my opinion, there was no other way to proceed than to establish a democratic debate and to give all political opponents the space they needed. That was the only way to see a true restoration of the Republic over the entire territory of Ivory Coast, so that each sector of the Ivorian population would know their security was guaranteed and that they would have access to an education, healthcare, a job, and all the benefits they are entitled to and deserve to receive.

These were my goals, this was my ambition. I thought I could provide certain guarantees to the opposition, that would give them a chance to build their own strongholds and assure their leaders and the International Community of my good faith....I was wrong. Soro Guillaume, the rebels' leader was heading my Ministers' cabinet. The

---

[54] Translator's note: Gbagbo was in the 'opposition' for thirty years (1969-2000), as he fought for a multiparty system of government in Ivory Coast. He was jailed several times, including in 1969, in 1971-1974, and in 1992.

rebels and our National Armed Forces had been integrated into a joint military.

Letting members of the opposition (in the end, willing to do anything to sabotage peace efforts) direct the electoral commission was a serious mistake. It allowed them to tamper with the election results and plan other maneuvers which I suspect were initiated by the French. Indeed, I had seriously underestimated Nicolas Sarkozy's unrelenting determination to do anything possible to bring his close friend Alassane Ouattara to power.

I began to have serious doubts about the sincerity of the French when I heard that they had appointed Emmanuel Beth as ambassador in Ouagadougou in Burkina Faso. He's a soldier, the former boss of the Licorne force stationed in Ivory Coast. He was known as being anti-Gbagbo and his brother was in charge of the COS, a structure for "special operations" in Ivory Coast.

His nomination came into effect a few weeks before the first round of the Ivorian presidential election. In the history of French diplomacy, never before has a military general been appointed ambassador. Well, that is what happened three months before the Ivorian presidential race. A military general close to Sarkozy and the brother of a person who had organized underhanded tricks for French intelligence was appointed ambassador to the country to the north of Ivory Coast. At that very moment, Ivorian mercenaries from Burkina Faso and neighboring countries were recruited, trained, and provided with arms in the Burkinabè army, before being transferred to the north of Ivory Coast. Some of them infiltrated into Abidjan even before the election took place. The remainder--organized under rebel leaders, were poised to flow down towards the southern part of the country. This is exactly what happened in 2011, with the rebels getting logistical and operational assistance from the French special services. When I raised the issue with Compaoré, he replied:

"Really? I didn't even know Beth was here [in Ouagadougou]*!"*

In fact, at that time, they were busy building their base as a back-up for the intervention of the French Special Forces. But we had to find a solution. I did not trust either Soro, Compaoré, or Ouattara. I knew their goal was to seize power in any way they could. Their objective was to have

Ivory Coast "melt" into a larger entity including Burkina Faso, with them taking the lead. People need to understand: the south of Ivory Coast is the fat milk cow of the entire sub-region. People migrate to Ivory Coast from the northern arid areas, where there are so few riches. In order to get real wealth, to have real power on the domestic as well as international fronts, you need to possess the south of Ivory Coast. Their goal was to use some of the many immigrants, some living in northern Ivory Coast, some from Burkina, Niger, and from Guinea. Today, they promote the immigration of tens of thousands of foreigners and offer them electors' cards in order to "swamp" the native Ivorian populations through sheer numbers. If the French had been in my shoes, I don't know how they would have dealt with such a situation. They themselves have not been able to integrate their Muslim population which is around 10%. In Ivory Coast, the problem is not the foreigners; they have always been welcome in Ivory Coast. The problem is that Compaoré and Ouattara want Ivory Coast to melt into Burkina Faso. Thinking about it, they both seem to want to somehow "get even" with Ivory Coast...

As for me, all I wanted was a pacified country, a country in peace where harmony between citizens would reign, no matter what each one's origin. You know, in my inner circle as well as in my family, many people come from the north. In Ivory Coast, inter-ethnic marriages are common. It was this balance we were trying to preserve. We tried to prevent some groups from aggressing other groups. It was in the interest of all of us to preserve this status, to preserve what made Ivory Coast a prosperous and ethnically rich country.

What do you think was the secret of my support among the people of Ivory Coast? It was because all Ivorians, whatever their origin, were opposed to violence, because they knew my policy of appeasement was the right way forward. It was because they wanted to preserve what they had acquired, be it collective (health, education, etc.) or individual (improvement of their standard of living, etc.) I had support from people from all walks of life. In the eight opinion polls conducted by Sofres in the last months prior to the 2010 election, I was always the favored winner.

The French Ambassador, Jean-Marc Simon claimed that these opinion polls were rigged and were meant to put me to sleep, to prevent me from seeing all the manoeuvers [to subvert me] taking place. In any case, all these polls ranked Ouattara third. If these opinion polls were rigged, why wouldn't they have ranked Ouattara second instead of third?

Whatever the meaning of all this, it helps us to see the truth of certain things and the forces at work which were trying to oust me from power. All this also reveals to what extent seemingly respectable political leaders or representatives of world powers are nothing but swindlers. What's worse, they dare to brag, even today, about their swindling. If Jean-Marc Simon and all the others tell the truth, they will have to admit they organized this all to be able to cheat, when they claim the contrary... I rather believe they loaded the dice because they knew I was likely to win. Just take a look at the map. In almost every region, from east to west and in the south, I was ahead, while Ouattara was ahead only in the north. It's up there that everything was played out, [as voters went to the polling stations] under the threat of armed rebel-militias.

Gbagbo, so used to storms and other dangers, probably became over-confident, though he would never admit it. He says:

I could have controlled the chain of events if the rules and institutions had been respected. My strategy was successful. I won the elections. But from the beginning, I was betrayed, in the first round and again in the second. They did what they had to do. Alassane Ouattara was never the runner-up in the first election, and thus he was not even qualified for the runoff. It was Bédié who was in second place and thus qualified. But Bédié was like Esau. He sold his birthright for lentil stew.

Information that was gathered at the time of the election and since then will enable people to understand why Ouattara and his supporters had no desire whatsoever for a recount or a final audit of the votes.

At the 12th Congress of the PDCI, the oldest Ivorian political party founded by Houphouët-Boigny, which took place on October 3, 2013, the ceremonies began with lots of fanfare, and then Henri Konan Bédié, its president, launched into a diatribe against the majority of Ivorian political leaders, including obviously, the *"dictator"* Laurent Gbagbo. It was a speech filled with bitterness and attacks, a speech in which he also took his own supporters to task, chiding them for hanging their dirty laundry in public. He also spoke of *"threats, bleeding and buying people off,"* terms intended to depict the electoral tactics used by the RDR party of Ouattara. It was indeed a powerful indictment against those attempting to drain the PDCI of its life's blood. But the most surprising note occurred right after he leveled his cutting remarks against an audience who hardly reacted. Then the bomb exploded when he said:

"After the first round of the presidential elections of 2010, it is important to realize that the ranking they gave me and which I accepted wasn't correct. Despite the bad organization and direction of my campaign, I have been able to establish, with concrete proof, that I was deprived of at least 600,000 votes. I informed different chancelleries in Abidjan, including the ONUCI, the Constitutional Council, and the Independent Electoral Commission which received my objections."

Doing some basic arithmetic, it is as easy as pie to understand the significance of this revelation. When the 600,000 votes stolen from Henri Konan Bédié are added to the 1,165,532 votes (25.24%) obtained for the first round, it puts him ahead of Alassane Ouattara with his 1,181,091 votes (32.07%). It also put him within reach or ahead of the 1,756,504 votes (38.04%) obtained by Laurent Gbagbo.

Looking at it this way, Ouattara shouldn't have ever been in the run-off election, as Bédié made clear in his public statement, which no one ever contradicted. Ouattara should have been eliminated. Between the two rounds, Bédié threatened to lodge official protests, but then, without anyone being able to explain why, he doesn't do it. Some kinds of negotiations go on. There are numerous rumors, some coming from those close to the candidates. Some speak of a possible meeting between Bédié and Gbagbo. People also talk about a phone call made by Ouattara to Bédié, where Ouattara "calls him to order." Others say Sarkozy put pressure on Bédié to let Ouattara be the runner-up. All this is mysterious, but Gbagbo confirmed this confidential information with just one sentence:

Sarkozy and Ouattara pressured Bédié to change sides.

Then what explains Bédié's determination to remain head of the PDCI even though he is eighty years old? Gbagbo's analysis:

He wants to keep being paid off.

When I heard this comment, I remembered what Ambassador Jean-Marc Simon told me at Berkeley, as he sipped his coffee:

"Bédié counts envelopes [containing pay offs].*"*

In October 2013, when the news about the 600,000 stolen votes came out of Konan Bédié's own mouth, there was an embarrassed silence among his political partners, but there was no protest inside Ivory Coast, and not a word concerning this appears in the French press. Maybe this was because the reason may have been that the electoral misadventures of Abidjan had already been poured in the concrete slap of conviction.

"Gbagbo did not expect Ouattara and Bédié to get along so well. It was if they did some secret magic invocation and it worked."

Jean-Marc Simon who made this statement did not believe a single word of what he said. He bragged to Jean-Christophe Notin about the fact that he had manipulated Gbagbo, with the complicity of Guillaume Soro, making him believe in his upcoming victory. According to Notin, Gbagbo's *"[...] longtime adviser, Bernard Houdin,"* "was singing the same song."

When I first saw Gbagbo again, meeting him in prison at The Hague and well before Bédié had made his explosive declaration, Laurent Gbagbo told me that fraudulent manipulations in the voting apparatus had first begun with Sagem, which affected the first round of voting. He also told me how between the elections, they had tried to set another trap:

The people at the Independent Electoral Commission wanted me to change the date of the second election. They wanted a week's delay. In fact what they wanted to do was to bring Burkinabè across the border, people who vote in their own country, so they could come and vote in Ivory Coast.

By then Bédié-Esau was out of the picture. The second round of voting on Sunday November 28 had barely passed, when the next day, Monday November 29, Young-jin Choi, representing the UN, and the Canadian La Tortue, representing the Francophone Observation Commission made the following declaration: *"In spite of some incidents, the elections went well."*

They hoped that: *"The turn out, inferior to the one of the first round, would nonetheless reach 70%."*

In December 3, 2010, an article published online at *Abidjan.net* had already reported that Youssouf Bakayoko had pointed out fraud in the north, of some 500,000 votes. The elections in this region (that is to say, 9.35% of the recorded votes) were cast in polling stations overseen by the armed rebellion.

After subtracting this "bonus" from Ouattara's score, a quick tally would give the following results:

Out of a total of 5,784,490 recorded electors, 70% of whom would have cast their votes in the runoff (i.e. 4,049,143 voters) Laurent Gbagbo received 2,107,055 votes, arriving at 52.04%, with Ouattara receiving 1,942,088 votes, i.e. 47.96%.

In one crucial area in the north, the Bandama Valley, the registers show that the RDR candidate Ouattara had a total of 149,598 votes, while the local Independent Electoral Commission reported to its central counterpart Commission the figure of 244,471 votes, i.e. with 94,873 fraudulent votes.

Ivorian newspapers close to Ouattara kept asking: *"Where are all the voters?"*

They saw the turnout for the second election and were worried about the abstention rate.

By late afternoon of the election's day, the Independent Electoral Commission announced a low turnout, that is to say, 70.84% in comparison with the first round which had mobilized the record figure of 83%. Amadou Soumahouro, one of the vice-presidents of the Independent Electoral Commission declared on Ivorian Public Television:

"The turn-out is around 70%...
"We are surprised that the turnout is so high, contrary to what we thought yesterday (Sunday). We were getting scared that voter numbers might not even reach 60% of the electorate."

Already Pascal Affi N'Guessan, speaking on behalf of Laurent Gbagbo, was lodging complaints for fraud in the northern region, where the armed rebellion supervised the voting.

That evening, the results of the Ivorian diaspora were publically announced, with the votes from France being subtracted, giving Ouattara the victory among Ivorians living abroad.

On Tuesday, November 30, the observers of the African Union, headed by Joseph Koffigoh, former Prime Minister of Togo, thanked the ONUCI for having freed three of their colleagues who were blocked and threatened by rebels, and who consequently could not achieve their mission. The AU observers declared that competent jurists would have to assess the impact of these incidents on the vote:

"The mission noted, with regret, serious acts of violence, including loss of life, physical aggression of individuals, illegal detentions, acts of intimidation, and abduction attempts. […] Moreover, the mission deplores the late opening of some of the polling stations, the lack of stickers in some of them, and the menacing atmosphere which prevailed around the polling stations. Finally the mission deplores the illegal detention of two of its observers and thanks the personnel of the ONUCI who intervened in time, to avoid the worst."

I was able to talk to Mr. Koffigoh by phone, as he was about to leave Ivory Coast as he awaited his flight for Lomé at the Abidjan airport. He said he was sickened by the contempt with which his mission [the representatives of the African Union] was treated by the representatives of the International Community, because, this group was *only composed of Africans.*"

There were rapes. Voters were prevented from voting. There were polling stations where Alassane Ouattara obtained 100% of the votes. This means that even the one pro-Gbagbo representative present at the polls would not have voted for his own candidate! Out of 20,000 polling stations, in 2,200 of the voting records, there were more votes supposedly cast than there were names on the electoral lists.

On Thursday December 2, at the Golf Hotel, Youssouf Bakayoko [head of the Electoral Commission] had decided to go "solo," a completely illegal move and made public not only the victory of Ouattara, but an incredible turnout of 82%. [UN representative] Choi outdid Bakayoko by announcing a turnout of 83%. The 70% turnout announced by the Independent Electoral Commission on Monday was a thing of the past. The figure for the turnout was officially recorded as 81.10% with 54.10% for Ado and 49.90 % for Gbagbo. A real magic trick!

The magical increase of the turnout by 12%, representing roughly 400,000 votes, is one of keys, but not the only one, to explaining the reversal in the outcome of the second round of elections, after the first election had already been rigged. The point was to make Ouattara the winner, not Bédié, not me. They knew that for Ouattara to win in the second round, they had to obtain 50% of the votes of the pro-Bedié camp, but many Baoulé voters abstained. That community had for a long time harbored ill feeling toward the RDR and Ouattara. They were the ones who abstained, so they had to do something to change the rate of turnout to make the victory of Ouattara statistically credible.

The other issue is Bakayoko's "solo" announcement of the election results at the campaign headquarters of my adversary[55], as he was appeared surrounded by both the French and American Ambassadors. It has been argued that he appeared alone and at the wrong venue as a result of the "pressure" prevailing at the headquarters of the Independent Electoral Commission. But this doesn't hold up. The UN was there to

---

[55] Translator's note: according to the Ivorian Constitution, the results must be announced at the headquarters of the Electoral Commission, by the committee, not by a single individual.

guarantee the voting. **They are the ones who should have seen that everything was in place [to carry out the procedure in the legal way]. On the contrary, what they did was far from legal and made no sense. What a hoax!**

In August, 2011, Ahoua Don Mello, a civil engineer with a degree from Ponts et Chaussées[56], former Minister and spokesperson of the last Gbagbo cabinet was also the head of Sils-Technology, a structure involved in the processing of the votes on behalf of FPI, has written a widely circulated document[57] providing his analysis of the election. According to his analysis based on transcripts provided by ONUCI, Sils-Technology, and the Independent Electoral Commission, including 19,041 official transcripts from 20,073 polling stations there are 1,032 missing transcripts which were never reported to the Independent Electoral Commission.

Don Mello asked that his study, which he carried out by going through each official record of each polling station, be compared with those documents held by the ONUCI, and the records of Sagem. All this was in vain, since none of these organizations were willing to "put their cards on the table." Troubled by the missing 1,032 voting records, representing 306,889 votes, and having tallied the number of fictitious or invalid votes, he came to the conclusion that it is the commissioners of the Independent Electoral Commission who were responsible. He notes:

> *"[They] were in charge of the areas under rebellion control [...] and they were the presidents of the local commissions, which let "disappear" 1,032 records from those polling stations, without providing any official explanation. When you realize that the quasi totality of these commissioners and the presidents of the local commissions are.... pro-Ouattara and that they had the results of the first round in hand, nothing prevented them from creating situations which would invalidate the official voting records favorable to their opponent, which is what happened in Paris."*

According to Don Mello, for the second round, there was a 71% turnout:

---

[56] Translator's note: Now known as École des Ponts ParisTech, this was the first engineering school in the world, founded in 1747. It is still one of the most prestigious engineering schools in the world.

[57] *Ma part de vérité* (My take on the truth), a document circulated on August 7, 2011.

"...a figure which roughly corresponds with the figure announced by the Independent Electoral Commission when the polls closed..." *"These figures are based on the signatures on the attendance lists, which are far from the 81% announced, based on the official polling records."*

For Don Mello, the results put Laurent Gbagbo, with 52.45% of the votes, ahead of Alassane Ouattara, with 47.55%.

It will be remembered that on December 3, 2010, the incumbent Ivorian president had been declared winner of the November 28 presidential election by the Constitutional Council with 51.45% of the electorate against 48.55% for his challenger, while the provisory results of the Independent Electoral Commission had made Ouattara winner with 54.1% against 45.9% in favor of the incumbent president.

Following the official complaints submitted by Laurent Gbagbo, the Constitutional Council declared void the votes of seven departments in the north under rebel control and for the reasons given by Paul Yao N'Dré who was immediately put under scrutiny since he had been appointed by Gbagbo. But the reasons of this massive annulation of these voting stations was clear: absence of representatives of the opposition in some polling stations, obvious stuffing of ballot boxes, absence of polling booths, the number of voters, often exceeding the figures on the electoral lists, i.e. the list of actual voters, as well as the transportation of ballots by non-authorized personnel. No one took up Don Mello's challenge, whose proposal had serious merit.

Anyway, how can one take seriously an election when, in the city of Bouaké...the stronghold of Ouattara, you end up with more than 250,000 people casting their votes for some 150,000 registered voters? Was that the kind of election that the International Community wanted?

Beyond the complicated calculations and in spite of the recount that should have taken place but never was carried out, the admission of Henri Konan Bédié made things clear once and for all, in his official, public and uncontested declaration. Ouattara did not win the presidential election in Ivory Coast in 2010. Henri Konan Bédié, Ouattara's "best enemy" and his political ally could not be lying. He had no interest in doing so. If we take Bedié at his word, then the conclusion is: a usurper today runs the country of Ivory Coast, and this usurper has sent Laurent Gbagbo to the International Criminal Court.

Lanny Davis, the former communication specialist of Bill Clinton, who worked briefly for Laurent Gbagbo in the U.S. during the post-electoral crisis, declared on CNN that the UN

> "[D]id not even take the time to read the text of the decision of the Ivorian Constitutional Council."

He said, Laurent Gbagbo wanted *"to stop violence and negotiate a peaceful solution."*

Likewise, Thabo Mbeki[58], in an unpublished report, recommended a recount. The American Senator, James Inhofe, would go far as to write to Hillary Clinton to also ask for a recount. But nothing happened, even after the clergy in Ivory Coast took a stance in favor of Gbagbo. Cardinal Agré said he was taking position for the Constitution, and the Ivorian bishops fell in behind him, asking ECOWAS (the Economic Community of West African States) and the UN to respect Ivorian sovereignty.

Author Jean-Christophe Notin, as usual, tells his own story [of course to ridicule Gbagbo], quoting an American politician he did not even know. He writes:

> *"Religious anathema is a classic in Gbagbo's behavior, and this even made its way into the U.S. where Pat Robertson, former candidate in the primaries for the 1988 presidential election [...] declared on CNN in April: 'The issue is that this country which was run by a Christian, will now be in Muslim hands. So now there will be another Muslim nation which will contribute an arc in the circle of the charia around the Middle-East.'"*

Everyone sees things through their own eyes. But at least we should be asking why all Gbagbo's proposals for direct dialogue and a carefully controlled recount were refused by Ouattara and his allies. The unheard of cost of these elections--261 billion CFA francs (369 million euros), 342 billion of which were paid by Ivory Coast, raised hope that there would be a better outcome than a war with thousands of dead.

As of March 30, 2011, a general offensive, including the shelling of the residence of Laurent Gbagbo, started. European economic operators, blocked for weeks by the embargo that was decreed to suffocate Gbagbo, warned that

---

[58] Former president of South Africa.

they could not hold out any longer than the end of March. After that date, they wanted to resume business as usual, whatever the politico-military situation. For Sarkozy and his allies, they needed to act fast, to do away with Gbagbo, who would have been saved by the resumption of economic activities in Ivory Coast. French military forces were already engaged, and their last military intervention, seemingly already won. This is what leads the supporters of Gbagbo say *"We won the elections but we lost the war."*

Chapter 15
"The Ouattaras are not a couple, they're an enterprise"

In this chapter both Gbagbo and Mattei give insight into who Alassane and Dominique Ouattara really are. Dominique Ouattara came to Abidjan as a beautiful blond-haired French national born in Constantine in the then-French Algeria. In 1975 she arrived in Ivory Coast with her first husband, Jean Folloroux, a high school teacher. She worked her way up from secretary to head of a major real estate firm in Ivory Coast during the reign of Houphouët-Boigny. She later set her sights on Alassane Ouattara, who had held several posts in important international financial institutions and who Houphouët later appointed--most agree under pressure from the International Community--as Prime Minister of Ivory Coast. Alassane Ouattara, though born in Sindou, Burkina Faso, spent his younger years in Ivory Coast being raised by his aunt until, at age 6, his Burkinabè father came to get him and put him into school in Ouagadougou. He later continued his studies in the U.S., travelling on his Burkinabè passport. This family history is at the bottom of the many conflicts surrounding Ado's nationality--with many claiming that Ouattara never was and never has been an Ivorian citizen.

In contrast to the Gbagbo's, Alassane and Dominique Ouattara are said to be immensely wealthy and owners of several homes, one in Nice on the French Riviera and another in Ivory Coast's luxury lagoon area in Assinie. Dominique Ouattara, along with her many brothers and sister, and children from her first marriage, headed up various real estate companies and other enterprises. Madam Ouattara also runs a charity foundation, Children of Africa, with offices scattered around the world. For the time being, not many questions have been asked concerning the origin of the Ouattara's great wealth, though some eyebrows have been raised over Madam Ouattara's past association with the Bongo family of Gabon, who themselves have been pursued by French authorities for "ill-gotten gains." Gbagbo has known the Ouattara's for years—he was even put in prison by Prime Minister Ouattara. Not one to delve into personal lives of those for or against him, Gbagbo simply says, "they're not a couple—they're an enterprise."

In this chapter, Mattei also underlines the extremely close personal ties that exist between former French President Nicolas Sarkozy and Alassane Ouattara. Nicolas Sarkozy was the sitting president when Gbagbo was "de-throned" and Ouattara put in his place. When Sarkozy lost the last French presidential elections to François Hollande, it is rumored that only one head of state flew to his side: Alassane Ouattara.

We think we know the facts but in reality we only see the vague appearance of things. The media doesn't write history. They don't have the means, nor the time, nor the calling. In France, very few of the media, especially audiovisual ones, can choose to abandon the single-thought highway flowing out of the high places of Nicolas Sarkozy's Elysée. The involvement of the French president would be even more heavy-handed than that of his predecessor, Jacques Chirac, in his wrangles with Gbagbo between 2000 and 2007. It is a question of style. Sarkozy's involvement was also more personal. The friendship that ties him to Alassance Ouattara goes back over twenty years. In the online journal *Le Post* of April 12, 2011, which at times tries to ask what role it might have played in the downfall of Gbagbo, Ouattara often evokes this privileged relationship:

> *"He [Sarkozy] and I are first and foremost friends. And we were friends well before the crisis. Whenever I travel to Paris, I always go to see him. To tell the truth, if I have five or six true friends around the world, he is one of them,"* declared the Ivorian president in *L'Express* magazine

[...] According to the same article, during the same month, on Canal+, Ouattara confirmed their 'longtime' friendship and notes he is also friends with Dominique Strauss-Kahn and Laurent Fabius, friendships which developed when he was deputy director at the IMF from 1994 to 1999. The article goes on to state:

> *"From 1990, when he became the Prime Minister of Félix Houphouët-Boigny, Alassane Dramane Ouattara entrusted the private markets of water and electricity in Ivory Coast to Martin Bouygues, a close friend of Sarkozy, which Bouygues held onto for a period of fifteen years. It*

was natural, then, for these two politicians to spend time together. They liked each other and became friends."

"Ouattara then became very close to Bouygues," Antoine Glaser, former chief editor of *La Lettre du Continent,* explains to *Le Post.* On August 24, 1991, Alassane Ouattara married Dominique, a widow of Folloroux, at the town hall in the 16th arrondissement in Paris. Antoine Glaser who attended the wedding remembers very well: *Martin Bouygues was seated in the first row.*

However, it was not Nicolas Sarkozy who performed the ceremony. *"This is an incredible rumor,"* says Antoine Glaser. *"Contrary to the persistent rumors spread over the Internet, the ceremony was performed by the deputy mayor of the 16th arrondissement."* The *Post* explains:

> *"From the time of Ouattara's marriage, against the background of their mutual business and political interests, Nicolas Sarkozy and Alassane Ouattara became even closer friends... Through Martin Bouygues, Nicolas and Cécilia became close to the Ouattaras."*

The *Post* also explains that Ouattara's wife, Dominique, a French national born in Algeria had become a mutual friend of Martin Bouygues and the Sarkozy couple. She is known as an influential business woman. She made her fortune through managing the considerable property holdings of Félix Houphouët-Boigny. It is true that she was very much appreciated by the first president of Ivory Coast whose fortune was estimated at the end of his life between 7 to 10 billion dollars. It is common knowledge that Félix and Dominique were on intimate terms with one another. A former close aid of Houphouët remembers the afternoons he spent playing pinball in the café around the corner as he waited for the "Old man"[59] who was paying a personal visit to Dominique in her Parisian apartment located on Avenue Victor-Hugo. When Ouattara became Prime Minister, thanks to Dominique, the young couple built its own fortune, based on Houphouet's fortune, with "Monsieur" doing the cooking and "Madame" taking care of the garden...until the "Old Man" passed away in December 1993. When Houphouët dies, there is no will—none is found or produced by anyone.

---

[59] Translator's note: In Ivory Coast, for almost everyone--youngsters to adults--Houphouët-Boigny was affectionately called *Le vieux,* that is to say, *Old man*, a term of respect used across Africa and especially in Ivory Coast. Such expressions are in no way derogatory, as they might be in many European languages.

Dominique Folloroux first arrived in Ivory Coast in 1975 and held modest jobs, such as working at the Ascott bar, then as a secretary at the Embassy of Canada. Her fierce determination to make something of herself, her charm, and her stunning blond hair quickly drew the attention of people in power. In 1979, she created and developed her own real-estate company, the AICI, thanks to the support of Abdoulaye Fadiga, governor of the BCEAO who also was a very close friend. Dominique managed to take possession of the personal properties Houphouët had entrusted to her, at a time when there was no difference between the Ivorian state funds and Houphouët-Boigny's private ones.

Then, she went off to manage the funds of Omar Bongo of Gabon. The now deceased Gabonese president entrusted her with the management of his "ill-gotten gains." Thus her name and that of her agency should have logically appeared in the files of Sherpa, a company involved in the search of embezzled public funds generally invested in real-estate businesses. Sherpa has recently focused its attacks on Denis Sassou-NGuesso, the president of Congo-Brazaville. All these ongoing investigations did not prevent "handsome Denis" from receiving as his guest in Brazzaville Christine Ockrent, who came for the launching of the magazine *Forbes Afrique*, or to play host to Bernadette Chirac in April, 2013, at the Parisian hotel Meurice[60].

Theodoro Obiang of Equatorial Guinea, along with Omar Bongo of Gabon, and afterward, his son Ali, are also targeted by the anti-IGG, ill-gotten gains crusade. Both presidents, Obiang of Guinea and Bongo of Gabon have asked the former executive of Publicis to "smooth out" their image in the West by organizing international economic forums in their respective capital cities. The actions of Sherpa are totally hypocritical, as they strangely pass over in silence the system which made possible hiding the misappropriation of funds, a system that facilitated embezzlements and often organized them, without mentioning those who could benefit from them.

When I paid a visit to his office on *la rue de Rivoli* on July 15, 2013, I asked William Bourdon, the specialist on ill-gotten gains why he never looked into the role that AICI, Dominique Ouattara's company, could have played in the case of Bongo's "ill-gotten" real-estate, a link which might legally qualify as complicity. He answered that a company cannot "seize" itself. He noted he would need a very precise dossier to pursue this.

---

[60] According to *La lettre du Continent* n° 657.

The financial holdings of Alassane Ouattara and the mystery of the origin of Dominique's immense fortune are still taboo and do not seem to fascinate too many people. This topic does not seem to interest the main stream media either. In the book *Queens of Africa, the True Story of First Ladies*[61], which cites a *"former adviser on Africa at the Elysée,"* one quote reads as follows:

> "[...] *it is possible that Dominique got hold of some of Houphouët's cash. At least that's what some of his heirs claim, who believe they were robbed.*"

It is true that in 1993, when Houphouët passed away, people weren't yet talking about ill-gotten gains. Only a complete biography of Dominique and Alassane Ouattara would be able to unravel the golden threads that weave their common history and tell us the origin of their fortune, as well as the secret of their success story. What facts we do know, however, give a kind of outline.

On the purported liaisons of Dominique Nouvian-Folloroux after the death of her husband, everything has already been said. She has denied it all. That a young blond widow would suddenly find herself at the head of a real-estate business covering vast properties of the head of state did not surprise those close to Houphouët-Boigny. According to Michel de Bonnecorse, the Elysée's adviser for African Affairs, Houphouët was very affected when Dominique later set her eyes on Alassane Ouattara and ended up marrying him:

> *"Jacques Chirac saw him [Houphouët] weep [...] This explains the consequent mistrust Houphouët showed towards Ouattara, the one who "stole" Houphouët's woman."*

Dominique Ouattara swears this malicious gossip *"wounded her"* and that she *"loved Houphouët"*...He considered her like a *"daughter."*

The Ouattaras were very skillful at making useful friends. From Michel Camdessus, General Director of the IMF for fifteen years, to Martin Bouygues or George Soros, the famous multimillionaire and speculator. Laurent Gbagbo notes: **Dominique Ouattara herself told me he [Soros] was one of their close friends.** His high position at the IMF allowed Ouattara to form a circle of

---

[61] Vincent Hugues, *Les reines d'afrique: le roman vrai des Premières dames* (Queens of Africa, the True Story of First Ladies), Perrin 2014.

powerful friends. In addition, Ouattara benefited from the intense public relations efforts of "Madame." This alchemy gives the couple every advantage. Dominique Ouattara communicates a great deal through her foundation, Children of Africa, whose patroness, Ira von Furstenberg, and all the "guests," all volunteers, such as Alain Delon, Adriana Karembeu and MC Solaar travelled to Abidjan for a charity dinner at the Hotel Ivoire February 24, 2012. On March 14, 2014, they are all off again... "Maman Dominique," as she is dubbed in a Figaro article dated March 21, 2014, flew in a charter-full of celebrities to Abidjan for a charity gala. This time it was to build a 115-bed hospital for children in Bingerville, 18 kilometers out of Abidjan. The guest list was impressive. The visitors gathered at the Palais des Congrès at Hotel Sofitel to enjoy a show inspired by Patrick Sébastien and his Grand Carbaret, an event which proved as impressive as the one in 2012. All the loyal supporters were there: Richard Berry, Adrianna Karembeu, the inevitable MC Solaar, Ira von Furstenberg and also Jean Todt, president of the International Automobile Association, the jeweler Edouard Nahum, the film director Alexandre Arcady, Professor Alain Deloche, founder of Chain of Hope, Professor Marc Gentilini, Miss France 2014 in the company of Miss Ivory Coast 2014, Ivorian singer Alpha Blondy, and Gary Dourdan, the American actor from the series The Experts. Best of all was the guest of honor: her Royal Highness Lalla Salma, wife of the King of Morocco, Mohamed VI.

Interviewed by the bi-monthly Afrique Education[62], Mamadou Koulibaly, in his capacity as president of his political party Lider, and a professor of economy, provided a vision different from that of the journalist who interviewed him. The journalist introduced the new First Lady as a person who is only concerned with social issues, not political issues, as was the case for Simone Gbagbo. Mamadou Koulibaly comments:

> "Did you say she's not involved in politics? The foundation of Children of Africa, the personal property of the First Lady, has been recognized as a service organization through a presidential decree[63] signed by her husband. This means that this foundation gets its operational funds from the Ivorian government. To be clear, the foundation is taking away money from the state and using it for charity. This is not good governance. Why can't the Ministry of Social Affairs

---

[62] Afrique Education, n° 348 of May 16 -31, 2012.
[63] Decree n° 2012-232 of March 7, 2012.

take this money and do this work? [...] Beyond that, on December 6, 2011, Mrs. Ouattara was promoted by her husband—and the 'Grande Chancelière' to the rank of Commander of the National Order of the Republic of Ivory Coast."

Mamadou Koulibaly ironically points out that neither Mrs. Houphouët-Boigny, nor Henriette Bédié, nor Simone Gbagbo--the three previous First Ladies had the honor of receiving the highest distinction in the country nor the advantages that go with it. Offices for Children of Africa have been set up in numerous capital cities, with bases in Paris and Abidjan, a parallel track for the flow of private finances, while the foundation is simultaneously linked to the Ivorian state budget.

All experts agree that Dominique Ouattara has played a crucial role in her husband's rise to power, beginning with his appointment as head of the BCEAO and then as Prime Minister of Ivory Coast. She helps him project an image which draws supporters--an image also projected through the French media. Her continual work in public relations gave an international flavor, even if a little too flashy, to the first part of her husband's reign in Ivory Coast. In addition, in 2013, the current First Lady was ranked by *Jeune Afrique* among the most twenty-five influential business women on the African continent. She has also created a powerful conglomerate of hairdressing salons and products in the U.S. under the mark *Dessange*. Her sister, her daughter, and her son are part of the family businesses. We know, of course, that Loïc Folloroux was the Africa-Director for the Anglo-saxon group Armajaro, specialized in cocoa. In that capacity, he had his say as to the new partitioning of cocoa profits after the fall of President Gbagbo. As for Ibrahima, a real spitting image of his brother Alassane, thus his nickname "Photocopy," he seems to be a kind of "shadow president," assigned to budget management and its allotment. With a smile, Gbagbo says:

The Ouattara's are not a couple, they're an enterprise.

Dominique Ouattara, like her husband, is a "fine talker," watching what she says, always mixed with bits of truth. However, her discourse often says the opposite of the realities meant to be communicated. She claims, for example, to have greatly sacrificed in giving up her businesses as soon as she became First Lady. With Dominique, categories often overlap: this "sacrifice" must be put into perspective, since through her link to important and devoted collaborators, especially members of her own family, she remains at the heart of a huge far-

147

reaching system, which she can easily monitor from the office of First Lady, where she is assisted by a staff of forty.

With Elisabeth Gandon, one of Dominique's most faithful friends, now head of Malesherbes Management, a property management complex currently overseeing 250 portfolios, as well as head of the real estate agency AICI (along with Nathalie Folloroux-Bejani, the elder daughter of her boss, Madam Ouattara), and on the Board of Directors of Children of Africa, it is clear that Dominique is never far from what interests her. The links between the different components of her galaxy are ensured. Her son Loïc has left the cocoa business and is now running Radio Nostalgia for Africa, another property which belongs to his mother. Dominique's sister, Nathalie, in addition to her functions in real-estate, helps Loic. As for Ouattara's son-in-law, Benedict Senger, husband of Fanta Catherine Ouattara-Senger (daughter of Ado), in 2013, he was granted a series of contracts involving customs, harbor, and airport control through Webb Fontaine, his company registered in Dubai with its head office in Geneva. In March, 2014, a mission of the IMF in Ivory Coast pointed the finger at the management by this company and the important losses the company had caused for the state of Ivory Coast: 46.36 billion CFA francs (70 million euros) foreseen in revenues have apparently "gone missing."…

"In the Nouvian family, among the brothers [...] Patrick is a general practitioner in Hyères in the Department of Var. Marc, fifty-three years of age, created, with his sister Noëlle, in 2012 (one year after the election of his brother-in-law Ado to the presidency), Sonecei, an international trade company specialized in the trade of cocoa beans, of which Ivory Coast is the world leader. As for Philippe, also in his fifties, he has left the management of the Gabonese branch of the AICI. Now, he controls Gecmo…involved in real-estate management. It is Philippe who was called upon to receive the bids for the hospital in Bingerville[64], the hospital so dear to his elder sister's heart. He has also been put in charge of the renovation work on the residence of the president[65]."

From charity to family business, things are well tied up. Evil to him who evil thinks…

---

[64] Translator's note: A college city in the eastern part of the suburb of Abidjan
[65] Vincent Hugeux, *op.cit.,* see footnote 61 above.

But besides all this, everyone keeps on living it up in Abidjan! Ten million dollars to see Rihanna on stage live December 29, 2012, for Ado's birthday party, which happens to coincide with the Koras, an African music celebration. The beautiful singer Rihanna was accompanied by her fiancé of that time, Chris Brown, who came to sing at the Houphouët-Boigny stadium-- in the end, only half full. Evidently the seats were too expensive for average Ivorians. Even when late in the evening, they announced free seats, no great crowds emerged. And while the two American stars were giving a private performance for Ado, and the fireworks were going off, there was a terrible panic and crush of people, leading to the death of 60 spectators and 200 injured. The organization and security measures were said to be insufficient. They claimed that Hamed Bakayoko, Minister of the Interior was responsible. Chris Brown did not show up at the Hotel Ivoire as scheduled to present the trophies at the Koras Ceremonies. He slipped away with his girlfriend, a little bit richer than when he arrived. This event was intended to "re-position" Abidjan as one of the concert capitals of the world.

Even before coming to power, the Ouattaras are known for behind-the-scenes action. François Loncle, former Socialist minister and lawmaker for the Department of Eure discussed the *"maneuvers"* that contributed to sowing discord within the French and Ivorian socialists, which caused the French party to position itself against Laurent Gbagbo [a socialist]. According to François Loncle, in a series of interviews recorded and broadcast on the Internet by the information officer, Nicoletta Fagiolo, it was the intense lobbying of Dominique Ouattara that was responsible, allowing her *"to reach her goals, thanks to her enormous fortune."* This intense lobbying of Dominique Ouattara made all the difference.

François Loncle has also mentioned names of well-known socialists who were in favor of Ouattara. For instance, Laurent Fabius, the current French Minister of Foreign Affairs and Dominique Strauss-Kahn. This network of friends that the Ouattaras were so good at building may explain the repeated refusals to set up a parliamentary commission to investigate France's participation in the Ivorian crisis, proposed by the Communist député Alain Bocquet. Another person who tried to propose this was Jean-Marc Ayrault[66]. The point was to clarify the role of France and its army in the coup d'etat against Gbagbo in September, 2002. But we should not fool ourselves: the

---

[66] Translator's note: Jean-Marc Ayrault was the leader of the Socialist Group in the French National Assembly from 1997 to 2012. He then became Prime Minister (May 16, 2012 to March 31, 2014).

transparency of the relations between France and Africa are still imaginary. Antoine Glaser recounts:

> *"Sarkozy became well acquainted with Ouattara in 1993 at the time of the devaluation of the CFA franc."*

As a matter of fact, the then-head of the Ivorian government, Prime Minister Alassane Ouattara, helped the then-French Prime Minister, Edouard Balladur, with this operation. It is at that time that Ouattara must then have first dealt with the Minister of the Budget, Nicolas Sarkozy. Gilles Labarthe notes:

> *"In 1997, Nicolas Sarkozy made his first trip in Ivory Coast. He was accompanying Martin Bouygues as his business lawyer to meet with Henri Konan Bédié, the Ivoiran president who served from 1993-1999. The goal of Sarkozy's presence in Abidjan was to defend the contracts his friend Martin Bouygues was bidding for in Ivory Coast. By that time Ouattara and Sarkozy were personal friends. Ouattara was already known in Sarkozy's family circle and it is possible they saw each other during this visit which was more economic than political."*

As time goes on, the bonds between Ouattara and Sarkozy become closer and closer.

> *"When Sarkozy was Minister of the Interior, he and Cécilia would often invite the Ouattaras to their home,* reports Antoine Glazer. *And since Sarkozy became president in 2007, Ouattara has stopped in at the Elysée at least four or five times for a drink.*

In August 2011, President Sarkozy was on vacation in the villa which belongs to the family of his new spouse, Carla Bruni, at Cap Nègre on the French Riviera. Exceptionnally invitded for dinner, the Ouattaras are one of their few guests.

On January 25, 2012, President Ouattara was invited for a state visit to France. He was welcomed with the great pomp of the French government: upon their arrival, the Republican guard on horseback escorted the couple to the *Invalides*--after being helicoptered in from the airport to their hotel.

For the New Year 2013, it was the turn of Nicolas and Carla Sarkozy to be warmly welcomed by the Ouattaras at their splendid seaside property in Assinie, a little paradise a few kilometers east of Abidjan.

Between the two men, the close relations have never weakened, even in difficult times. Still in a state of shock after his defeat on May 6, 2012, there was only one head of state who rushed to the Elysée to comfort Sarkozy: Alassane Ouattara. According to Alpha Condé, president of Guinea-Conakry, Ado did not make that trip just to see his friend... The Guinean president is still outraged that he has yet to receive the five million euros France had promised him. According to Condé's interview in the *Challenge*[67] Alassane Ouattara *"who dropped by for a private visit with Sarkozy the day after his defeat, left with 150 million."* Nobody contradicted the Guinean president's declaration.

Also, Ouattara and Sarkozy let the inflammatory statements of El Hadj Cissé, frequently appearing in Ivorian press, slide by without comment. This unruly man has a reputation of knowing every detail of Ouattara's life. Like a griot telling the saga of Ado, he often says he is Alassane's uncle, not by blood, but in the true African sense. The reality is that Cissé's sister, Nabintou Cissé, is married to a Burkinabè who is the biological uncle of Ouattara, who used to live in Dimbokro in Ivory Coast. When Alassane's mother died, the young Alassane Dramane was left in the care of Nabintou Cissé. According to El Hadj Cissé, Ouattara was born in the village of Sindou in Burkina Faso, in December, 1941, not in Dimbokro, or Kong in Ivory Coast as noted on a second birth certificate--forged to permit him to run in the 1995 presidential election in Ivory Coast. Ouattara was thus brought up in Dimbroko until his father came to get him when he was six years old. This would explain why there are no traces of Ouattara's youth in Ivory Coast. He went to school in Ouagadougou, Burkina Faso, then through a scholarship, continued his studies in the U.S. His professional career, as a Burkina national also began far away from Ivory Coast. Opponents of Ouattara say:

"Every Ivorian constantly refers to his village and often goes back there and builds a home. Ouattara never did that, because he can't."

El Hadj Abou Cissé was involved in Ouattara's story from the beginning and he claims to know every detail of it. No one in Ivory Coast would doubt his word, especially since Abou Cissé is one of the founding

---

[67] *Challenge*, n° 301 of May 17 to May 23, 2012.

members of the RDR, Ado's political party. In the past, Cissé has often been presented as a "wise old man." One day Cissé told people *"In the 1990's, he sold two houses to help him* [Ouattara] *when he had problems with Bédié."* This man known for his "big mouth" has also publicly reprimanded Ouattara for having sent Gbagbo *"to whom he owes everything"* to The Hague. Likewise, he reprimands him *"for having hidden fourteen billion in the Cayman Islands,"* and hiding *"three ships"* he acquired during the time he was Prime Minister in the 1990s.

Feeding the streams of unverified rumors that are always flowing everywhere in Africa, Abou Cissé also recently said Ouattara is the *"banker"* of his friend Sarkozy. As the saying goes, only rich people get loans...

> *"[…] The gold mine which the former French president possesses is in Ouattara's care. It's Ouattara whom Sarkozy chose to oversee the financing of his campaign for the French presidential election [...] Ouattara is the one who is going to coordinate everything[68]."*

Furious against Ouattara for the shameful transfer of Gbagbo to The Hague, Abou Cissé continues to publicly attack the one he calls *"the beggar of Abidjan."* Laurent Gbagbo has known Abou Cissé for a long time...

We met in the late 1990s. He was a member of the RDR which had been created in 1994 by Djeni Kobina who was a friend of mine. At the time, we had a good relationship with that party until the death of Kobina in 1998. Ouattara took over the control of the party and colonized it with his own people. During the hard times when we were all sent to prison, Abou Cissé saw me personally help members of the RDR, taking care of them and being their friend. Afterward, I kept in regular contact with him and some of the others, usually by phone. What makes Cissé react against Ouattara is not anything political. Rather it's from a feeling of injustice, on the human level. Abou Cissé saw me in action. He knows I never harmed Ouattara. On the contrary, I allowed him to become eligible for the presidential bid, and I always took care of his security. So Cissé doesn't understand why people have developed such bad feelings against me. Abou Cissé is a free person that nobody dares to contradict. Isn't this perhaps due to the fact that there is something at least partially true in what he says?

---

[68] This is a quote from the online journal *Lecridabidjan.net*.

"Some people have advised him [Abou Cissé] *to move out of his house for his own security. He has refused to do so. Because he believes that he is in the truth and that his life is in God's hands,"* writes Yacouba Gbané in the Ivorian daily newspaper, *Le Temps.*

Abou Cissé has refused to obey the different delegations sent by Ado asking him to quiet down and stop his stormy declarations. Since then, Abou Cissé has received several anonymous death threats. But he hasn't changed his address or what he has to say. And nobody has yet brought legal action against him or officially denied what he has claimed. From an African viewpoint, this passive attitude gives weight to his accusations. In the daily *Quotidien d'Abidjan* of May 16, 2014, he once again hit very hard, accusing the Ouattara clan of being responsible for the disappearance of the journalist André Kieffer in 2004.

Let us try to answer the question posed in *Le Post* which asks whether, in fact, the long-standing friendship between Sarkozy and Ouattara *"favored the ousting of Gbagbo."* Avoiding African rumors, fantasies and stories that tend to run like the wind, one may wonder about the repercussions of such a strong personal relationship, especially since none of the contracts signed between big French groups and Ivory Coast were revisited or threatened by Gbagbo. It doesn't seem possible that the French anti-Gbagbo stance comes from the bosses of these big groups, even if Martin Bouygues is a friend of Ouattara. It is even said that Vincent Bolloré, who was on good terms with Gbagbo, would not have minded seeing Gbagbo re-elected. Gbagbo notes:

I have never opposed the work or the interests of French companies [working in Ivory Coast]. To say that I was, that I am, or that we are anti-French is a misuse of language. Anyway, if that were the case, word would have gotten out. All I did was to defend the interests of my country. If foreign companies make money here, Ivory Coast should be making money too. Our policy was to encourage entrepreneurs to be inventive, provided they abide by the laws and provided that free competition is established and enforced. For example, Ouattara's son, Loïc Folloroux, entered into the cocoa business at the beginning of 2000 and he had no problem whatsoever.

I have always let [Ivorian] institutions do their work. I never mingled in business affairs. No doubt we had gloomy periods: In January 1993, during one extraordinary session of the Ivorian National Assembly, the lawmakers of the PDCI of Bédié criticized the way the contracts for

153

Ivorian electricity and water were given to the Bouygues's group by Prime Minister Alassane Ouattara. They had raised questions concerning the financial conditions of the transfer which were, to say the least, murky. There is a record of it, and it is easy to get hold of it in the archives of the [Ivorian] National Assembly.

I remember that 2005 was the date for the end of the contract with Bouygues, which had been signed in 1990. The group was told that I didn't want to renew the contract. Martin called me and sent me his son Olivier. I told him that I had nothing against Bouygues. I added that I would let the normal process take place, but I made the point that the Ivorian state would from now on be present on the Board of Directors of the Ivorian National Company in order to double check the figures provided to the Ivorian administration. Until then, nobody had ever obtained credible and verifiable figures from the Bouygues's group.

I had seen enough with the problems concerning oil. When I took office, Ivory Coast was receiving only 12% on every barrel. With Bouygues, we were able to work something out, even if their Ivorian Director, Zadi Kessi, overtly took position against me. I did not exclude the idea that Bouygues wanted to have some of his men in the Ivorian government. Zadi Kessi did not hide that he wanted to become the Prime Minister.

So who was so bitter against Gbagbo, if it wasn't the Elysée? The unsolicited answer came to me during a lunch meeting with Jean-Marc Simon on March 19, 2013.

"If Nicolas Sarkozy had not been there, obviously things would have gone differently. There would have been sharing of power, a gas plant," he told me.

For once, Laurent Gbagbo agreed with the Ambassador's opinion.

I do not think anyone else but him [Nicolas Sarkozy] would have acted with such brutality. Sarkozy is someone who doesn't not know how to step back, how to assess events in retrospect. I recall an interview that I gave to the French newspaper *Le Figaro* on January 27, 2011, right in the middle of the post-electoral crisis. The next day, Sarkozy called me, he was very angry, he wanted an answer, it was as if I had addressed him personally...

If I had wanted to talk to him, I would have done it. That was not my intention. But he always relates everything back to himself. It was like he treated anything to do with Ivory Coast as a personal and private matter...

He was the friend of Ouattara and he did not like me; that I always knew. I offended him by not accepting his invitation to the France-Africa Summit held in Nice in June, 2010 and also his invitation to the July 14 celebrations *"to commemorate the fiftieth birthday of the independences."* Which independences? African independences? with military parades of African troops on the Champs-Elysées [in Paris]? I was the only African president who missed the roll call. And he got angry. He got angry because he doesn't take the time to think. I had my reasons. How is it possible to invite Ivorian troops and an Ivorian president who are accused by the French authorities of having caused the death of nine French soldiers during the bombing in Bouaké in November 2004? I want to be told the rationale behind this. In the hours that followed, the French army massacred dozens of Ivorian demonstrators, all civilians, in the streets of Abidjan. So we had things to talk about, some questions to be answered before we could go to a parade in Paris. The incoherence in Sarkozy's behavior surprised me. This was for him a supplementary reason for wanting me dead.

Chapter 16
"My conviction is that we need to build solid democratic institutions in Africa"

As Laurent Gbagbo stands before his accusers at The Hague, it is not as a broken prisoner but as a statesman. He waxes well and long on the importance of democracy, the importance of respecting the Constitution and laws in each country. He points out that, traditionally, African cultures have many and varied ways to appoint their chiefs and kings and many different means of governing. Democracy is needed, he argues, not because the West thinks it is a good system, but because it is the way to unify peoples of different cultures, giving each one a voice in the running of the country. In front of the Court, Gbagbo stands tall and declares: "It is my conviction that we need to build strong institutions in Africa," almost an echo of the words pronounced by U.S. President Barack Hussein Obama who declared in a speech in Ghana in 2009, "Africa doesn't need strongmen, it needs strong institutions."

Unfortunately the American administration seems to have forgotten these words, or has perhaps been led astray by the French, who along with a group of rebels overthrew a democratically elected president. At the very least, the U.S. could have allowed what they allow in their own country: a recount. One of the few "in the know," U.S. senator of Oklahoma, Jim Inofe, wrote in March, 2011 to Secretary of State, Hillary Clinton:

"I am aware that my position is different from that of the Obama Administration, which has recognized Alassane Ouattara as the winner. I ask, however, that you change your position in light of the evidence… that you call for a new election." *He continues that such a move would be* "consistent with our American dedication to the principle that democracy works best when it works for all and not for some. I am convinced that only through a new election will the people of Ivory Coast end the increasing bloodshed, stop another civil war and ensure free and fair elections." *Sound advice, but words left unheeded. As the Ouattara Administration has taken shape, observers have been shocked at his appointments. Many high posts have been filled with rebels—many well known for their brutality and viciousness.*

Every since I began my life in politics, my conviction has been, and I never swayed from this, that we need to build solid institutions in Africa and respect them, even if those who manage them make mistakes. Am I going to criticize the Constitutional Council that declared Sarkozy the winner? Jean-Louis Debré was the one who proclaimed François Hollande president. He was appointed by Chirac. I was proclaimed the winner of the 2000 election by a relative of Robert Guéi. Government institutions are supposed to put political life above the circumstances of the moment and to put the interest of the state at the heart of political life. This is the bottom-line for progress. Tribalism and clans, with the life of people and votes being based on ethnicity is an African reflex which is still very alive and dangerous, since it causes conflict. Some exploit this tendency; some even water it, like a weed. It is only solid democratic institutions and a strong state that can transcend political life, through multi-ethnic parties and institutions with universal values. De Gaulle used to say that above political parties and above clans, it is the law that must reign in the general interest, against mafias and external interference.

Daniel Mayer, a French humanist and politician, president of the League of Human Rights and president of the French Constitutional Council between 1983 and 1986 used to say:

"The Law only expresses the general will within the limits of the Constitution."

More recently, on July 4, 2013, François Hollande indirectly reminded Nicolas Sarkozy of this undeniable truth, when the latter criticized their Constitutional Council after fraud had been detected in Sarkozy's campaign accounts during the presidential election of 2012. The next day, July 5, from Tunis, Hollande declared:

"The Constitutional Council must be respected, completely respected, and no one can raise suspicions or doubts about this institution without questioning the validity of our whole set of institutions."

Hollande added: *"Their* [The Constitutional Council's] *decisions must be applied to all."*

We'll always wonder why no one in France established a link between the declaration of François Hollande and what happened in Ivory Coast two years earlier, when the decision of the [Ivorian] Constitutional Council designating the winner of the presidential election was considered null and void, under the pretext that the president of the Constitutional Council had been appointed, according to the law, by the president of the Ivorian Republic, Laurent Gbagbo... A waste of time...Only the supporters of the "deportee at The Hague," as they call him, will have noticed the double standard. To be frank, African institutions are not considered as having the same weight as those in the West. It is elsewhere that this episode of African history was written: in Paris, in Washington, in Brussels but not in Abidjan.

Today, Francis Wodié reigns from the throne of the Constitutional Council of Ivory Coast[69] without any complexes, legally appointed by his longtime friend Alassane Ouattara. The other six members of the institution, Laurent Gbagbo and Konan Bédié former presidents of the Republic are ex-officio members, have also been nominated by the current Ivorian president. No one would even dare to question the competence of this institution, certainly not the French friends of Ouattara who might have argued that Wodié and the current head of state are too close. This is what people reproached Gbagbo for during the run-off election when the president of the Constitutional Council declared Gbagbo the winner of the presidential election. They said that the president of the Ivorian Constitutional Council, Paul Yao N'Dré, was Gbagbo's personal friend. Yesterday, as today, it is the president of the Republic alone who is authorized to designate the person to head up the Constitutional Council, in order to guarantee the stability of this institution. That was the case for Paul Yao N'Dré, nominated by Gbagbo, and for the lawyer Noël Némin, from Bedié's inner circle and even director of his presidential office, who was nominated by that president [Konan Bédié].

---

[69] Translator's note: While speaking on RFI on January 12, 2011, Francis Wodié, a constitutional scholar, asked President Gbagbo to step down. In so doing, the Ivorian scholar took the side of Alassane Ouattara. Despite his pro-Ouattara stance, on February 3, 2015, Wodié was politely dismissed from the chairmanship of the Ivorian Constitutional Council where he had served for the past four years. Most observers believe that Wodié stepped down because he did not want to "twist" the Constitution, to allow Ouattara to run for president once again. Ouattara was made an exceptional candidate for the 2010 presidential election by virtue of Article 48 of the Ivorian Constitution that the then-sitting president, Laurent Gbagbo used. Ouattara can't apply this constitutional provision to himself for the 2015 presidential election.

Since the advent of the French Constitution in 1958 under the Vth Republic, from Pierre Mazeaud to Jean-Louis Debré, designated by Jacques Chirac, from Daniel Mayer, to Robert Badinter, to Roland Dumas, all designated by François Mitterrand, the same tradition of a certain closeness between the president and the one he entrusts with the mission to run the "Council of the wise" has been respected. And yet Gbagbo only chose some members of the Council. The others were nominated by Mamadou Koulibaly, president of the Ivorian National Assembly and number 2 of the Gbagbo's regime. Whereas, without exception, Ouattara chose all the persons currently serving on the Ivorian Constitutional Council. This is the Council which will validate the upcoming elections of 2015 and proclaim the winner.

The Ivorian Constitution clearly stipulates that the Constitutional Council is the only entity authorized to proclaim the final results of a presidential election, as is the case in France. But like at the casino, it's the one who throws the dice, deals out the chips, and counts the points, who always wins. And it is always the player who loses, especially if the one throwing the dice is not his cousin. Gbagbo understood this only when it was too late. He was the only one to believe that Western democracies would not dare to trample the highest institution in the land, the symbol of the sovereignty of Ivory Coast. A friend of mine from Togo, one of the countries where France--so concerned about democracy in Ivory Coast and Libya--allowed that the son of a dictator to take over from his father, because the father was one of the most docile francophone African leaders with respect to Paris, said about Gbagbo:

> *"He [Gbagbo] doesn't get it. Doesn't he know that Houphouët-Boigny sold his country to France fifty years ago? He [Gbagbo] thought he was the landowner, but he was only the renter, or at best, the manager!"*

In order to survive and remain in power, many African politicians have accepted the path of submission. They have accepted dependency [to colonial powers]. Their defeatist attitude is part of what Jean-François Kahn calls, in his article, *"Media-Loathing,"*[70] the *"mental pre-structures."* At The Hague, on February 28, 2013, Gbagbo repeated:

> *"Our countries, our states, and it will be my last point, are fragile. And each time a European or Western head of state told me to 'ensure*

---

[70] *L'Horreur médiatique* is literally Media-Loathing.

democracy in Africa,' I would say, 'We need democracy, not because you say so, but because we ourselves need democracy to build our countries.''

As he addressed the International Criminal Court, Gbagbo said:

"Madam, look at Ivory Coast. If we do not use democratic methods, how are we going to choose our head of state?

"To the east, along the Ghanaian border the Akans have their own way of choosing village and regional chiefs and their own way of choosing their kings. We in western Ivory Coast have a decentralized system of power. In the north, we have the Islamized Malinkés who are grouped around mosques, and next to them are the Senufos who go to the sacred forest.

"[With all this variety] which electoral method will be used?

"Democracy helps us. Because it makes a clean sweep of all these systems and gives to every individual who is a citizen the right to vote. That is why I became involved in the struggle for democracy. [...]

"But democracy is not only about voting. It is also about who declares the results. That's part of democracy as well.

"When, on a given night, you go and grab the president of the electoral group, the Independent Electoral Commission, and you take him to the headquarters of one of the candidates, and invite foreign television reporters, and tell him to talk, and you film him, and then you broadcast this the next morning, this is not very democratic. This is not democracy.

"Democracy is the respect of the written texts, beginning with the respect of the most important provision of the law: the Constitution. Anyone who doesn't respect the Constitution is not a democrat.

"Madam, it is because I respected the Ivorian Constitution that I have been brought here. So I am here now, and I am counting on you. I am counting on you because I want all Africans who support me, those who are outside [right now] in front of this Court, in front of this prison, or who are in their various countries, staging demonstrations and marches, I want all these Africans to understand that the salvation of our African states is the respect of the Constitution, constitutions which we ourselves formulate, and the respect of the laws flowing out of them."

But that day, who heard Laurent Gbagbo? Besides *Jeune Afrique,* whose business is based on such things, very few newspapers or magazines even took the trouble to send a journalist to cover the trial held on February 28, 2013. Gbagbo comments:

Ouattara didn't understand that tribalism is a thing of the past. Who built the Republic and who destroyed it? We had an army and a police force. Ouattara put them aside and replaced them with tribal militias. The new chiefs of the army supervise tribal militias: people like Cherif Ousmane, alias "the Cheetah," one of the main rebels who organized the first putsch against me in January, 2001, the putsch they called "the plot of the black Mercedes." Today, he is in charge of security at the presidential mansion.

Alassane Ouattara has promoted many rebels. In 2002, Koné Zakaria, an initated Dozo, was at the head of 1,500 Dozos called "the warriors of light." According to the International Crisis Group, in May 2003, in Mankono, Koné Zakaria is said to have had thirty traditional women dancers killed, along with civil servants. When he was in charge of the camp in Adjamé [in one of Abidjan's neighborhood], it is said he tortured and put to death many civilians. This is the man Ouattara put in charge of the military police.

As for Wattao, he is suspected by the above-mentioned NGO of having, on repeated occasions, destabilized the peace process, through targeted attacks. In 2007, he was responsible for massacres in Bouaké. In 2008, Wattao drove Koné Zakaria out of his zone, so he could take control of the diamond mines located there. Ouattara later appointed him second in command of the Republican Guard.

Losseni Fofana took control of Duékoué, in the north-west on March 29, 2011, and his men massacred hundreds of people in the neighborhood called "Carrefour." He was promoted to commander, and he is henceforth one of the bosses of the Ivorian Special Forces.

During the 2002 crisis, Ousmane Coulibaly, alias "Ben Laden," and his men were responsible for several massacres, acts of torture and rapes against civil populations in Man, also in the northwest. Well-known international organizations for the defense of human rights have denounced these crimes. In May, 2011, Ben Laden was appointed by Ouattara commander of the former camp of the BAE in Youpougon [a western suburb of Abidjan]. He had people arrested arbitrarily and tortured. On August 15, 2012, Ouattara placed him at the head of the troops conducting military operations in Dabou, outside of Abidjan, where numerous civilians were arrested without cause, tortured and assassinated. On September 26, 2012, Ouattara appointed him as *Préfet* of the region of San Pedro, in the southwest.

Soumalia Bakayoko was the army chief of staff of the *Armed Forces of New Forces* (FAFN) with his headquarters in Bouaké, in the center of the country. He was in charge of the army and the administration, in parallel to what had been put in place by the rebels in the north. Under his watch, the *Nouvelles Forces* set fire to buildings, looted, racketed, robbed, and killed. On July 7, 2011, Ouattara appointed him army chief of staff of the *Republican Forces of Ivory Coast* (FRCI). This is the highest position in the armed forces in the Republic of Ivory Coast, a position he still holds till today.

Chapter 17
"Whenever I was in Paris, François Hollande would drop by to my hotel"

Laurent Gbagbo, as his father before him, is a socialist. But oddly, many French socialists turned a deaf ear to Gbagbo. But he is open-minded and appreciated those who at least listened to him and heard what he had to say, people like Dominique Strauss-Kahn and Jean-Louis Borloo, even if they did not support him.

Gbagbo's relationship with socialist President Hollande is more enigmatic. Though Gbagbo notes, the current president of the French Republic, Hollande, who used to "come by his hotel," untill today, has made no move to acknowledge, let alone undo, what France did in 2011 or prior. It is socialist Lionel Jospin who Gbagbo respects most, as a man of reflection and integrity.

As for Sarkozy, obviously the relationship between him and Gbagbo is almost non-existent. Sarkozy has never shown respect for Gbagbo and indeed declared war--in the very literal sense of the term--against the Ivorian president. Like all politicians Gbagbo can speak out in a loud voice, but he is not impressed by outward appearances and turns away from displays of arrogance seen in French right wing leaders like Sarkozy and Villepin.

The way France reads and interprets African Affairs is imposed from "high places," namely from the Elysée, and news reports always fall in line with the economic, strategic and political interests of France. This was also the case during the tenure of Mitterrand, who wasted no time appointing his son Jean-Christophe to head the African Office at the Elysée, an entity he openly criticized during the time of De Gaulle. With François Hollande, there is no more African Office, but the French president has a firm hand on Africa who is *"the most visible theater of the partnership between France and the U.S.,"* as noted in a rather frank joint communiqué from the Elysée and the White House, issued right before Hollande's trip to the U.S. in February 2013. At least, the notion of "interests" is made evident here. Is "Atlantiquafrique" more practical and open than "Françafrique"? Gbagbo comments:

Whenever I came to Paris, François Hollande always dropped by for a visit. I had never expected anything from him, and I do not expect anything from him now. Ouattara's lawyers at The Hague are the current French president's close friends: Jean-Paul Benoît and Jean-Pierre Mignard. And Ouattara obviously did not choose them by chance. He knows the meaning of lobbying ...

The French socialists have a hang-up... They want to make people believe that they govern France like the right-wing does. From the outset, in the early years of 2000, Villepin manipulated all of them, and told them all what a monster I am... They were afraid of getting "dirtied" and they dropped me. "Gbagbo is not respectable" Hollande said at that time... because I didn't want to organize elections in a country occupied by armed men. They wanted me to go ahead with the presidential election in a country which was in a constant state of war, in a country where the electorate was ill-defined because no census could be carried out, due to that war. To carry out a credible census, I needed the cooperation of the rebels, and they only came on board in 2010. Even so, it was a trap because the company which organized the census "overlooked" the registration of thousands of fraudulent voters. It was a French company who carried out the census, and they were of course obeying the French authorities.

I am accustomed to being judged ahead of time on my "intentions." For me nothing has changed since 1990. Upon return from my years of exile in France, when I dared to challenge Houphouët in the first multi-party presidential election [in the history of post-indenpence Ivory Coast], the gentler of my socialist "friends" estimated I would get 1% of the electorate... But in fact, I obtained 18.3%... After that, they all started to invite me...

But I do have some socialist friends, about whom I will say nothing bad, even if they didn't support me, people like Dominique Strauss-Kahn (DSK). He knew Ouattara better than he knew me because of the IMF. I met him twice to deal with some issues when he was IMF director. The first time was in Ouagadougou during the meeting of the leaders of the West African CFA zone. The other time was when I talked to him on the phone and asked him to come to Abidjan to discuss some serious problems we

166

were having with the Ivorian debt. DSK came and we had a wonderful working session with my government ministers. He is brilliant and works hard. He had a good command of all the dossiers and things went well. He was not arrogant nor did he try to intervene in the African dossiers. I spoke with him before the French presidential election of 2012 and asked him if he *"was going to go for it."* He said he needed to speak with Martine Aubry[71] first. He wanted her opinion about it. He was someone who listened to me, who heard me, even if he wasn't for me.

It was the same with Jean-Louis Borloo whom I met in Yaoundé on May 20, 2010. I travelled to Cameroon at the invitation of Paul Biya for the fiftieth anniversary of the Reunification of Cameroon. Borloo suggested we meet. I gave him my suite number at the Yaoundé Hilton and he came by, with no protocol. We exchanged on various subjects for about forty-five minutes. Neither Borloo nor Strauss-Kahn would have bombed my home.

I also had a good relationship with Dominique Paillé, a UMP député. He is an open person and a good listener, like the other two I just mentioned. Their approach is different from that of Mitterrand or Chirac or even De Gaulle, who all held to old ways of thinking. Strauss-Kahn, Borloo and Paillé all knew something about our dossiers and their culture allowed them to not be chauvinistic. Even if you're not their favorite, they still listen to you, hear you and respect you.

Sarkozy is a whole different story. I met him for the first time in 2007 in New York at the UN. Robert Bourgi suggested I make the effort to meet with the new French president, after all the problems I had had with Chirac. So I had no negative feeling beforehand--on the contrary. But as soon as he saw me, he left the area reserved for the five members of the Security Council, came over to shake hands with me, and said *"President, and these elections? When are you going to have them?"* He just blurted it out like that... I responded that we needed to be patient, that I was not the only one involved[72]. That discussion took place right there, both of us standing across from each other, and that was the end of the conversation. For Sarkozy, arrogance takes the places of ideas. George W. Bush was the perfect symbol of this type of person. They are individuals who don't have

---

[71] Translator's note: Daughter of Jacques Delors, Martine Aubry was the first female Secretary of the French Socialist Party and the first female Mayor of Lille, in northern France. Her father, Jacques Delors, served as president of the European Commission for three consecutive terms from 1985 to 1995.

[72] For the elections to move ahead, it had been stipulated that the rebels would disarm.

deep thoughts. That's the category I put Sarkozy in, along with Villepin: arrogant people who use their arrogance instead of their brains. They think by acting this way they show that France is great, while all they are proving is that their country has lost its stature. As for us, we are not great, we are small and weak. And those with big muscles think they're more intelligent than we are. But what is at stake here is crucial-- we're talking about our country!

Since the fall of the Berlin Wall, political thought has also "fallen" in the West. In Asia, South America and Africa there are still a few politicians left with some aspirations, who want to search for meaning, who try to have vision ... The comedy of French political life saddens me. Your public debates and your societal concerns only show how low your pedagogy and the general cultural level have dropped: Marriage for all? Didn't Emperor Cesar say he was *"the man of all women and the woman of all men?"* The West is scared of Muslim jihads but there have also been Christian jihads, during the time of the warrior monks and the Templar Knights. The Americas were conquered and colonized in the name of Catholic kings and in the name of Christ...

The last truly political person in France, among those in power, who I have come to know, is Lionel Jospin. He had a sense of political thought, he had an ethic. As for Chirac, he was just happy to win elections, he wasn't really governing.

I got to know Lionel Jospin when he was Prime Minister. He refused French military intervention when Bédié was overthrown, and in this, he did well. He let us manage our problems by ourselves: we put in place our Constitution and moved forward. He used to say, if I remember right, "Do not remain indifferent but do not interfere [in domestic affairs of others]." He carried out his ideas, his principles, and he was a man of integrity. At least, no one can imagine *him* picking up the phone and calling Africa to ask for a little cash...

Concerning Lionel Jospin, Guy Labertit reported in *A Farewell to Abidjan-on-the-Seine!*[73], that Lionel Jospin displayed a total mistrust concerning African affairs. He notes also that François Hollande once said:

"In Africa, we can only get in trouble."

---

[73] Guy Labertit, *op.cit.,* see footnote 34 above.

When De Gaulle defied the powerful nations by saying that France would acquire an atomic bomb and with it its own independence, and when Mitterrand spoke at the German Bundestag about obtaining mid-range missiles, another kind of politics came into play. I reread the works of De Gaulle and the book on Mitterrand written by Roland Dumas. Boy, have times changed! I never bore a grudge against Mitterrand for having always supported Houphouët-Boigny. They belonged to the same government and they were friends. In Africa, Houphouët served France in any way he could. Besides, there was the Cold War, East vs. West, and the whole Western world was supportive of Houphouët and forgave him for everything he did. It was really a different era…

In 1970, there was not a single French protest when Robert Guéi, acting on Félix Houphouët-Boigny's orders, wiped out the Bété uprising in the Guébié region, opposing the Bété's and the Baoulé's, Houphouët's ethnic group. The government forces killed between 4,000 and 6,000 people. It was a genocide whose survivors still ask in vain for an acknowledgement and retribution. Who would have dared to bother the "Old Wiseman of Africa" for such a small matter?

Chapter 18
"Sarkozy looked everywhere, but they found nothing: no hidden fortune, no ill-gotten gains"

Gbagbo laughed out loud when the ICC officials came to ask him how he would pay for his lawyers' fees. They certainly didn't believe him when he said he had no money, his accounts being frozen by the International Community. Mattei and Gbagbo tell how the officials at ICC, and even Sarkozy himself, sent investigators out all over the world to uncover hidden bank accounts—to no avail. Gbagbo had "no hidden fortune" and certainly "no ill-gotten gains."

Many rumors have been spread about Gbagbo, but of course most are unfounded, like the belief that he is some kind of religious fanatic. He tells how people laughed at him when he closed his state addresses with the phrase, "God Bless Côte d'Ivoire," and then explains that he heard Americans say "God Bless America" at a Republican convention in the U.S. and decided to take up the expression....

Gbagbo is also regularly accused when any one disappears mysteriously, as in the Keiffer affair, a journalist who was certainly "taken out" by those he was investigating in the cocoa business, or in the abduction of four individuals from a swank hotel in Abidjan in April, 2011, when Gbagbo himself was under siege.

Despite all this, Gbagbo luckily keeps his sense of humor. When people began looking for what he owned in France, he just laughed: "I don't own anything in France—not even a studio apartment—not even a parking space!"

I arrived at Scheveningen, a suburb of The Hague, on Saturday June 3, 2012 at 1:30 PM. It was my first visit to the most famous prisoner there. I had to go through a glass door, to the first checkpoint, have my passport checked and have my name verified on the list of *bezoekers*...visitors... With my badge in place, from that point on, I was constantly surveyed by cameras, big fish-eyed globes followed me everywhere. I went through another remote-operated door and entered another place filled with lockers, where people are supposed to empty their pockets....You take off your shoes before going through the metal detector ....then more doors leading to a waiting room. A guard in a dark blue uniform comes to get you, leading you through still more doors. You cross a big courtyard....to finally arrive at the political prisoners' block, surrounded by heavy walls, surrounded by more doors... There is a new checkpoint, the badge and my ID are checked once again, then, another metal detector. I remove my shoes, my belt, my watch, still being escorted by the huge Dutchman in his blue uniform. He opens the last door, marked on the top with two large letters, a B and an O. A long corridor runs alongside the common room where families are admitted and monitored by two special guards, sometimes women, one of them pumped up with muscles, piercings in her ears, tattoos on her arms.

The *bezoekamers*, the private visitors' rooms, are small and contain a sink, an electric kettle, and a wooden table with two chairs. It's there he came and sat down in front of me. All my visits lasted about three hours, minus the time taken for all the control procedures under the camera's dark eye.

Each time, I would go through the same ritual. After having escorted me to the room, the guard would leave me there and go get Laurent Gbagbo and bring him from his cell.

This time, dressed in an Adidas jacket, canvas pants and jogging shoes, he sat down with some difficulty on the little wooden chair, being careful not to lean too hard on the table.

My wrists hurt, my back and shoulders ache too, he told me right away, as if he wanted to divert my questions. **But at least I feel better than when I first arrived at the end of 2011.**

I think the first time I smiled was the day the International Court officials came to ask me how I was going to pay for my lawyers' fees. I told them that my bank accounts, where I received my only income, my salary since I became president in 2000, had been frozen and I had nothing else. They certainly didn't believe me, so they decided to launch a careful investigation on the international level. I joked about it and told them that if they found anything, they could keep it. They looked everywhere: in France, in Switzerland, in the U.S., in various financial paradises... They did everything they could, but they found nothing: no hidden fortune, no ill-gotten assets hidden on some foreign soil. Likewise, Sarkozy did his utmost: his people were looking everywhere... Of course, they found nothing, because I just don't have that much. When I was a professor at the university, I was able, like all the other professors, to get a loan at a

good rate, and that allowed me to buy a small house in Abidjan. In my village [upcountry, in Mama], I had inherited a plot of land belonging to the family, and I built a modest house for my mother.

If there is anybody who knows that I am not a greedy person, that person is Ouattara. Every time he came to Abidjan to see me, and that was very often, he would call me by phone, and I would assure his security, because he was always fearful. He used to say to me:

> *"Do you know what surprises businessmen? You never ask for anything for yourself."*

He himself was surprised at my behavior. Because it was so hard to prove that I had amassed wealth, my enemies tried to make me out as a violent person. That's what they said about the Kieffer case, the journalist who disappeared in Abidjan in April, 2011. They say the same about the French people who were abducted from the Novotel Hotel[74] in Abidjan and were later murdered. I barely knew Guy-André Kieffer. I met him one time and saw him once more from a distance surrounded by a bunch of journalists during a press conference. When he disappeared, Ivorian judicial authorities ordered an investigation to be carried out within a 100 kilometer radius of Abidjan. I don't know what more we could have done. I know that several journalists started their own investigations on Kieffer's death, each one following a different lead. According to them, when Kieffer was killed, he was investigating scandals in the coffee-cocoa sector.

It is worth noting the French judge in charge of the Keifer case, Patrick Ramaël, at the Paris *Tribunal de grande instance,* seems to have been obsessed with Gbagbo as the main suspect; he ignored all the other leads. And in 2013, this very judge became an advisor to Alassane Ouattara. Amazing, isn't it? Gbagbo continues:

As for the victims of the Novotel, this incident occurred right in the middle of the battle of Abidjan. Maybe it would be more helpful to look in the direction of those who were on the ground at that precise place on that particular day: namely the rebels. But, it is easier to blame everything on us. I knew the people at the Novotel for ten years; they were my neighbors.

---

[74] Translator's note: A four-star-hotel in downtown Abidjan, in the commercial neighborhood of *Le Plateau.*

The story of the Novotel abduction boils down to this: Yves Lambelin, CEO of Sifca, the largest private company in the country (with 27,000 wage earners), Lambelin's associates, along with a Malaysian Chelliah Pandianand, and a Beninois man, Raoul Adeossi, as well as Frantz di Rippel, the manager of the Novotel, were all abducted on April 14, 2011. After being captured, they were apparently tortured and executed, and their bodies thrown into the lagoon. The body of Yves Lambelin was found two months later and officially identified. Despite various stories circulating at the time, the judicial officers of those who had just come to power immediately placed the responsibility for these four murders on the supporters of Gbagbo. In his book published in Paris in 2012[75], the repentant rebel colonel Séméfia Sékou, alias "Colonel Sékouba," an important member of the invisible commando of Abidjan, provides many details and accuses the rebel forces of having perpetrated these murders. He claims his own people and those of Koné Zacharia carried out this punitive operation. His testimony is signed and submitted. Can you believe it? Sékouba was never summoned by anyone in the Ivorian justice system or by the International Court, no one who could have verified his testimony. We need to ask why this was never done.

They tried to make us forget the death of Philippe Rémond, the French teacher at the Yamoussoukro Houphouët-Boigny Polytechnic Institute, assassinated in his hotel room, March 31, 2011, following the rebel forces' entrance into that city. At that point, no fighting had begun in that city. Philippe Rémond was the representative of Europeans living in Ivory Coast and also an ardent supporter of Laurent Gbagbo, a sin he paid for dearly. Many times on Ivorian television, Rémond used harsh language as he spoke of the 2004 atrocities committed by the French army in Abidjan, resulting in the death of more than sixty Ivorian civilians. He also criticized the general policies of the French which he called "scandalous de-possession of Ivory Coast." His widow has begun legal proceedings in Paris, but the French media has remained silent, perhaps because they are embarrassed? The question is: Will the French continue to pick and choose among the French victims, examining their [political] opinions, before they decide which assassinations are worthy of interest and which are not? Philippe Rémond was not an adventurer, just a simple prof who overtly expressed his opinions, which happened to be contrary

---

[75] Information made available in his confession to the journalist Germain Sehoué, *Le Commandant invisible raconte la bataille d'Abidjan* (The Invisible Commander tells the story of the combat in Abidjan,) Paris, L'Harmattan 2012.

to those of the rebels and the Elysée. That's what killed him: assassinated first by a bullet in Yamoussoukro, he was killed a second time by the indifference of the French authorities who simply forgot he existed. Gbagbo comments:

The method of "selective indignation" and "selective investigation" is the hallmark of the Ouattara camp and of the French authorities. They don't say a word about the hundreds of deaths caused by the rebels during their coup d'etat in 2002. The phrase "death squads," imported from South America, was uttered for the first time on our soil by Alassane Ouattara, the very day of the coup d'Etat he initiated. There has been no word about Dagrou Loula, a colonel of the state police, who was shot in the back in his Bouaké home during the rebels' offensive. There has been no word on the murder of Dali Obré, another colonel of the state police, killed in his sleep in Korhogo, or again, on the death of my Minister of the Interior, Boga Doudou, shot down while he was trying to flee his home... There has been no word on the October 2002 murder in Bouaké of about sixty unarmed *gendarmes* [state police], along with their spouses and their children, assassinations carried out by Guillaume Soro and his men. The list of the names of these poor people are available and the facts are there. The *gendarmes* have taken a heavy toll. Their headquarters were small and vulnerable. For months, the rebels kept going after these people, not just because they opposed them, but because, as officially recognized police agents, they could investigate their crimes and protect the Ivorian population. These *gendarmes* were systematically murdered in the most horrific way.

And I haven't even begun to start talking about massacres, shootings in cold blood of specific populations. The rebels' goal was to spread terror, drive people off their land, so they could take hold of the land themselves. The genocide in western Ivory Coast against the *Wè* peoples is documented, the torture of the *Guéré* group, as well. The mass crimes committed for ten years by the rebels in power today in Abidjan are countless. But we have to remember the first populations to suffer are those from the north. From 2002 to 2010, the rebels systematically bled the north, the territory they occupied. Their crimes are recorded. In 2010, just after the elections, rebel groups infiltrated Abidjan and attacked civilians. In March 2011, with the assistance of the French army, squads of mercenary rebels poured down from the north into the south. They committed numerous killings in the southern regions. Has there been a single investigation of any of these incidents since the rebels took power?

In order to make the unjust de-legitimization look flawless, French media depicted President Gbagbo as a "goody-goody" Christian. Nothing is further from the truth. Laurent Gbagbo is an intellectual--Cartesian in his thinking, nurtured by the French principle of "laïcité."[76] He is a rational believer, what we would call in France, a left-wing Christian. Gbagbo comments:

When they recall that I am a Christian, they dub me as some kind of religious freak, a "religious extremist." Religious fanaticism is worse than savagery. But they spared nothing in their caricatures of me. For instance, when I said at the closing of my public addresses, "May God bless Côte d'Ivoire," they made fun of me, saying who do you think you are: God's chosen one? The truth is so simple. I heard the expression *God bless America* in the U.S., at a Republican Convention, when they were choosing their candidate for the presidential race in 1980. I liked the expression and I adopted it.

As for my religious practices, [at home] it usually consisted of a Sunday worship service and a prayer on Sunday afternoon when the pastor came over to my house for a visit. Those who wanted to demonize me in France, which is still a country with a Christian tradition, never dared to criticize heads of state who are Muslim, who slipped quietly out of [international] conferences to go say their prayers five times a day. When I went to visit the president of Benin, Yayi Boni, sometimes he would say: "Brother, let's pray," right in his office. Wade and Gaddafi used to organize their meetings according to the hours for prayer. No one told them not to do it, it is their right... I do not steal, I do not kill people, I'm not rich, even if no one will believe what I say because I am an African head of state.

In January 2011, during the post-electoral crisis, the American Treasury announced that it would:

> "...freeze the U.S. accounts of the Ivorian president, his wife and three close associates."

---

[76] Translator's note: Related to but going further than the American principle of separating church and state, the French principle of "laïcité" prohibits the exhibition of any kind of religious symbols in state institutions: crosses, stars of David, or Muslim veils.

But nobody ever heard much more about this mock freezing of assets. On the 5 of the same month, Michèle Alliot-Marie, who had not yet been pursued by French justice because of certain real estate investments made by her family in Ben Ali's Tunisia[77], managed to get an interview on the American TV show *60 minutes*. When asked about the possibility of Gbagbo obtaining asylum in France--it was precisely at this stage that both Gbagbo and Ouattara declared themselves elected and were shooting daggers at each other--Alliot-Marie answered with a tone many know her for:

"If he [Gbagbo] would leave office in a normal way, why not? I believe he [Gbagbo] has properties in France..."

A statement sure to be repeated in the press. Go ahead and spread lies, there will always be something left over! Gbagbo had a good laugh about what she said:

I have nothing in France. I mean nothing, not even a studio apartment, not even a parking space!

On December 28, 2011, when the emptiness of the accusations concerning his purported assets was finally demonstrated, it was admitted that President Gbagbo was unable to pay his legal fees and was accorded judicial assistance.

For months, the Prosecutor of the International Court, supported by intelligence agencies of great powers, had undertaken investigations to find any trace of hidden riches, but with no success. After that, other investigations were launched, but nothing was found, despite the intensive efforts of pseudo experts acting on behalf of the UN, who claimed they had found several hidden bank accounts in Ivory Coast. It must be noted that Gbagbo's lawyers have provided us with clear explanations for those accounts:

"Careful evaluation of the experts' final report sheds some interesting light. They claim that President Gbagbo had several bank accounts on which appeared, up until recently, financial transactions. But even the most basic analyses show that these affirmations are false, and represent at best, errors of analysis which reveal serious

---

[77] Translator's note: Ben Ali whose full name is Zine El Abidine Ben Ali succeeded Habib Bourguiba as the second president of Tunisia. Habib Bourguiba is considered the "father of the nation" in modern Tunisia.

incompetency, and at worse, a deliberate attempt to fabricate charges against President Gbagbo.

[...]The experts claimed President Gbagbo had at least eight bank accounts. [...]

If we examine the numbers inscribed on the two accounts of President Gbagbo listed on the printouts of the accounts reproduced in Annex 47, we realize that they are a pure duplicate of the two numbers in the accounts listed in Annex 68. [...] The point is that these are the same accounts which the experts said were frozen anyway.

In fact, the numbers mentioned in Annex 47 are a simple duplicate of the numbers listed in Annex 68. Therefore, on the purported eight accounts, it is obvious that two of them are inexistent since they are the accounts mentioned in Annex 68, whose numbers are exactly the same as the numbers in Annex 47. For the two other accounts, [...] the experts did not provide any new information. Finally for the two accounts of Annex 68 whose numbers are not exactly the same as in Annex 47, the point is they are not bank accounts per se. They are only simple accounting operations for the purpose of making transfers.

[...] The only accounts shown to exist are first, the account which received the monthly salary of the president of the Republic and second, the account to which President Gbagbo transferred his salary for the purpose of earning interest. In any case, these two accounts were frozen, as the experts have stated."

Gbagbo's honesty and his seeming indifference to the accumulation of wealth can be contrasted with the greed which all of those who have worked for his downfall are known. We are not even referring here to Alassane Ouattara's entourage, who takes a "tithe" from each transaction and financial operation carried out in Ivory Coast. Not to speak of the rebel leaders who are currently recognized as state authorities, but who systematically bleed the state. They are currently destroying, piece by piece, what was, until the ousting of Laurent Gbagbo, one of the rare examples of a functioning sub-Saharan state in Africa.

But turning now to the French: the former French Minister of the Interior and General Secretary of the Elysée now has a branch of his law firm in Abidjan, where he travels to frequently from Paris, expanding his own business and the business of his son-in-law, Jean-Charles Charki, who himself has become a counselor to Alassane Ouattara. Likewise, the former French Ambassador to Ivory Coast has become a consultant and spends a great deal of his time with Alassane Ouattara. The French military chiefs themselves have also become "consultants" and have been entrusted with modernizing the Ivorian army. Not to mention Judge Ramaël who has settled in Abidjan. Without forgetting the scores of military aids, lawyers, advertising executives, communication experts, etc. You have more of a chance to find these guys in Abidjan than in Paris. A journalist, ex-manager of TV channel France 24 is now in charge of the restructuration of the Ivorian television station and of the organization of a defense and security exhibition in conjunction with Phil Media[78].

---

[78] La *Lettre du Continent*, n° 681 of April 30, 2014.

Chapter 19
"I wanted this moment to go down in history"

> *Gbagbo uses this phrase to explain his participation in the 1990 presidential election, the first democratically organized election within the thirty-year life of the Republic of Ivory Coast since its independence on August 7, 1960. While the other candidates bowed to intimidation and withdrew from the race, Laurent Gbagbo retained his candidacy and ran, because as he tells it, he wanted that moment "to go down in history."*
>
> *In this chapter Mattei and Gbagbo explain important facts concerning Ivory Coast's history, its first steps towards independence and its eventual emergence as a sovereign state. Up until 1990, elections were held but only one candidate ran: Houphouet-Boigny. Laurent Gbagbo dared to enter the race--the real beginning of democracy in the country. Mattei and Gbagbo describe what happened when Houphouet-Boigny, the Father of the Repubic, died: how this same Alassane Ouattara tried to usurp "the throne" from Houphouet's designated successor, Henri Konan Bédié. They describe how Bédié himself fought to have the Constitution changed to prevent Ouattara (or any other foreigner) from ever becoming Ivorian president. Intrigue upon intrigue...*
>
> *Once again, in these pages, Gbagbo reiterates his strong belief in the democratic process and describes some of the efforts he made to create a healthy political environment where everyone's voice could be heard.*

Why, am I so hated by France? No one can understand this if they don't know the history of Ivory Coast, my country, and its specific relationship with France since its independence in 1960...

Just before independence, in 1956, the Defferre Reform Act[79], named after a French Socialist politician, created a territorial assembly,

---

[79] Translator's note: Gaston Defferre was a leading figure in the French Socialist Party in the 1950s. During his tenure as a French overseas Minister, he drafted a bill called *la loi-cadre* [framework law], because it empowers the French government to rule by decree in an area usually reserved to the legislation.

which included all the French African Colonies. Each Colony, which had its own government, was functioning under the tutelage of a French governor. That was our autonomy, the first step on the road to political independence. The leader of the major political party would become the Vice-president of the council presided over by the French governor. In Ivory Coast, that man was Auguste Denise, whose father was Antillais and whose mother was Ivorian. He was the person Houphouët delegated and also the General Secretary of Houphouët-Boigny's party, the PDCI-RDA. Houphouët-Boigny himself headed to Paris to become a member of the Guy Mollet government at "Abidjan-sur-Seine," as my friend Guy Labertit jokingly calls Paris.

In 1958, in the newly created Franco-African Community, the heart of Françafrique, the territorial assemblies continued to exist but the government of each territory was run by a local Prime Minister. The president of the French Republic was also the president of the territorial community. Local governments ran the colonies, except for the domains of Foreign Affairs, Defense, Currency, and Higher Education. For all these, France had full control, in accordance with the provision of Article 12 of the French Constitution, which dealt with all issues related to the Franco-African Community. Few French people are aware of this unusual situation. This same Article 12 still exists within the texts of the current French Constitution…

In 1959, Félix Houphouët-Boigny became Prime Minister of our country, Ivory Coast, and then, in 1960, the head of state, at the time of the "independences."[80]   There was no election. De Gaulle had to force Houphouët-Boigny's hand for him to accept the independence of Ivory Coast, which was planned alongside the "independences" of Upper-Volta[81], Benin, and Niger. Houphouët didn't really want independence for Ivory Coast. But at that time France no longer had a choice: with American and Russian pressure on the one hand, and the disasters in Indo-China and Algeria, on the other, France was in an extremely weak position. It was under those circumstances that French authorities decided to proclaim

---

[80] Translator's note: In France and Africa, people often refer to the "independences" (plural form), because so many African countries became independent at approximately the same time.

[81] Translator's note: Upper-Volta changed from its colonial name to Burkina Faso on August 4, 1984, under former President Thomas Sankara killed in a coup d'etat by his brother-in-arms, Blaise Compaoré.

independence for their various colonies. But these declarations of independence were a mere formality. Houphouët became president within a system of total dependency on France, the Francafrique system of which Houphouët himself was one of the pillars. Houphouët contributed to the drafting of the Defferre plan and to the drafting of the French Constitution of 1958... From then on, there was no [real] election in Ivory Coast for thirty-three years.

In October, 1990, who changed this? His name is Laurent Gbagbo! I ran against Houphouët who, for the first time in the history of modern Ivory Coast, was compelled to accept pluralism, a concept for which I had been fighting for a long time as a leader of the democratic opposition, and for which I had even gone to prison. Various international upheavals, as well as the dismantling of the iron curtain played in our favor. The Ivorian internal opposition, but especially my party, the FPI, obtained in the end the organization of multiparty elections. But the people in power wanted to control these elections. They asked me to withdraw my candidacy. All the other candidates stepped down, but not me. I maintained my candidacy. They told me the elections would be rigged, and, of course, they were. Yet, I wanted to make a mark in history. That was, in fact, my "original sin," the reason why I am now here at The Hague. By obtaining more than 18% of the electorate against Houphouët, I became someone who had to be reckoned with. I became the officially recognized leader of the Ivorian opposition. Already I was someone who threatened the schemes they had to maintain Françafrique...

In December, 1993, when Houphouët passed away, it was that continuity, organized by Houphouët himself and France that remained, with Bédié as Houphouët's successor. There was to be no election. Due to an amendment to the Constitution, Konan Bédié, president of the National Assembly was to automatically become president.

Immediately Bédié clashed with the then-Prime Minister Alassane Ouattara, who tried to usurp Bédié's "right to succession." You must remember that Houphouët had taken Ouattara on as Prime Minister under pressure from the French authorities. But he never intended that Ouattara would be his successor. It's Ouattara's wife, Dominique, who projected a place for him in the nation's destiny. Ouattara fought with Bédié, trying to be the one to announce Houphouët's death. Ouattara rushed to make that announcement, but Bédié reacted immediately, and Ouattara was obliged to back down...

In his interviews which were turned into a book entitled *The Paths of my Life*[82], Henry Konan Bédié was the first Ivorian leader to write the story of Ouattara's political intrigues and his attempts to push ahead of him to seize power. Bedié writes:

> *"Alassane Ouattara knew very well that the mission he was entrusted with [as Prime Minister] meant he shouldn't get mixed up in political issues, all the more so, since he is not an Ivorian citizen."*

Ouattara had a passport from Burkina Faso, and thus did not meet the criteria defined by Article 35 of the Ivorian Constitution, as amended by Bédié in 1994. Acccording to Article 35, to qualify as a presidential candidate, a person has to be born of both an Ivorian mother and father. The concept of "ivoirité", finely "woven together", as Ouattara would point out, was created by Bédié to prevent him from setting his sights on the Ivorian throne. Bédié also explains in his book:

> *"The President [Houphouët] had made it clear to him [Ouattara] and had made it clear to me, as well as to several other Ivorian and foreign personalities [...] in very clear terms and through precise facts. Soon after his nomination, the President [Houphouët] asked Alassane Ouattara to travel to the capital cities of neighboring countries to insist on the purely economic nature of his mission [as Prime Minister]. The fact that the President [Houphouët] asked him to allow his post as head of the Central Bank or BCEAO to remain vacant, proves that Houphouët viewed Ouattara's post as temporary. For two years, that position was empty and Charles Banny was only the interim director of the Bank."*
>
> *"But had he [Ouattara] taken Ivorian nationality?* [the interviewer of Bédié's book asks. Bédié immediately answers:]
>
> *[...] President Houphouët had granted him a diplomatic passport when he was in trouble with the authorities in Burkina Faso. He was then working at the Central Bank which serves seven countries in West Africa. A diplomatic passport, you know, is not a document recognized as an official document of a given country [like an identity card, birth certificate or passport of that country]*

---

[82] Henri Konan Bédié, *Les Chemins de ma vie* (The Paths of my Life), Paris, Plon, 1999.

184

Nevertheless he [Ouattara] had been Prime Minister *of Ivory Coast and in that capacity, head of the government* [the interviewer argued and Bédié continued]:

It was not the first time in the history of his presidency that President Houphouët-Boigny called on technical competencies from outside the country [...] In any case, by his father, Ouattara was a Burkinabe and he still held onto his Burkinabè citizenship. Thus it was not for him to meddle in our issues of succession [...]." Gbagbo comments:

Before the 1995 election, Bédié had the electoral code modified. This additional provision blocked Ouattara, because of his Burkinabè nationality, and Ouattara eventually accepted that fact. Anyway he had just been granted an interesting position at the IMF. Sometimes I made fun of these fights over origin. One time when I was in Paris, I made the comment that all those of our generation who were over forty, which was the minimum age required to compete for the Ivorian presidency, were all born before 1960 and thus before Independence. So, in fact, we all had French nationality...

For the presidential election of 2010, Bédié was able to present his candidacy only because President Gbagbo accepted to sign an exceptional authorization in his favor. Bédié was already one year over the age-limit to run for the presidency. He was seventy-six years old. This measure was taken by virtue of Article 48 of the Ivorian Constitution, the equivalent of the French Article 16 in the French Constitution. Laurent Gbagbo took this decision, despite the misgivings of many of his political friends, because he thought this would contribute to appeasement in Ivory Coast. He did all this within the framework of a democratic debate, hoping the greatest possible number of political leaders could express themselves. President Gbagbo thus also issued a special decree, in accordance with the same Article 48 of the Ivorian Constitution, to allow Alassane Ouattara, who did not meet the criteria set by the Ivoirian Constitution, to exceptionally run for president [for the 2005 presidential election which actually took place in 2010]. It was a courageous gesture--or suicidal, according to some of his friends--a decision that was difficult for many of his electors and supporters to accept. Today, the Ivorian Constitution remains unchanged:

"The president of the Republic [...] must be Ivorian by birth, born of both a father and a mother of Ivorian birth. He must never have

renounced his Ivorian citizenship. He must never have availed himself of another nationality. He must have resided in Ivory Coast continuously during the five years preceding the date of the elections and must have totaled ten years of effective presence in the country. [...]The candidate to the presidency of the Republic must present a complete report on his physical and mental well-being, duly determined by a set of three physicians appointed by the Ivorian Constitutional Council from a list proposed by the Council of the Order of Physicians. These three physicians must take an oath before the Constitutional Council. He [the candidate to the Ivorian presidency] must have good morals and be known as a person of solid integrity. He must declare his assets and account for their origin."

Morality... because of his age, Konan Bédié did not meet the established criteria, nor did Alassane Ouattara, because of his nationality. If the Constitution is respected, neither would be able to run in the 2015 presidential election. We know that constitutions and principles in Africa, as elsewhere, evolve according to need and circumstance. If the illness he suffers from does not prevent it, Alassane Ouattara will in all likelihood run. Yet, in order for him to do so, the constitutional text would have to be modified, a text he himself approved in July, 2000. As the song says, "What will be will be."[83]

In 1995, to show our solidarity with Alassane Ouattara, chased away by Bédié, and to enable a true democratic exchange, allowing for a real opposition to express itself, we formed the Republican Front, with a view to grouping all opposition parties. I boycotted the presidential election that took place that year. Without Ouattara and without me, Bédié became a quasi-unique candidate. He was elected with more than 95% of the electorate, with the support of Jacques Chirac and his party, the RPR. The general delegate of this right-wing French political party, Jean-Pierre Bazin, came to Abidjan to publically support Bédié.

---

[83] Translator's note: Very recently, during a state visit in south-western Ivory Coast, Alassane Dramane Ouattara told Ivoirians assembled there that there was no need to amend Article 35 of the Ivorian Constitution. In the following days, there were media reports arguing that Article 48 could be used to qualify Ouattara as a presidential candidate for the upcoming election of October 2015, since it had been previously evoked by Gbagbo allowing Ouattara to run in 2010. Ouattara and his "spin doctors" argued that President Gbagbo had set a legal precedence which could be used again. According to the opposing camp, that stipulation was clearly limited to that one particular instance and was not to change in any way the Constitution.

I have often asked myself why a man as sharp as Houphouët chose Bédié as his successor. Is it some deep seated tribal reflex? They are both from the Baoulé ethnicity, but that does not seem a sufficient reason... Actually, they were other young Baoulés waiting in line, some of them very gifted, even brilliant. I regularly visited Madam Houphouët because we were on very good terms. Each time she was asked if the declared preference of Houphouët for Bédié could be explained by the fact that Bédié was in fact his son [out of wedlock, a rumor that persists till today], she would answer with a laugh:

> *Oh dear, no! You know he* [Bédié] *is too ugly to be the son of my husband!"*

It was during that time, in August, 1994, that the Ivorian Constitutional Council was created and put in place with the mission of arbitrating possible electoral disputes. The ICC was presided by Noël Némin, former Minister of Justice during Houphouët's tenure and former director of Bédié's presidential office. Six of the nine personalities on the Council were nominated by Bédié himself, and three others by his friend Charles Donwahi, president of the Ivorian National Assembly. It is good to remember these facts today. From that period on, the Council, in its capacity as the country's supreme jurisdiction, was in charge of controlling Ivorian elections. Their job was to see that the candidates were qualified, of course, but also to proclaim the results of the elections, to evaluate appeals, and to finally give various verdicts.

I have said it before and I will repeat it again: in Africa, we need our institutions to be respected, even if people are hesitant about the leaders who embody these institutions or their mode of functioning. Otherwise, the states of Africa will collapse. I had already criticized Jacques Chirac because he did everything he could to by-pass my authority and to empty our Constitution of its content, our Constitution which was adopted by 86% of the Ivorian electorate in the 2000 referendum. In 2003-2004 Chirac put pressure on us to give way to the rebels, thus emptying Ivorian institutions of their meaning. The total indifference of the French towards Africa just stares you in the face. In October, 2006, the then-Ambassador of France to the UN, Rochereau de la Sablière even dared to draft a Resolution that said:

"The decisions of the Security Council take precedence over the Ivorian Constitution and the legislation of the Ivory Coast."

Other members of the Security Council, China, Russia, as well as the U.S., opposed this annulation of our Constitution. You realize, of course, that whether through the use of force or through diplomatic pressure, any attempt to question the democratic expression of a people and any attempt to deny the legitimacy of the holders of these institutions inevitably lead to questioning the very existence of these institutions and to the destruction of the foundation of the state.

Don't the French realize that a victory for the pro-Ouattara's camp, through a violent coup d'état attempt in September 2002, or the diplomatic and political threats we were submitted to in 2003 at Marcoussis, lead to the same result: the collapse of the Ivorian state? You cannot support those who do not respect state institutions; you cannot praise those who do not play in accordance with the rules of democracy. You cannot undertake all this and think that it will not have a profound impact on our state institutions. You cannot pretend democracy will be preserved.

Marcoussis, the great "masterpiece" of Villepin, was a model of perversity. You create *ex nihilo* pseudo opposition of political parties which are but smoke screens behind which are hidden armed rebel groups. These armed rebel groups are those who are invited to make it look like a solution is being discussed freely, when this "solution" had already been conceived by Villepin's advisors, even before the arrival of the representatives of the "opposition parties" in Marcoussis. And to be sure he would reach his goals, Villepin was careful not to invite to those "discussions" the sitting president of Ivory Coast, the representatives of the government, and those who run legally recognized parties in the country.

In other words, it was just a bad joke told by amateurs. France always did everything it could to save my opponents from their electoral defeats and failed putsches. This is what I qualify as a plot against Ivory Coast and a plot against me. France needed to by-pass the Ivorian Constitution and by-pass me...before they could get rid of me.

Chapter 20
The Many Coups d'Etat

> *In this chapter Gbagbo and Mattei refer to the many coups d'etat which have plagued Ivory Coast since 1999. Most believe Ouattara was behind even the first coup d'etat by General Guéi against sitting President Bédié. Rumor has it Guéi was supposed to step aside, but he became enamored with power and declared himself president. Elections were eventually held in 2000 pitting Guéi against Gbagbo. When Gbagbo won, Guéi made moves to "re-take" power, but the world was watching and the people were not behind him. Guéi and his wife were later assassinated at the beginning of the next coup in 2000, in the cathedral where they had run to for protection—many believing he knew too much.*
>
> *The second coup thus was launched and semi-succeeded, since rebels took over the entire northern section of the country, effectively dividing the country in two. There is ample evidence that Ouattara was also behind this second coup d'etat.*
>
> *On the African continent, statistics are thought-provoking. Out of the 67 coups that modern African states have endured for the past half a century, 45 or more than 60% were perpetrated in former French colonies. Today no one doubts France's role in bringing to power Alassane Ouattara—the one who said "I will make this country ungovernable." The irony is that it is Gbagbo and not Ouattara who is sitting in The Hague waiting for his trial for crimes against humanity. It is obvious that what was and could easily be hidden yesterday to the view of many ordinary people is hard to be concealed in today's world of alternate media. It is furthermore in the stubbornness of nature that anything that is born to this world is expected to grow, reach a limit, and relentlessly enters into a process of waning before dying.*

The timing of the first coup d'etat in Ivory Coast was unambiguously announced by Alassane Ouattara on Saturday September 11, 1999, from his "fief" in the northern part of the country. In front of members of his RDR party, he delivered a speech, part of which he would probably wish today people would forget, especially those quotes which remain famous:

> *"When the time is right, I will strike this corrupt power, and it will fall to the ground like a ripe fruit[84]."*

Ouattara laced his speech with the plans and means to carry out this goal. Three months later, on December 24, 1999, Guéi's soldiers overthrew Bédié and fled the country... Gbagbo comments:

At Christmas, 1999, more precisely on December 24, Bédié was overthrown by General Robert Guéi, head of a military junta made up of people close to Ouattara, including Ibrahim Coulibaly (alias IB), who had been Ouattara's body guard. Guéi was Ouattara's military tool, who carried out the coup d'etat on his behalf. But instead of stepping aside, Guéi developed a taste for power. He took over, called together all the political parties, and formed a transitional government which lasted ten months, until the elections in 2000. A Constitution accepted by all became official, setting up electoral laws and procedures. The referendum took place in July, 2000. Strangely, Ouattara accepted the new Constitution. He voted "yes" for the referendum, even though, according to the terms defined by Bédié in 1994, the new Constitution with its Article 35 excludes Ouattara from standing as a candidate in the presidential race, since he was not born an Ivorian. It is the issue of the famous concept of "ivorité" invented by Bédié. Ouattara lets everyone believe that he is not interested in power. But he was already busy preparing something else...

In exile in Paris after the coup d'etat, Bédié preferred not to return to Ivory Coast. But the Ivorian Constitution stipulates that candidates for the presidency must undergo a medical check-up in Ivory Coast. Bédié had his check-up in France and so was excluded from the race. So I was Guei's challenger, along with three other candidates. Ouattara said: *"Guéi is going to win."* But I won in the first round with 59% of the votes (Guéi got 32%). They were all surprised. They were so sure of themselves they had not even made strong arguments against me. Robert Guéi took up arms and tried to oppose the results but was unsuccessful: the people were simply not behind him. That was the only truly democratic election which

---

[84] Translator's note: *Le Patriote* is an Ivorian daily newspaper close to Ouattara and his political party, the RDR. The quote ascribed to Alassane Ouattara appeared in the September 13, 1999's issue of the newspaper.

has ever taken place in Ivory Coast since the 1960s until now. True, there were troubles in the streets following my election caused by supporters of Ouattara. They wanted to redo the elections. But when Bédié opposed them, they calmed down. So there really was a kind of real consensus, a real link between those elected and the electorate.

One explanation of the seeming "fair play" of Alassane Ouattara, who at that time said he wanted to respect Republican law, was inadvertently given by Francis Wodié. This brilliant law professor, himself founder of a political party, Ivorian Workers's Party (PIT), was an experienced Ivorian politician, showing the battle fatigue of several electoral defeats. He obtained 3.5% of the electorate in the 1995 presidential election, then a little more than 5% against Laurent Gbagbo in 2000 and 0.29% in 2010. In a book of interviews recently released in Abidjan under the title of *My Combat for Ivory Coast*[85], Wodié recounts that for the 2010 presidential election, he had sought the support of Ouattara and his electors. Some of his closest friends had gone for Gbagbo, for whom Wodié nurses an entrenched hatred. In veiled terms, Ouattara evidently promised Wodié the leadership of the next transitional government, telling him in confidence that he:

> "...was convinced that the regime in place, voted in at the urns, would not last long."

These words foreshadowed a future destabilization. It is true that since 1993 and his failed attempts to become Houphouët's heir, Ouattara was lying in wait, pretending to get in line behind the others. In reality, he was nursing his resentment.

So having just been elected, Laurent Gbagbo becomes the target. He needs to pay for taking advantage of the disagreements between Bédié and Ouattara, squeezing in-between the two favorites of France and the United States. **From that time on**, Gbagbo notes, **they never stopped trying to get rid of me.**

On January 7-8, 2001, there is the first attempted military coup (called "the coup of the black Mercedes") against newly elected Gbagbo, only two months in office, carried out by Ibrahim Coulibaly (IB) [former body guard of Ouattara]. This coup failed.

---

[85] Translator's note: Francis Wodié, *Mon combat pour la Côte d'Ivoire* (My Combat for Ivory Coast) , Abidjan, NEA-CEDA, 2010.

On March 21, 2001, as always speaking from his favorite region, the north of the country, Ouattara made a public statement: *"I will make this country un-governable."* The following coup took the shape of a military attack, on September 19, 2002. That coup d'état succeeded in splitting the country in two. More than half of Ivorian territory (60%) was occupied by rebels, mainly Guillaume Soro's MPCI forces, the armed branch of Ouattara's RDR party. According to the then-RDR mayor of Bouaké, Fany Ibrahima, who claims without any scruples to be the *"rebel mayor"*:

> *"The MPCI is a military force we are proud of. Who says "MPCI" says "RDR" and there is nothing else to say..."*

The "math" looks like this: Ouattara (political head of the rebellion) + Soro (military chief of the rebellion) = coup d'état of the rebellion. Everybody knew this equation. The International Community, with France--the 'expert' of the Ivorian dossier--taking the lead within the UN Security Council, hurried to back this "equation." Gbagbo comments:

Over a period of ten years, Ouattara suffered repeated defeats in his attempts to seize power. The French finally decided to impose him by force in 2011. They first forced the organization of the presidential elections, while they simultaneously re-armed the rebels. All of sudden, Ouattara had the support of France, which, under Chirac had supported Bédié, but now favored Ouattara, thanks to Sarkozy and also to the support of the U.S., where he had carved out his niche in the financial realm. Most notably, Ouattara benefited from the active support of George Soros. Sarkozy took a different approach from his predecessors, as far as the Atlantic alliance was concerned. France no longer had a problem supporting a candidate also favored by the Americans. If it had been an earlier period of history, Gaullism would have prevented French authorities from supporting Ouattara. But Sarkozy had abandoned Gaullist policies which had "declared independence" from the U.S.

But in order to be president, you must 'do politics.' Firing from a bazooka does not make you president. So in 2000, after I won the election, Ouattara protested there had been a 'hold-up,' because the Constitution that he himself had approved a few weeks earlier, had prevented him from running. He called publically for a new election and urged his supporters to go down into the streets in protest. Despite this, I allowed him to come back

to Ivory Coast by cancelling the arrest warrant Bédié had launched against him for forgery and use of false documents. Then I did all I could to ensure his re-integration into the political scene and give him the chance in 2010 to [exceptionally] run for the highest post in the land, and what does he do? He refuses a simple recount of the votes!

Ouattara is praised by the International Community on pretext that he brought the Ivorian crisis to an end. But he was the one who provoked the crisis twelve years ago. He was the one who nurtured the crisis for ten years. He was the one who threw Ivory Coast into chaos. He is the one who is currently bringing tribalism back into our political discourse in the name of what he calls *"catching up ethnically,"* choosing people from the north to fill *all* the administrative posts in our country. He is the one who impoverishes the people while he repeats, *"money is [hard] at work, it's just not in circulation."* He is the one who wants, in one fell swoop, to naturalize hundreds of thousands of Burkinabès and other foreigners (more than 30% of the overall population living on Ivorian soil are foreigners) so that they can become part of the electorate favorable to him. From neighboring countries, they drop them off by the truck-load…

Chapter 21
"The steamroller advances and Gbagbo will be crushed"

The above heading is not a quote ascribed to President Gbagbo. François Mattei attributed it to a journalist, one of his friends very familiar with the methods of the Ouattara team. Alassane Ouattara's henchmen did not hesitate to go ahead with the financing of an expensive and preposterous film, whose ultimate goals were to do damage to the reputation of President Gbagbo.

By African standards, the film ought to be an important production since it was endowed with a tiddy budget of 180 million CFA francs (about 165,000 euros). The film produced in December 2013 strangely resembled the 2001 documentary ("Ivory Coast, identity time-bomb") of the Belgian sociologist Benoît Scheuer which was mysteriously financed. In that 2001 documentary-film, the coup of September 19, 2002 was announced and justified in anticipation of the seizing of power by violence. Remember that in January 2001, hardly seventy days after his election, President Gbagbo had to face a failed coup whose mastermind was a certain Ibrahim Coulibaly alias IB, one of the body guards of Alassane Dramane Ouattara. Likewise in December 2010, the same IB became the leader of the much-talked about "Invisible Commando" that launched deadly attacks against the lawful armed forces and civilian populations of Abobo, a northern neighborhood of the city of Abidjan.

During the past twenty years, IB was an active member of many attempted coups. He was immediately eliminated when Ouattara took power, because certainly he knew too much and was expecting a big share of the cake as a payment for services rendered. The French professor of political science, Michel Galy, has depicted the semantics of Ouattara's system as being one in which words are the reverse of things, a system in which "peace" means "war" and "irreversible democracy" means "continued repression." This is what this French professor of international relations and expert on Africa calls the "communication-disinformation."

195

It was a man dead-tired and frozen to the bone that Gbagbo's lawyers welcomed to the Scheveningen prison. To prevent his state of health from worsening, they rushed out to buy him warm clothes and a suit for his first appearance before the judges of the International Court. President Gbagbo has been through it all: the outbreak of war, the bombing of his residence by French Armed Forces, murder attempts, his own capture amid the screams of the wounded and the groans of the dying, intimidation from his jailers at the Golf Hotel, his transfer to the north of the country, illegal detention in horrendous conditions--perhaps a programmed physical exhaustion--a complete judicial farce as they authorized his extradition to The Hague, his hastened transfer to Scheveningen, while his lawyers' appeals had not yet been examined, and finally his arrival in a flimsy cotton shirt in a country where the temperature was below 0°...

His health seemed to be affected. He confirmed to me as time went on that nothing was done to follow the recommendations of the medical specialists who had visited him. He still seemed shell-shocked, even though it had been months since his residence had been bombarded. His eight-month detention in Ivory Coast in particularly difficult conditions did not make things any easier. He still seems to suffer physically. Eight months without seeing the sun, without knowing what was going on outside the little room where he was held prisoner by the men of Commander Fofié, a warlord close to Soro, who is accused by the UN of "frying" his opponents for hours in a metal container until they died. In some way, if President Gbagbo can sit in front of me today, it is because of his courage and his internal strength. Any other human being would never have survived. As usual, whenever Gbagbo fights for his ideals, he just looks straight ahead and endures. He says wryly:

Well, at least nobody can say I ran away.

There was no single line in the French press on the scandalous conditions in which President Gbagbo was detained in Ivory Coast, despite the communiqués of his lawyer, one on August 10, 2011, speaking of President Gbagbo, an "ill-treated hostage," and another on September 16, 2011, where he reports "President Gbagbo's lawyers are again prevented from seeing their client." There was not the slightest move to alleviate his sufferings. Yet, the French Ambassador as well as the French civilian and military leaders knew all about the disgraceful conditions of his detention.

There was no word either on the fact that Gbagbo's son, a French citizen, was also imprisoned for months in dreadful conditions. And there

196

wasn't a single word on the hundreds of political prisoners held by Ouattara's regime today--victims of what is called "justice for the victors." Yet the French state knows about all of this and is continually notified of the situation. The fate of the "big fish" is the main subject of discussion of Alassane Ouattara, his close aids, his French advisors, and the representative of French authorities.

Little by little, Gbagbo seemed to be getting better. Would the state of health of President Gbagbo justify a temporary release? Every time his lawyers requested it, some event would occur, as if by chance, a few days before the audience. The ICC Prosecutor would rush to inform the other judges of some detail to dissuade them from granting the requested release. And each time, the Prosecutor would try to scare the other judges, saying, if you release him, you will be responsible for the inevitable clashes which will take place in Ivory Coast. She would tell them: Gbagbo's supporters are ready to do anything, even provoke a bloodbath, to put their leader back in power. To give credibility to these predictions, the Prosecutor would pull incidents "out of her hat," incidents which always occurred exactly a day or two prior to the judges' decision. There would be all kinds of incidents, armed clashes, crimes committed at the border between Ghana and Ivory Coast… This last set of events was mentioned the first time the request was made. All this stopped the debate, allowing the judges to avoid even making a decision.

Gbagbo is presented as a "danger to the public," someone who, from his prison cell in The Hague, is manipulating the tentacles of a huge network throughout Africa. The same scenario occurred when the appeal for this decision was made public on October 26. On October 24, Gbagbo's supporters, imprisoned at the MACA [in the south of the country], were transferred to the north 48 hours before the decision, suggesting civil unrest or even an imminent coup d'état. The prisoners were brought back south on October 30. Nothing happened in between except for a new refusal to release Gbagbo. The procedure was so familiar it seemed to be taken from a book entitled "The Best Recipes of Fatou Bensouda."

The next time the request was made, still in the same year, an alleged plot was suddenly discovered to be carried out by Gbagbo's friends in exile, including Marcel Gossio, former head of the Abidjan port. Fatou Bensouda took at face value a UN report and newspaper articles whose authors obviously preferred not to carry out any investigations. The lawyers of President Gbagbo almost enjoyed showing the invalidity of these various accusations, revealing the inconsistencies and the people behind all the 'talk.' The ones who were the quickest to jump to conclusions about these incredible subversive activities in the end had to agree that such plots never existed, that Marcel Gossio had never left Morocco where he now resides nor did he plan any such operation. On other occasions, the Prosecutor would discover a network of activists fed by inexhaustible funds. Here again, President Gbagbo's lawyers uncovered the hoax and dismantled the ridiculous accusations. As for the president's inexhaustible hidden cache discovered by pseudo experts to the great joy of the Prosecuter, would be shown to have never existed.

To continue down the list of accidental happenings that show the feverishness of the Prosecutor and the sabotage carried out against Gbagbo's defense team, can be added the Prosecutor's announcement of the discovery of Gbagbo's eight *"hidden bank accounts"* in the *Société Générale Bank* of Ivory Coast, discovered by investigating UN experts. They spoke of *"**hidden accounts**"* which nonetheless bore his name and could be found in his own personal bank! How strange!

During the actual hearing, James Stewart, one of Bensouda's deputies, seems to develop a whole scenario, which collapses like a house of cards, after a simple counter-investigation by Gbagbo's defense team. First, the defense team made it obvious that the experts mistakenly mentioned twice two accounts, which leaves six instead of eight accounts. Among these six accounts, two of them are entirely empty: no recorded transaction, there is not a single franc in either of them. Of the four remaining, one is where the salary of President Gbagbo (8 million CFA francs or about 12,215 euros) was deposited each month until the transfers were stopped in February, 2011.

Did the investigators talk about *transactions* after the arrest of Gbagbo? The answer is no, since the *transactions* in question turned out to be nothing but bank charges. Another account, a savings account, was fed from the first, where interest was accrued. This account was for the other *transaction*s detected by the experts. There was an account which served as go-between between the checking and the savings accounts. Finally, there was a last account used by the bank for a selective operation. In this account, there was the amount of 3 euros. This is the complete story of the *hidden accounts* that the UN experts discovered[86]. End of story for the *"eight secret accounts"* of Laurent Gbagbo. They only needed to do a little checking, something the International Criminal Court chose not to do. Unless perhaps the ICC changed its strategy and was trying to buy time and maybe wear down the defense team, after having pushed

---

[86] Translator's note: Actually $200 was discovered under Gbagbo's name in Los Angeles which had been forgotten. It was an account for one of his daughter's education fees.

so vehemently for an acceleration of the trial, to get it over with. The extra time granted to the Prosecutor might give her time to glean *"more evidence."*

What about the funds available to the pro-Gbagbo's in exile in Ghana? It is widely known they have no money whatsoever and struggle just to stay alive in a foreign country. It is not because such or such refugee tries to forge ahead to either obtain refugee status or some refugee subsidy that it means a *"network"* exists.

Concerning the supposed network of pro-Gbagbo's supporters who, according to the Prosecutor, are waiting to destabilize Ivory Coast, that network does not exist. There is no more a pro-Gbagbo underground network than there is a chocolate factory in Ivory Coast, a country which is the world leader in the production of cocoa beans. In its issue of October 28 *Jeune Afrique* reports on a UN report which concludes that:

> *"There is no evidence of the existence of a cleverly prepared political and military plot…"*

The Prosecutor, either through ignorance or bad faith, continues to deceive the ICC judges by raising the spectrum of these much talked-about supporters of Gbagbo. More than anything, this talk allows her to avoid speaking about true Ivorian realities…. For the Prosecutor, it is much better for international public opinion to continue to ignore that Ivory Coast is being deprived of its resources by the warlords who, after having conquered the north in 2002, conquered the south in 2011. These warlords destroy state institutions by racketeering and by imprisoning and killing innocent victims, while they themselves are almost never brought to justice. And so the widespread insecurity continues and is even intensified by the presence in the country of several thousand unemployed pro-Ouattara combatants who remain armed. Mercenaries from Burkina Faso and Niger who remained in Ivory Coast hang out with gang members, former soldiers of the rebel forces and thousands of traditional hunters, the Dozos, who try to get "a return" on their 2010-2011 investment from Alassane Ouattara. These Dozos are sadly related to the infamous Kamajors who ran wild in Sierra Leone, cutting off people's hands.

> *"In Charles Taylor's trial at the Special Court for Sierra Leone, it was specified [...] that the Kamajors ate people who were accused of being supporters of the RFU[87]."*

All these former combatants are bitter, frustrated and abandoned—but also armed. They multiply their attacks and racketeering activities which exploit people. They plunder and seize land, as the former Burkinabè rebel leader Amédé Ouérémi did in western Ivory Coast. Luckily, his arrest in May, 2013 resulted in a decrease in terrorist acts and an improvement in security in that part of the country.

The illegal seizure of land by new-comers is another crucial issue. That is the real hotbed of tension in Ivory Coast, which could even lead the country to its ruin. Every day, hundreds, maybe thousands of immigrants from Burkina Faso and some neighboring countries, who are members of the same ethnic groups as the rebel warlords and as Alassane Ouattara, are brought in to the South and the West, to reinforce those who have confiscated rich agricultural lands from their legal owners. They settle in a place, bring their families to join them, and then push the indigenous peoples further and further away. An excellent article by Fanny Pigeaud in the September 2012 issue of *Le Monde diplomatique,* entitled "A Territory out of Control, War for Cocoa in the Ivorian West," describes the unceasing rumbling of vehicles, loaded with immigrants coming from Burkina Faso and the dire consequences of trying to substitute one population for another.

Coming back to the possible temporary release of President Gbagbo on November 24, 2012, new events occurred. Two days beforehand, November 22, the secret on the arrest warrant of Simone Gbagbo was unveiled. Up to that point, Fatou Bensouda denied the existence of such a warrant, while it had been in effect since February 29, 2012. The press, getting hold of the information, began, right on time, to talk about the "death squads." The spouse of President Gbagbo has been slanderously accused of being linked to death squads. When you attack Simone Gbagbo, in an attempt to refuse to release Laurent Gbagbo until charges can be confirmed, it just shows what everybody knows: we are dealing with a two-headed monster. Besides the media hype that it created, the Prosecutor also saw this as a means of weakening the defense team, even before

---

[87] Translator's note: This was the hearing on the confirmation of the charges held in February 25, 2013. The RFU is the English acronym of the Revolutionary United Front. This group fought an eleven-year war in the West African country of Sierra Leone, without success. The war then spilled over into the neighboring country of Liberia.

the trial. There was no mention of the French Court decisions in 2006, which declared that accusing the Ivorian presidency of putting death squads in place was considered as slander.

Also, the Prosecutor paid little attention to the fact that President Gbagbo's lawyers had demonstrated before the Court in February, 2013 that since 2002, Franco-Ivorian lobbyist groups have been conducting slander campaigns against Laurent Gbagbo to enable the rebels to take power legitimately. The same thing happened again in 2010: the same people maneuvering on the French side and the same people executing the acts on the Ivorian side.

All these pretexts nourished the mistrust deliberately planted like land-mines on Gbagbo's road in order to destroy him. These underhanded tactics and practices have been part of the Ivorian crisis from the beginning and continue to weigh in on the pending case.

At the end of 2013, a Cameroonian journalist, Said Penda, formerly of the BBC, produced a film of two times fifty-two minutes, entitled *"Laurent Gbagbo or the Anti-Neocolonialist: Word and Blood."* One may wonder what motivated this author-director. Indeed the Cameroonian public as well as their media have been predominantly in favor of Gbagbo during the post-electoral crisis and opposed to his transfer to the ICC. Yet, Said Penda declared in an interview in the daily *Le Patriote,* a newspaper close to Alassane Ouattara:

> *"I myself do not understand why the ICC would have any trouble finding concrete evidence against Laurent Gbagbo, concerning his liability in what occurred in Ivory Coast, when investigative work by journalists like myself have revealed solid proof that Laurent Gbagbo gave orders that send shivers down my spine, that his people should put down any attempt at opposing his power."*

Was Said Penda's goal to provide the ICC with arguments, if not evidence, or was his goal to discredit this international institution in anticipation of its failure? We need to recall that on June 3, 2013, the judges of the ICC declared they did not consider that the Prosecutor had not produced sufficient evidence in support of her argumentation, allowing them to order that a trial be held.

The author presented his film before a panel of journalists at the Abidjan Press House in December, 2013. Some sceptics were astounded by the huge amount of financial support made available to him to produce the film. He was generously endowed with an unheard of budget of 108 million CFA francs, about 165,000 euros, which, in Africa, is a huge production. It is hard to see how the producers, Sentinelles Productions, a little-known company in Abidjan, even if endowed with such resources, would break even. This expensive film, done in such bad taste, reminds me of a remark made by one of my journalist friends familiar with Ouattara's team. While we were talking about Gbagbo's upcoming trial at The Hague, he warned me:

"Gbagbo will be crushed because the people across from him will unleash a steamroller against him. They have all the financial means and all the connections to do it."

Communication and disinformation, along with all its techniques are part of Michel Galy's teaching domain. He is a political science professor at the Institute of International Relations (ILERI). He is very critical of the way in which France treats Ivory Coast and Laurent Gbagbo. Now he is focusing in on the Ouattara regime. He denounces a *"Goulag"* where 800 political prisoners are arbitrarily detained and their most basic rights denied. He points to a lie or a 'cover up' spread by various communication agencies at great expense.

Michel Galy notes that in Ouattara's system of semantics, *"words represent the reverse of things."* They may mean the contrary of what they designate in the real world. Thus, *"war"* stands for *"peace,"* and *"irreversible democracy"* designates, in fact, *"continued repression."*

For those who remember past events in Ivory Coast, this also resembles the 2001 appearance of a documentary coming out of the blue, by the Belgian sociologist, Benoît Scheuer, entitled *Ivory Coast, Identity Time-Bomb*[88]. This documentary was hostile to a newly elected Gbagbo, whom no one had yet charged with any crime. It too was mysteriously financed. An association called "Genocide Prevention" tried to communicate the idea, one still put forward by Soro today, that Gbagbo's entourage was planning a genocide of the Muslim populations in Ivory Coast. The living proof of this discrimination, according to Scheuer, was of course, that Alassane Ouattara was prevented from running for the presidency because he was a Muslim. Like an unleashed devil, this film announced and justified in advance the armed coup d'etat to come, that of 2002, against Gbagbo in Abidjan, which itself succeeded another coup in January, 2001, when Gbagbo had barely been in office seventy days. Carried

---

[88] *Côte d'Ivoire, la poudrière identitaire* (Ivory Coast, Identity Time-Bomb).

out by the late IB, Ibrahim Coulibaly, one of Alassane Ouattara's body guards, this coup attempt failed. In 2010, the same IB would become the leader of the much-talked about "Invisible Commando," based in Abobo, a suburb of Abidjan. From December, 2010, IB launched several deadly attacks against the Ivorian regular armed forces and against civilian populations. Previously, he had distinguished himself at the sides of General Guéi, "*Father Christmas in combat fatigues*," in the military coup that overthrew Henri Konan Bédié on December 24, 1999 and brought Guéi to power, on behalf of Ouattara, before Robert Guéi discovered his own "national destiny." As for IB who was involved in all the Ivorian coups over a period of twenty years, he knew far too much and was hoping for a too big piece of the pie, in payment for past services. When his boss Alassane Ouattara acceded to the throne in 2010, he was immediately "liquidated."

Chapter 22
The deliberate blindness of
the International Community

As the International Community's attention is diverted by the word "genocide," pronounced in heavy tones by rebel leader Guillaume Soro on a French television station in May, 2005, the French authorities and the UN are pushing Laurent Gbagbo to go ahead with the presidential elections. The problem is: the rebels, under Soro's command, have refused to disarm, so how can free and fair elections take place? Here Laurent Gbagbo describes his catch-22 situation: "damned if you don't, damned if you do." He knew going ahead with the elections was a mistake, but he also knew if the elections didn't take place, they would find another way to oust him.

Today he humbly admits to having committed two serious errors: going ahead with the elections without disarmament (the latter not being under his control), and giving in to the request that the Electoral Commission be made up of a majority of representatives from the opposition. While admitting his errors, he notes his only goal was to find a peaceful solution to the Ivorian crisis.

In this chapter, Gbagbo also recounts how he first met Soro, a university friend of his son Michel. But Mattei goes on to describe what Soro's troups are doing, while he is busy in France promoting his book and giving TV interviews. His rebel troops are, in fact, committing true genocide, massacring dozens of Guéré in the west (killing old people, men, women and children). Mattei also comes back to an earlier massacre carried out by the rebels: that of the 2002 slaughter in Bouaké of over sixty gendarmes, along with their wives and children.

As Soro talks about his "civilized rebellion" and a few "slip-ups," the International Community turns a blind eye, as they have done to all the cover-ups carried out by pseudo human rights movements richly funded by billionaire George Soros, who openly declares that closed societies (those trying to run their own affairs) should be overthrown....

Standing at the foot of the rebellion's "sacred tree," decorated by the International Community, people wondered if it is not the Christmas tree itself that needs to be planted in The Hague, in the yard of the Dutch-based International Criminal Court. The violent history of those now in power as well as the brutal methods they are still using, were, for a very long time, well-kept secrets of the International Community and the media. Guillaume Soro, in his book, *Why I Became a Rebel*[89], presents the movement he led with others as "the camp of the Good" which defeated "the forces of Evil." With the help of a colleague from RFI news, Soro writes that it was:

> "...a civilized rebellion, which surprised journalists, NGO representatives and other organizations, because of our commitment to respect human rights" with the brigades of "street sweepers in their pink tops" which intervened three or four times a week.

During May, 2005, when he appeared on a TV set in Paris for the promotion of his book, Soro announced, like a romantic hero in a combat against tyranny,

> "There is a serious risk of genocide in Ivory Coast. That is why I had to sound the alarm."

The buzzword "genocide" is pronounced, for the exclusive attention of white audiences and the ears of the West traumatized by Rwanda[90]. Guillaume Soro: arsonist in Africa and firefighter on the banks of the Seine. Obviously, in his TV interview, the man only reveals one side of himself. Like so many others, journalist Thierry Ardisson, had not done his homework, so he had no information to counter Soro's propaganda "intox." Ardisson could have found the information he needed in a book written by Georges Neyrac, *Nude Ivory*[91], published in March, 2005, with Soro's being published in April, one month

---

[89] Guillaume Soro, *Pourquoi je suis devenu un rebel* (Why I Became a Rebel), Paris, Hachette, 2005.

[90] Translator's note: In the East African country of Rwanda, from April 7 until July 15, 1994, the Hutu majority slaughtered between half to one million members of the Tutsi minority ethnic group. This Rwandan mass murder was the first case of genocide in modern Africa except for pre-WWI genocides which occurred in present-day DRC, South Africa, Zimbabwe and Namibia.

[91] Georges Neyrac, *Ivoire Nue: chroniques d'une Côte d'Ivoire perdue* (Nude Ivory: Chronicles of a lost Ivory Coast), Paris, Editions Jacob-Duverne, 2005.

later. Based on the same subject matter, the rebel's book received rave reviews from the media, whereas the book by Neyrac, a French soldier, providing a narrative of what he observed close up, full of undisclosed information, was ignored. Though splendidly written, it does not coincide with France's political stance. What can we make of all this?

In an interview with a journalist of *France-Soir* on May 13, 2005, Guillaume Soro justified his refusal to disarm his men, even though the agreements signed at Marcoussis in 2003, those signed in South Africa in 2005, as well as the peace treaty he signed with President Gbagbo in 2007 in Ouagadougou, all stipulated that his troops had to disarm. Soro maintained his position until 2010, not respecting a single agreement and none of the UN resolutions which demanded disarmament by the rebels in exchange for the concessions made by President Gbagbo. All the UN resolutions [18 in total] imposed the disarmament of the rebels in exchange for Gbagbo's concessions, including majority membership of the opposition in the future electoral commission, the agreement to exceptionally allow Bédié and Ouattara to run in the next presidential race (despite their non-qualification according to the Ivorian Constitution), and the rebels' participation in the government, with Soro as Prime Minister. In making some of these concessions, President Gbagbo had to go against some of the provisions of the Ivorian Constitution and some of the people in his own camp.

Soro responds to the journalist of *France-Soir*, saying that disarmament *"is an extremely sensitive and delicate matter and we need time."* Well, it was truly a sensitive and delicate issue, since the rebellion never disarmed. President Gbagbo comments:

I made two [fundamental] errors: first, I went ahead with the presidential election without the promised disarmament of the rebels, and second, I yielded to the demand of the opposition to have a majority on the Electoral Commission. My supporters criticized me for doing this, but I wanted to move on quickly to the elections, as early as 2005, so that reconciliation could take place as soon as possible. I took this decision in good faith, in April and May, 2004, during the meetings in Pretoria, South Africa, to find a way to end the crisis. During the talks in Pretoria, people seemed to be leaning toward reconciliation, at least, that is what I thought.

In South Africa [for peace talks], I was the only "pure" Francophile [the one fond of anything French]. Bédié and Ouattara spoke in English with Thabo Mbeki, the South African president. I always refused to use

English, and it was Ouattara who translated for me. But for the French, I was always the black sheep... I still would like to know the reason why!

After Pretoria, Soro asked me: *"And us, what do we get?"* I had just granted Ouattara and Bédié the possibility of running for the presidential election without any pre-conditions. I understood that Soro's "we" referred to Compaoré and himself. So we organized the Peace Conference of Ouagdougou in Burkina Faso to satisfy them both. I was always the one who tried to please everyone else. I did my share in the process of bringing peace to the country, but they did nothing in return. They never kept their promises.

What about the disarmament? In every single agreement, it was always stipulated that the rebels were obliged to disarm. In all the UN resolutions, and God knows there were a lot of them, the disarmament of the rebels was a key condition. Yet, we were pushed to carry out the presidential election without disarmament being achieved... The pressure was incredible: *"Go ahead with these elections,"* we were told by the International Community, with Sarkozy in the driver's seat. It is only today I realize they were looking for a brutal and final end to the Ivorian crisis.

I was wrong to have accepted to go ahead with the 2010 presidential election without having achieved disarmament beforehand. But in any case, it is clear they would have found another reason [to bring about my downfall]. The attack would have occurred on the pretext that I refused the elections. My country was in a deadlock, and I wanted, at all costs, to help the country get out of that situation.

Did someone call this "a civilized rebellion?" From 2002 to 2010 the pro-Ouattara warlords carved up the territory in the north of Ivory Coast. They destroyed state-owned infrastructures and tormented the population. There was intimidation, racketeering, property seizure, theft, arbitrary detention, torture and murder. The documented evidence on the crimes of the rebellion chiefs today in power in Abidjan is abundant and accessible. Curiously, the French press hardly ever talks about it. As the saying goes, *"There are none so blind as those who will not see."*

We must say that if the reader were given the opportunity to have a clear understanding of the truth, it would mean calling into question all that has been said, everywhere and anywhere, to demonize President Gbagbo.

When the same journalist of *France-Soir* pointed out to him [Soro] that his name is on a list of 80 persons released by the UN naming those *"suspected of serious violations of human rights,"* the Ivorian rebel chief, Guillaume Soro, doesn't bat an eye. Obviously, he thinks he will not be subject to judicial pursuit. Isn't Soro Guillaume the hero of the International Community, the valiant knight that Luis Moreno Ocampo, the former ICC Prosecutor, congratulated when he was named president of the Ivorian National Assembly? Isn't he the one who is warmly received on July 2, 2012 by his counterpart Claude Bartolone at the Palais Bourbon in Paris?[92]

Soro calmly states *"When you are at the head of a rebellion which controls 60% of the territory and you are the one who covers its administration, you can imagine there might be a few slip-ups."*

In fact, on May 31, 2005, as Soro returned from the parties and book signing sessions of his Parisian promotional trip, in another place, far away from the French TV studios, in the villages of Petit Duékoué and Guitrozon, in western Ivory Coast, more than one hundred and twenty peace-loving inhabitants (men, women and children of the Guéré ethnic group, supporters of Gbagbo) were being massacred in the night: cut with machetes or burned alive. According to testimonies received, it is Soro's MPCI men, as well as the Dozos who are implicated in this mass murder. In 2007, a certain number of the rebels were sentenced with up to twenty-years in prison. But are people in France also aware that during the attack of September 19, 2002, when more than half of the Ivorian national territory was occupied by the rebels, crimes were perpetrated by the hundreds and even the thousands?

All the evidence concerning the involvement of Soro's men are in the report on the investigation, which registers the complaints filed by the families. It is all there in the office of the Prosecutor in Abidjan, where I consulted the dossiers.

Another sinister "exploit" to put on Soro's "account" is the massacre in Bouaké (already mentioned above by Laurent Gbagbo) of the sixty *gendarmes* [state police], their children and their spouses, after they had been taken hostage by the members of the MPCI. The website *Afrique2050.com* provides a good synthesis, from which the following excerpt comes:

> *"After a thorough investigation, Amnesty International was able to retrace, on the basis of direct testimonies, the circumstances of this massacre. The gendarmes arrested on October 6, 2002 at the Bouaké*

---

[92] Translator's note: The Palais Bourbon is the counterpart of the American Capitol Hill, the seat of the House of Representatives in the American Congress and the equivalent of the British House of Commons.

staff office of the Third Legion were not killed during combat. They were killed in cold blood, shot down by armed elements of the MPCI while they were detained with around fifty of their children and some civilians in the prison at the military camp of the Third Infantry Battalion of Bouaké. It would appear, moreover, that some among them, including the injured, were probably shot down at the site of the communal grave where they were compelled to bury some of their comrades. The survivors of this massacre had their life spared thanks to a last minute order given by one of the leaders of the MPCI. Finally, the dozen or so gendarmes still detained in December 2002 were released, after having paid very huge ransoms."

In reality, this nebulous group of armed men called "the rebels" was built up through a kind of wild fray: armed clashes between factions, internal fighting, rivalries among leaders, and physical elimination of some. Corporal Kassoum Bamba, alias "Kass", one of the *com'zone* (commanders of zone) and a close ally of IB [Ibrahim Coulibaly], was killed and his mutilated body discovered on June 21, 2004. He was a victim of the rivalry between his friend IB and Soro, the "fraternal enemies" of the rebellion. Likewise, Adams, another militia chief of the Ivorian rebellion, was executed a year later in an internal "settling of scores." In the same context, and this has been mentioned earlier, nearly eighty of their men (young people randomly recruited to go to war for CFA francs) would die from suffocation inside a container where they were locked up. Martin Fofié Kouakou, a militia chief, who later was to be Gbagbo's guard after his arrest, had ordered his men to leave his rivals in the sun in Korhogo. Fofié has been the object of UN judicial proceedings since 2004 for different crimes including the enlistment of child soldiers. *Le Monde* of December 25, 2013 stressed the last report of Amnesty International which stated that *"victor's justice"* and impunity enjoyed by former rebels, liable for mass crimes, but nevertheless promoted to positions of responsibility by Alassane Ouattara, *undermine the reconciliation."*

Ibrahim Coulibaly, better known by his initials IB, was not yet the auto-proclaimed "General IB," but already a professional putschist arrested and detained in Fresnes, France[93] in 2003 for attempted subversion in Ivory Coast. Strangely, he was released by the French judiciary after twenty days in jail, and

---

[93] Translator's note: Fresnes is a suburb south of Paris located in the Department of Val-de-Marne.

then he vanished into thin air. In 1999, IB had already been involved in the military coup against President Konan Bédié. In 2007, he teamed up with a Frenchman called Jean-Paul Ney in a new and incredible attempt, a completely half-baked project, to overthrow the government in Abidjan. In 2009, an international arrest warrant was issued against him, but he continued to travel all over Africa unhindered. He kept weaving his spider's web, thinking perhaps that he would one day come out ahead of his political partners and, who knows, maybe come to power himself.

On April 27, 2011, hardly a few days after the military victory over Gbagbo, it was IB's turn. He was killed by some men associated with his own "companions," Soro and Ouattara. His body was released to his family only several weeks after his death. Ouattara refused any autopsy, confirming that IB had been killed in combat and not assassinated, as his friends in Abidjan have claimed, pointing to the particularly horrible state of his corpse.

Thus comes the final act in the struggle between rebel rivals looking for power, a struggle which has not yet delivered all its secrets. On June 29, 2007, rockets and bursts of Kalashnikovs were shot against Soro's plane, at that time Prime Minister in Gbagbo's government of *cohabitation*[94]. Four members of Soro's escort were killed. One of the rebel chiefs, Issiaka Ouattara, better known as "Wattao," continues to claim he knows the name of the instigator of the attack, but he has never let the secret out. Likewise Soro never said who he suspected, even if he says he has *"his own idea about the issue."* In Abidjan, a name is on everyone lips: Ibrahim Coulibaly, the famous IB…

The promotion of Soro within the government of his sworn enemy, Gbagbo, did not please IB nor a lot of other rebels who felt cheated. The death of IB in 2011 was probably the outcome of a long mutual hatred.

The underground career of Soro bewildered some of his partners and deceived many of his opponents. This is hardly surprising since Soro moved from the armed rebellion against Gbagbo, whom he had denounced as a

---

[94] Translator's note: The term "cohabitation" comes from the French Constitution of the Vth Republic which was established on October 4, 1958. The advent of this new French Constitution brought about the beginning of a semi-presidential regime in the French government system by which the President of the Republic and the head of the president's cabinet share executive power. An example is when Socialist President, François Mitterrand appointed Jacques Chirac, from the Right, as Prime Minister because it was the latter's party who had the majority in the French National Assembly. This French "sharing" of governmental powers has undoubtedly been perverted under the African tropics where rebellions are created, *ex nihilo*, for the sake of applying the "cohabitation" rule.

dictator, to the position of the Prime Minister in this same government (which he had declared so horrible), following the signing of the peace accords in Ouagadougou in 2007. Then, at the end of the controversial election of 2010, Soro picks up his luggage and his guns and moves into Alassane Ouattara's camp. Of course, the truth of the matter is that Soro never stopped working for Alassane Ouattara.

A former student in English, Guillaume Kigbafori Soro, possesses no university diploma. He first was trained to be a union activist and later became head of the Student Federation, the FSCI. Then he goes into politics. Close to General Robert Guéi during all these years, Soro was, in fact, a mole for Ouattara, taking on the hat as "political chief" of the rebellion. Today, Gbagbo remembers how he made Soro's acquaintance.

It was my son Michel who one day brought home for lunch his student friend Guillaume Soro. That's how I met him.

As soon as he entered the government of the national union, Guillaume Soro kept a watchful eye on Gbagbo, and after the peace agreement of Ouagadougou, without hesitation, led a brilliant and permanent double political life.

After his own accession to power, Ouattara has words of praise for Soro, especially at public meetings in the north, proving the obvious complicity between the "Father" and the "Son" in the symbiosis of the "Holy Spirit": the Rebellion. A few months earlier during an interview on *Africa 24* during the campaign of 2010, Ouattara affirmed that he had *"condemned"* the rebellion since day one, and he said that *"violence never brings about any final solutions."* This contradictory stance evidently shocked no one, not even Ouattara himself.

On July 1, 2013 in Kong, Guillaume Soro made public *his long-standing tie to Ibrahim Ouattara*, Ado's "photocopy." This Soro's old pal works today for his brother as the Minister of Ivorian Presidential Affairs. People think of Ibrahim as president number 2. Ibrahim and Soro, both students, became friends in the 1990's. Soro is on record as saying that he then got closer to Ouattara and made a pact with him when he met him in 1998. He also spent a lot of time with General Robert Guéi. Thus, on his roulette race to power, the young Soro placed chips on several numbers. In his book, he offered the following explanation: *"Given my young age, it is like I am the son of several Ivorian politicians…"*

But he finally recognizes that he only has one father: Alassane Dramane Ouattara, whom he met through the brother, Ibrahim Ouattara.

"One day [...] I told him" "Well, Ibrahim [...] I promise you: from now on, I will support your big brother [Alassane Ouattara] *and I will fight with you for him." Since that day, I remember that it is Ibrahim Ouattara--as we returned here from our travels in 1998--who was instrumental in my decision to support Alassane Ouattara. That is the historical truth."*

Nothing can be said that is more convincing and definitive than this: Alassane Ouattara is truly the "godfather" of the rebellion who introduced and maintained the civil war in Ivory Coast for a period of ten years. Guillaume Soro never stopped being Alassane Ouattara's faithful lieutenant even when, between 2007 and 2010, as Prime Minister of Gbagbo, he simulated perfect loyalty to the sitting president. As soon as the results of the disputed presidential election were known in December 2010, with two presidents instead of one, Soro "came out of the woods." He made a statement in favor of Ouattara by *swearing on his Christian faith* that the latter had truly won the election. And this time, not surprisingly, the rebel forces officially joined their occult chief, who had been their chief from the beginning. These rebel forces would become, in March 17, 2013, by virtue of Ouattara's decree, the army of the country under the name of Republican Forces of Ivory Coast [better known under its French acronym FRCI], replacing the regular Ivorian army. President Gbagbo comments:

Soro owes his position to his use of weapons. He should be worried if, one day, he no longer has them with him.

In the history of Ivory Coast, a change of president had never brought about a change in the army. Governments change, but the country's army remains. Regardless of what is said about the old Ivorian army, it was rooted in the legitimacy of the Republic, with its high ranking personnel and officers of high standing. The new army is made up of a heterogeneous mix of uncontrollable former rebels, putschists, and militia. Thus, it won't be surprising if the French army ends up staying a very long time in Ivory Coast to protect Ivorians from their own army, who are not capable of holding themselves back from plundering. The [Franco-Cameroonian] journalist, Théophile Kouamouo, comments with irony on this situation in his contribution to the online journal, the *Gri-Gri International:*

"It is the French tax payer who will pay to ensure police protection in a country that has been independent for fifty years!"

Sure of himself and of the impunity he enjoys, as well as the constant support of the International Community who chose him as president of Ivory Coast, Ouattara finally admitted his complicity with his "faithful son," Soro, and this, in Korhogo in front of a crowd of supporters in late July, 2013, hardly three years after having made a contrary statement in an interview on *Africa 24*:

"Of course, at a given time, Soro decided that we, the elders, had taken a path which was, maybe, too long—it would take too long for us to win our fight.

"[…] Soro showed proof of courage and his sense of sacrifice when he fought for the populations of the north to recover their dignity by being granted their Ivorian nationality […]."

Addressing convinced supporters, Ouattara could not help tantalizing his audience with some juicy tidbits, quite daring comments for someone who had sparked off three coups d'état and two wars:

"[…] Today, I am with my own relatives. Thus, I would like, once more, to appeal to and invite our brothers of the FPI [the party of Gbagbo] *to enter into the peace process…*

"…The FPI must have the strength to ask for forgiveness from the victims and their relatives …"

Koné Djakaridja, alias Zakaria, one of the rebel commanders, currently appointed as chief of military police by Alassane Ouattara, had let the cat out of the bag and let the secret filiation of the rebellion be known in a speech in a Malinké[95] film, made public in 2002[96]. It was at a time when Ouattara was careful enough not to acknowledge, let alone claim, any link with Soro's people and with the other chief rebels. In his speech, Zakaria clearly designated Ibrahim Coulibaly alias IB, as the military chief and Ouattara as the political leader, the one *"who bought weapons,"* with France as an accomplice. As for Zakaria's threats against some other chief rebels, they were written in blood.

---

[95] It is the most spoken lingua franca in Ivory Coat and better known as "Dioula."
[96] In *Alassane Ouattara, the Father of the Rebellion,* a film by Thierry Legré.

214

In October 16, 2010, *"from the outset of the war,"* recounts *Notre Voie*, a daily newspaper close to Gbagbo:

"...[T]he members of the Ivorian rebellion travelled all over, in all the towns and villages in the north of Ivory Coast, to explain the validity of their bloody actions and to make themselves understood among their own people.

One of the main "singers" in the armed violence, Koné Zakaria, assembled the "chiefs of the land" in Séguéla[97] to tell them who was behind their movement, who financed it and why all of them, inhabitants of the north, should support that person.

Here are some revealing excerpts:

"All those who will betray the politics of Alassane Ouattara will have a tragic end, and IB is well aware of it. We had asked Kass to reconsider his stance...If you support the MPCI, do not do it for Zakaria or for IB or for someone else. Do it for the one who bought our weapons and ammunition, that is to say, Alassane Dramane Ouattara. [...] Sixty of us were obliged to go into exile [...] At the time, IB was our leader. We agreed that he would not be a candidate for the presidential election. Even if Laurent Gbagbo was killed, the person we would need would be someone who could look after our relatives in the north. We had planned to put in place a security council presided over by IB with the participation of France.

"Me, Koné Zakaria, I was in charge of recruiting gendarmes [state police] and military men for the cause of the rebellion [...]. We took weapons, but it was not IB who bought them. Everyone needs to know the truth today. When we were in exile, I was the one overseeing the whole group and I was ready to die for my brothers. I was the one who infiltrated the combatants and brought weapons into the country, from Korhogo to Abidjan.

If you support the MPCI, don't do it for Zakaria or for IB, or for someone else, except for the one who bought our weapons, i.e., Alassane Dramane Ouattara. When we were in exile, it's Alasane Ouattara who took care of us. Each month, he regularly provided us with rice and 25 million CFA francs. Soro, IB, Adams, and I, the four of us were housed at the same place. God was our strength. We were

---

[97] A town located in Northwest of Ivory Coast.

215

angry at the RDR because IB had for a long time hidden from us the fact that all the money he had in his possession was from Alassane Ouattara.

IB and I went to Paris where we were received by the rich guy, Zanga Ouattara and by Zoro Bi Ballo. We were each given one million CFA francs. Zanga promised to regularly send us money. But we don't know where this money has gone. Only IB knows. Zanga can testify to this because he's not dead. We swore on the Koran, and no one had the right to betray that oath, whether civilians or military men or even Dozos. I was the one who recruited them. So I know what I am talking about. I ask you to support us because it is for Alassane that we took up our weapons, not for IB or Soro."

When will the sly detectives of the International Criminal Court finally discover those responsible for the new massacres in Duékoué in 2011? On March 28, 29 and 30, 2011, while the two presidents were staring each other down in Abidjan in a face-off that became more and more dramatic, the forces of Alassane Ouattara launched a huge offensive towards the south heading towards Abidjan, in perfect synchronization with the French Licorne force who began bombing the capital city, starting with the barracks where the *gendarmes* [state police] families were lodged, the RTI TV network, and Laurent Gbagbo's residence.

The rebels entered Duékoué, a city wedged between the north and south. After the first battle, there was a huge civilian massacre. The traditional hunters, the Dozos, and militias of all nationalities invaded the city and the surrounding villages. They sorted through the population and gunned down those belonging to the Guéré ethnic group. One or two thousand men, women and children were raped, beaten. Their throats were cut; some were burned alive.

Was the propaganda-making machine out of order? This time, we expected to hear about the massacre in the French and international media. As Laurent Gbagbo said to me, weren't these the real "death squads"? Less than a year and a half after the Duékoué slaughter, while Ouattara's new regime had been legally in place for more than a year, 2,500 survivors of the Duékoué massacre who took refuge in the Nahibly camp and were supposedly protected by UN troops, whose base was located 500 meters from their camp, were again attacked and massacred by the thousands.

In ten years' time in Ivory Coast, these massacres are the killings that qualify as "genocide." They were committed under the direction of Guillaume Soro and Alassane Ouattara. Both of them misled the West by denouncing the danger of an imaginary genocide in order to better hide the genocide their own troops carried out. Not satisfied with "covering up" the assassins, they then pretended that, due to their action, the worse was avoided! It is a technique of systematic perversion of information, mastered to perfection since the outset of the crisis, as the French political science scholar, Michel Galy, has explained.

In April, 2013, Salvatore Sagues, a researcher for Amnesty International for West Africa, came to the following conclusion:

> *"…[D]espite its promises of justice, the [current] Ivorian government has made hardly any headway in the investigation on the crimes committed during that attack."*

Who, then, will see that these investigations are carried out and get to the bottom of things? Various incidents opposed the ICC Prosecutor and the lawyers of Gbagbo, who were accused of politicizing the issue when they described the nature and acts of the rebellion and tried to show how they were linked to Alassane Ouattara. However, the prime responsibility for the infringements on human rights must, first and foremost, be charged to those who began the crisis, even if this might involve amnesty for some involved in the criminal acts. But in the end, even the supposedly neutral NGOs obviously favor the victors, since they consider the crimes of the victor and those of the loser to be on the same level. It seems that it is only the victim who was aggressed who is taken to court and likely to be indicted. The victor is blamed, for appearance's sake, but accusations against him are quickly forgotten, and all this is carried out by entities without any coercive power but with a strong influence on media, international institutions and public opinion.

These NGOs are not all neutral. Yet they are able to orient the outside world's perception of these events to the advantage of powerful interest groups. Through the public communication they practice, by designating who is in the right and who is in the wrong, they have, at times, a hidden agenda, a secret strategy lurking behind their actions in the field. Thus the Human Rights Watch has as its main backer George Soros. *La Lettre du Continent* of November 25, 2010 reveals:

"Ado, who had been planning this for fifteen years, was able to count on his [Soros'] personal fortune accumulated over a period of two decades.

Beyond that, the American billionaire George Soros reportedly made available for Ouattara a "Grumman 4" renamed "RHDP Solutions." But Nerrati Press also comments:

"George Soros gave Ouattara a lot more than a private jet."

This journal gives its own analysis on Soros' objectives for Ivory Coast and suggests reading Léandra Berstein's article on "The Secret War Throughout the World of George Soros, the Misanthropist." The first paragraphs, quoted verbatim below, are indeed very enlightening:

"In The Deficiencies of Global Capitalism, in *On Globalization*, 2002, George Soros declares: *"Democracy and open society can only be imposed from the outside, because the principle of sovereignty stands in the way of external interference. [...] Admittedly it is difficult to interfere in the domestic affairs of sovereign countries, but it is important to acknowledge the issue."*

For a very long time, the action and money of George Soros have become instrumental in dismantling national sovereignty of several states by filling up the tills of organizations which are supposedly "philanthropist" or "advocates" of human-rights. We will briefly examine here one aspect of this operation.

At the time of the first action brought against him before a criminal court for manipulation of the stock market in 1979, George Soros launched the "Open Society Fund" intended to "open closed societies." Today, he is active in 29 countries. Stating that "states have interests but not principles," Soros explains that "an ideal open society would cancel the specific national interests because an international political and financial structure would take over the responsibility to defend the good of the people." This explains his unrestrictive admiration for the "United Nations (especially the Security Council), the "OMC" and the "World Bank" and his working together with these institutions. [...] To carry out his goals, Soros endows his philanthropic organizations with a financial cash-flow which then "buys" important sectors of the population which turn against and try to overthrow any government which strives to maintain a "closed society."

"If a nation wants to control its own natural resources, it is a closed society. If a nation wants to develop its economy and its workforce with the help of customs tariffs and regulations, it is a closed society. Any nation which rejects globalization, the imperialism of free-trade, is also condemned as a "closed society", and will be subject to attacks by Soros' organizations, including the secret ones."

"Among the British-style organizations under the supervision of Soros, there is the "Open Society Institute (OSI), "Human Rights Watch," the "Soros Foundation," and the "Initiative for Transparency among extractive industries."

"In 2002, Soros admitted having paid out more than 2.1 billion U.S. dollars in five years to these philanthropic enterprises. He wrote this about them: "When they can, they work with the government, and when they cannot, they work independently. Sometimes, they are completely opposed to the government. When these foundations can cooperate with the government, they are more efficient; when they cannot, their work is all the more necessary and appreciated since they offer an alternative source of financing for civilians. As a rule, the worse the government is, the better the foundation can work, because it has the commitment and the support of civilians not in power."

"George Soros has poured 100 billion U.S. dollars to "Human Rights Watch" over the past ten years to engage the services of this "NGO" whose investigations have had a crucial influence on the media whose task is to demonize President Gbagbo.

"The latest tactic of George Soros was the sordid attack against the producers of Ivorian cocoa by the lobbying group "Avaaz" closely linked to Soros, according to the Canadian Minister John Baird. George Soros has not just set his heart on Ivory Coast, but also on numerous other African countries that he destabilizes with a view to letting them fall into the hands of Anglo-saxon speculators."

George Soros dreamed the dream, but it is his Ivorian champion and friend from the IMF, Alassane Ouattara, who made it happen in Ivory Coast. Through guns and blood, the Ivorian market has henceforth rejoined the world market.

"The factual elements provided are verifiable but the analysis is up to each one. But everything indicates that the introduction of 'democracy

219

imposed from outside' as advocated by George Soros has succeeded in Ivory Coast."

The very day following the Ivorian presidential election, Human Rights Watch, mostly financed by Soros, denounced the purported crimes committed by the supporters of Gbagbo. During the whole post-electoral crisis, Human Rights Watch did not seem to clearly denounce any crimes committed by the supporters of Ouattara, to such an extent that it is mostly thanks to these accusations that the Prosecutor of the ICC built her indictments. Various exchanges took place in international conferences dealing with international justice, where the representatives of the Prosecutor spent time with representatives of these NGOs, notably those of Human Rights Watch. Moreover, in the ICC, there are several employees who used to be members of NGOs such as Human Rights Watch. And who "monitors" the trials brought before the ICC? The answer is: the institutions financed by Soros. And who organizes the conferences on international criminal justice? The answer again: the institutions financed by Soros.

Today, all the ignorance of the International Community is contained within these contradictions. This International Community is capable of politically covering for war criminals because they have, in fact, supported them, and because they are also held hostage by them, something Guillaume Soro has well understood. Thus, will history be written in the shadow of "international justice"?

> *"If one com'zone* (chief rebel in charge of a zone) *required to appear in front of the ICC was not handed over, it would raise a problem for the International Community."*

This was a declaration by Phillip Carter III, the U.S. Ambassador in Abidjan, during a limited press conference attended by only few, on February 6, 2012. Vincent Hugueux, from *L'Express*, who always had harsh words for the Gbagbo regime, told me himself: *"there should be representatives from the Ouattara camp at The Hague."*

And why not Ouattara in person, whose rebels were renamed by him as the Republican Forces of Ivory Coast, and who committed crimes and atrocities under this name during the battle of Abidjan?

Chapter 23
"They mocked our 'government of professors'"

    By trade, President Gbagbo is a history professor, and when he was elected, he surrounded himself with well-educated professors, engineers, and other professionals to help him govern. This is in direct contrast to the rebels, many of whom are part of the actual government today. Former French army spokesperson, Georges Peillon describes these men as "uncouth....covered in amulets," men who took pleasure in terrorizing and plundering the Ivoirian population. It is these men who have been rewarded with high posts and important assignments within the Ouattara administration.

    Peillon, the French solider turned author, tells a story very different from any official French version. He describes the mismatch between the vision of the French military on the ground in Ivory Coast and the French authorities calling the shots from Paris. As the events unfolded, Peillon is so disgusted that he decided to end his military career.

    Against the backdrop of the descriptions of the rebel chiefs and their rewards, Mattei asks:

- *Who paid for the rebels' heavy artillery which they had in hand in early 2011?*
- *Why wasn't the UN embargo against arms trade enforced?*
- *Who paid for the troops trained in Burkina Faso to be transferred down to the north of Ivory Coast, and who helped them deploy to the south for the assault on Abidjan, an assault that cost so many civilian lives?*

    Noting the complexity of such a military operation and despite his French nationality, journalist and author Mattei points the finger at France and closes with chilling warnings to that nation, whose own economy is struggling. Couldn't France benefit from mutually profitable projects in Africa? As Mattei sees it, France's "brutality" and "violence" in Ivory Coast may have done irreparable damage to the Ivorian "psyche" and created so much mistrust that Ivorians, along with many other Africans, might prefer to "go it alone."

For the very important hearing of February 2013, Jennifer Naouri, the youngest member of Emmanuel Altit's team, was in charge of highlighting the fact that, from the outset of the Ivorian crisis, there were obvious links between the current head of state, Alassane Ouattara, and the major chief rebels he nominated to positions of responsibility. How could he refuse anything to the armed people who opened the way to power for him?

On September 26, 2012, the Ivorian government appointed three former rebels from the *New Forces* (FN) as regional prefects[98]. Ousmane Coulibaly, alias "Ben Laden," was nominated for the regional prefect's position in San Pedro, Ivory Coast's second largest port and a major administrative town in the *Bas-Sassandra* region. Up till then he had been in charge of security in Yopougon, a western suburb of Abidjan, after he had reigned as a zone commander of Odienné, the town where Simone Gbagbo[99] was imprisoned from the time of Gbagbo's fall in April, 2011.

The second military man on our list, Tuo Fozié, was appointed regional prefect to Bondoukou, a major administrative town in the *Zanzan* region in north-east Ivory Coast. After the talks at Marcoussis, he served as Minister of Youth and Civic Services in the national union government. The third new prefect is Commander Koné Messamba, former director of the paramilitary forces of the FN. He took up his post in Guiglo, in the extreme west at the frontier with Liberia in the *Moyen-Cavally* region. These three nominations are all in high security regions.

How about the "son" of Ouattara, Guillaume Soro? He was the boss of the *Patriotic Movement of Ivory Coast* (better known under its French acronym of MPCI), a major Ivorian rebel movement which would later become the *New Forces*. According to President Gbagbo, **Soro was imposed by Blaise Compaoré [the former president of Burkina Faso] to head the rebellion.**

---

[98] Translator's note: In the French governmental framework, besides the centralized executive, there are also local executive entities that go by the name of "territorial collectivities." A regional "prefect" is a link in the administration chain. He is the custodian of the state authority over a geographical region, somewhat like a governor of a U.S. state although the U.S. "dual federalism," which looks at the federal system as a sort of "layer cake" is quite different from twin concepts of *déconcentration* and *decentralization,* two key principles of the French governmental framesork.

[99] Translator's note: After three years of imprisonment in this far north-western part of the country, Simone Gbagbo was brought to Abidjan for a trial before the Assize Court of Abidjan. This trial started February 24, 2015. The former First Lady and university researcher, now 65 years old, was condemned to 20 years in prison for, among other things, supposedly attempting to destabilize the Ivorian state.

Jennifer Naouri reminds us:

Soro had *"under his command the Republican Forces of Ivory Coast (FRCI), who perpetrated numerous massacres, for instance in Duékoué [in the extreme west of the country] where, on March 29 and 30, 2011, at least 800 persons were killed. He is currently, the president[100] of the Ivorian National Assembly, a post which ensures him parliamentarian immunity."*

As the lawyer Emmanuel Altit emphasizes, Ibrahim Coulibaly, alias "IB," was the body guard of Alassane Ouattara and one of the principal actors on the ground of the ex-rebellion [now in power in Abidjan]. Gbagbo's defense team notes that IB was the chief of the "Invisible Commando," the main armed rebel group in Abobo, a northern suburb of Abidjan, which targeted civil populations and the orces of law and order from February, 2010 until March, 2011. IB was eliminated by his own friends.

As for Soumaila Bakayoko, he became the Chief of Staff of the Republican Forces of Ivory Coast (FRCI), created by Alassane Ouattara during the post-electoral crisis. Gbagbo's defense team points out that prior to this Soumaila Bakayoko was the Chief of Staff of the rebellion and therefore one of those who profited most from extorting and exploiting the Ivorian population.

Ousmane Coulibaly, nicknamed "Ben Laden," was the commander of the *Movement for Justice and Peace* (MJP*)*, another rebel movement based in Man in the western part of the country. During the battle of Abidjan, this Ivorian "Ben Laden" was the most active rebel chief in Yopougon [western neighborhood in Abidjan], where a huge massacre of civilians took place. Ousmane Coulibaly's links with the former president of Liberia, Charles Taylor, are well known. In 2012, Ousmane Coulibaly was appointed as prefect of the administrative region of San-Pedro, the first port in the world for cocoa.

Cherif Ousmane, surnamed "Daddy Cheetah," or "the Cleanser," is accused of *"serious blood crimes"* in the western part of Ivory Coast. As for [Issiaka Ouattara] nicknamed "Wattao," he became famous when he was accused of being one of the most important diamonds traffickers in the region. Through his father, Wattao currently reigns over the region of Doropo where he drives around in his Maserati, flaunting a watch worth $40,000, all the while

---

[100] The position is the equivalent to the U.S. Speaker of the House in the American Congress.

continuing to extort money and possessions with total impunity. He lives in a sumptuous villa, with a garage full of Ferraris *"bought in the U.S. and resold in Ivory Coast,"* a point he made to Christophe Hondelatte and Jacques Langlade, authors of a broadcast on the 13th Street TV channel. He is also deputy chief at the *Center for the Coordination of Operational Decisions* (CCDO), a new police unit in charge of security in Abidjan. As for Gbagbo, he has always lived a little differently:

I never had a weapon in my hands except when I was doing my military service. As for gold, I don't have any. I don't wear and I have never worn jewelry: necklaces, rings, or even a watch!

The famous golden pistol about which there was such a fuss in the press was actually stolen from the house of Lida Kouassi, Gbagbo's former Defense Minister. Lida Kouassi had received this pistol as a gift from his counterpart in an Arab country who visited him in Abidjan.

Wattao is an upstart on the rise. He is violent, boastful and self-confident. A mafioso-type who introduces himself as a *"close collaborator"* of President Ouattara *"of whom I am one of the sons,"* he said to journalist Hondelatte. *"For the time being, the warrior and the president remain faithful to each other,"* the journalist added. The former Ambassador of France to Abidjan, Jean-Marc Simon, told me in Paris that *"Wattao is very much at home in the presidential mansion."* According to Théophile Kouamouo, who made an online comment about this report, the fortune of Wattao probably started with the robbery of a branch of the BCEAO bank in Bouaké on September 24, 2003. During three full days, the rebels, in a very organized manner, emptied the tills of the bank, taking with them--we don't exactly know how--several billion CFA francs. According to the November 21, 2003 issue of *Jeune Afrique*, some witnesses saw Wattao on site. A month later, still in the stronghold territory occupied by the men of Soro and Wattao, on October 28, the branches of the same bank were held-up in Man and Korhogo at 24-hour intervals. According to the local press, one of the attacks succeeded, while the other failed.

Georges Peillon, the former media officer of the military Licorne force in Ivory Coast during 2003-2004, author of *Nude Ivory*[101], under the pen name Georges Neyrac, remembers this episode and the fights among the rebels, with heavy machine guns, along with some of the local population who were trying to get their share of the loot. By the time French troops intervened, there were 30 dead and 30 injured. In the field, Peillon was able to assess in detail the

---

[101] *Ivoire Nue* (Nude Ivory), op.cit., see footnote 92 above.

Ivorian situation and the role of French authorities. What he learned led him to leave the military. His experience during the Ivorian conflict provides precious information. He remembers the ambiguity of French policy in Ivory Coast and the malaise of the French military chiefs there. He was told that the release of his book greatly angered Dominique de Villepin, who exclaimed *"Who is this idiot who mixes himself up in our politics?"* Here is Peillon's testimony:

> *"Michèle Alliot-Marie, who was the Minister of Defense, came to see us on December 31, 2003. General Joana, who then was the commander of the Licorne operation, was waiting for the go-ahead to put into effect the defense agreement with Ivory Coast signed in 1961. We knew that there were barbaric acts perpetrated in the north. We also knew that we needed to unify the country which was completely split in two. Everything was ready with a swift offensive planned on three fronts, and we had all the means we needed to deploy. With the professionalism of our units, recapturing the north would have been a very simple thing to do. Within thirty-six hours and without causing too much damage, it would have been all over. But the decision to support Gbagbo's legitimate government, to re-establish peace and stabilize the country was never made.*
>
> *"France approved this partition of the country and General Joana, who was our commander, understood that we did not have the same conception of our mission as the political powers in Paris.*
>
> *"I had spent time with the "Forces Nouvelles" during the negotiations on disarmament and during the talks concerning opening the territory up for free circulation. Except for one or two, these men were uncouth, their arms covered in [fetish] amulets. These were not soldiers. They were heads of bands of thugs. I said one day "gang chiefs," and I stand by that statement. They fear neither God nor man. They maintain their power through violence and terror which they imposed in the north of the country. The daily life of the populations was sheer hell. When I learned that Abidjan had fallen into the hands of these guys, I told myself the bandits have taken over... I still wonder: What kind of deal was made between President Ouattara and these gang chiefs?[102]*

---

[102] ibdem.

Gbagbo says with a sigh:

When I think that they used to make fun of our "government of professors," where people of high ranking worked together: Pascal Affi N'Guessan, Engineer in Telecommunication, Mamadou Koulibly, Professor of Economics[103], Emile Boga Doudou, Associate Professor of Law, Oulai Hubert, a licensed lawyer[104], Bohoun Bouabré, Doctor in Economy, Aké N'Gbo, Professor in Economy[105], Ahoua Don Mello, Civil Engineer, and so many other university graduates...

As hallmark of the rebellion, it is rather the number of killings which are recorded as their highest achievements. There you will find Tuo Fozié or Ousmane Coulibaly appointed as prefects. Also, you will find the former corporal and kitchen assistant, Koné Messamba, promoted as prefect of the administrative region of *Bas-Cavally*.[106] They constitute the first choice of Alassane Ouattara's victorious regime. They have invited themselves to the royal banquet of the one they made king, and the king is unable to refuse them anything.

At The Hague, the names of the Ivorian warlords, now executives of the current Ivorian regime are mentioned only by Laurent Gbagbo's defense team, never by the Prosecutor's team. The Prosecutor acts as if all these individuals suspected of killings never existed, their names have been erased so as to allow Alassane Ouattara to appear as the champion of democracy. But Losséni Fofana, alias "The Bold Loss," reigns in the west, along with Martin Fofié Kouakou, commander of the *Compagnie Territorial* of Korhogo (CTK), Koné Zakaria, and many others...Their names are quoted and their "achievements" recalled by Gbagbo's lawyers.

The defense team of Laurent Gbagbo calls out the names of each of the warlords and repeats the accusations lodged against them by organizations for the defense of human rights. Who benefitted from their atrocities, their extortions, their crimes? Emmanuel Altit's assistant, Jennifer Naouri pounds away:

---

[103] Translator's note: In the original text, these men are said to be *agrégé*. The *agrégation* is a French competitive examination which allows the selection of the best candidates for teaching positions in secondary schools and institutions of higher learning including the best universities within the French educational system. Within that system, the *agrégation* constitutes the most prestigious achievement possible.

[104] ibdem, previous footnote.

[105] ibdem, previous footnote.

[106] Low-Cavalla River

"The rebels were perpetrating all these barbaric acts on behalf of one man: Alassane Ouattara."

This defense team member reminds the audience that in the video Koné Zakaria explains that the chief rebels acted on behalf of Alassane Ouattara, who transferred funds to them to that effect. She emphasizes the contribution of the chief rebels to the success of Ouattara. What is the proof of the complicity between these thugs and the former deputy director of the IMF? The proof is that, as soon as he took office as president, Alassane Ouattara rewarded these people with posts [in the government] and their respective salaries. Nevertheless, these people are not immune to facing criminal charges for crimes of war and crimes against humanity...unless they have nothing to fear [because they are still covered by someone higher up].

To dissipate suspicion, Fatou Bensouda lets it be understood that charges *might* be lodged against some of them. Thus, in *L'Express* of July 17, 2013, in answer to Vincent Hugeux's question asking why only Gbagbo's camp is charged, Fatou Bensouda weighs her words:

"The case against Gbagbo is the first for Ivory Coast; it will not be the last."

As Jennifer Naouri explains, the warlords in the north of the country were protected by the French authorities. In addition, the mercenaries recruited in 2010, trained in Burkina Faso by foreign military advisers, made up a large part of the rebel army that was to capture the south. But we must ask: who paid for the weapons and the heavy artillery in their hands in March, 2011, in total violation of the embargo issued by the United Nations? Who paid them? Who paid for their transfer from Burkina to northern Ivory Coast during the entire year of 2010? Who organized them logistically in view of a huge sweep through southern Ivory Coast in March, 2011? Who opened the way for them to move forward? The traces of French intervention are multiple. And this is what Emmanuel Altit's team has started to bring forward. They are ready to give all they have, to dig as deep as they can, providing proof, if they are given the chance during the trial.

It becomes clear that such an operation aimed at seizing power by force, whatever the outcome of the presidential election, had to have been prepared and organized a long time in advance. It is the realization of a definite plan of action designed to overthrow President Gbagbo. In a context so complex, where

227

numerous representatives of French authorities are involved, in the political, diplomatic, and military sectors as well as other government officials, the decisions could only have been taken at the highest possible level of the French state. One of the lines of the offensive consisted in preventing Ivorian authorities from having access to their own funds in various banks and more specifically, the *BCEAO*. A troubling question then arises as to how the president of the French Republic and some French advisers and a few military chiefs could destabilize an entire foreign country, could build up from next to nothing, a rebel army, could launch military attacks against that country's regular armed forces, and could overthrow a legitimately elected president, all without anyone batting an eye? All these preparations were carried out openly, even if some French leaders of the time and the current ICC Prosecutor try to camouflage this in what can only be described as awkward manoeuvers. Isn't it shocking to see that the French parliament wasn't even consulted and that the French military hierarchy was by-passed? The case of Ivory Coast points out the defects and malfunctioning of the French political system which allows special interest groups to pull it "off track."

What's worse, this operation was conducted against all common sense. Its brutality may alienate forever some of France's "francophone family." The violence of the military intervention and the obvious contempt concerning a government and foreign institutions may have inflicted irreparable damage on the African psyche and thus on the Franco-African relationship. In a 2013 report written by former Minister Hubert Vendrine and the franco-beninois financial expert Lionel Zinsou [Prime Minister of Benin since January 19, 2015], at the request of Pierre Moscovici, then Minister of Economy and Finances, Africa is seen clearly as key to the future of France. In the global context of fierce competition and economic wars, France, overburdened with debt and unemployment, needs to work with Africa. But as Ahoua Don Bello, the former spokesperson of the Gbagbo government, now in exile, comments:

> *"If Africa is the future of France, many Africans today consider that France is Africa's past."*

Chapter 24
"I accepted every possible compromise"

This quote underlines how willing Laurent Gbagbo has been to accept "all possible compromises" and all possible negotiations. He was willing to do so because he feared not doing so would lead to deep-seated tensions and hatred among the Ivoirian people. Criticized by his opponents and oftentimes even by his own supporters, he sees compromise as a way of moving toward peace.

This chapter will be for many the saddest part of the book as President Gbagbo recounts in great detail his ousting from power in April 11, 2011. It begins with a description of the difficulties surrounding his swearing in on December 4, 2010. Gbagbo tells how, as he is preparing to make his way to the ceremony, he receives an enraged phone call from French president Sarkozy. "It was at this precise moment," Gbagbo recalls, "...that I got the feeling that everything might spin out of control."

In a section that might be entitled "Twelve days in hell: March 31-April 11," Gbagbo describes his and his family's "lock-down" in his own home, snipers positioned and firing into the interior on the innocent civilians who had taken refuge there. He tells how he tries to remain calm when the first bomb explodes right over his head. He forgets no detail: one of his best friend's mother...90 years old...sitting in the dark basement as the bombs fall, the smoke making breathing difficult, the killings before his eyes, his cherished library collected over a lifetime reduced to ashes...

In a flashback we learn how France tried to strangle the Gbagbo administration by cutting off its financial circuits--all to no avail. We hear how they airlifted heavy artillery and armored tanks into the country and how Gbagbo is warned by cell phone that armored tanks are making their way to his front gate.

Finally we hear how the rebels captured Gbagbo and his family among the ruins of their home and moved them to the Golf Hotel, from where Gbagbo was taken by helicopter to Korogho in the north. His former Prime Minister [Guillaume Soro], in on the coup, tells him, "[you will be going to] a house that belongs to me. It will be ok"....ok for eight months of detention...

In this chapter, one French-French exchange stands out: when Mattei asks another French journalist how it is possible to justify this invasion of a sovereign state and the throwing aside of the Ivorian Constitutional Council's ruling, Jean-Christophe Notin responds: "For Paris, it was [only] a puppet Constitutional Council." Mattei does not miss a beat and asks: "By puppet, do you mean nigger?"

The sadness of this chapter makes one ask: did all this really happen? And if it happened, how is it possible the world knows nothing about it?

[In this complicated game, there are lots of 'cross-overs' and lots of speculation]. Jacques Chirac's former adviser, Jean-François Probst, has been an overtly staunch supporter of Laurent Gbagbo for a long time. On the other hand, some strange usurpers, lawyers who are unfamiliar with the Gbagbo dossier, have spoken up in the media claiming to speak in the name of President Gbagbo... when it isn't some of Gbagbo's own too well-intentioned friends spouting off...They are among those who, during the post-electoral crisis, could not even envision the French army's April, 2011 attack. For instance, Jacques Vergès was convinced that *"Ivory Coast would be the tomb of the French Army."* Other advisors basked in boastful optimism, never believing France could ever take such a belligerent initiative ...

Having learned from past experience, and not being able to intervene himself to correct his visitors' misuse of language once they exit his prison doors, Laurent Gbagbo has had to let party members and close friends try to 'cover the bases' ...

In The Hague, his visitors, including Nady Bamba, his third wife, can see that President Gbagbo is still clear-minded and courageous despite what he endured during his detention in Korhogo. Guy Labertit notes:

"The first time I saw him on January 19, 2012, I found a man who was still marked by the eight months he had spent in Korhogo in disastrous conditions. He told me himself that he had not been allowed out of his cell except for the visit of Desmond Tutu, Mary Robinson, and Kofi

Annan. Kofi Annan actually dared to tell reporters that Gbagbo was being well treated, a very scandalous remark given the conditions he actually lived in. President Gbagbo had also been pushed around quite a bit when he was arrested and later, as well, at the Golf Hotel, contrary to what has been claimed. He still bears the marks of his mistreatment, for example, he still couldn't close the fingers of his right hand."

From the presidential mansion, where I had first met him in 2005 during the long interview sessions partly published in *France-Soir,* to his besieged residence in Cocody, to the house in Korhogo where he was detained, and finally to the prison of Scheveningen, the successive shocks have been brutal. The memories come back, one after the other, with accuracy. President Gbagbo remembers all the steps leading up to his arrival at The Hague. Laurent Gbagbo spoke calmly without bitterness, as an old man accustomed to adversity and hard times. He had already been jailed from March, 1971 to January, 1973, when he was in the opposition against Houphouët-Boigny. In 1992, Alassane Ouattara, the then-Prime Minister, had Gbagbo arrested, after he had run for the 1990 presidential election against Houphouët-Boigny, in the first multiparty elections since independence, after he became head of the opposition, and then a member of the Ivorian parliament under the label FPI. Gbagbo was sentenced to two years' imprisonment, but was released six months[107] later in the month of August, 1992.

From his prison in The Hague, Gbagbo recalls:

I took the oath of the office on Saturday, December 4, 2010 at the Ivorian mansion after the Constitutional Council had given its ruling on the official complaints we had lodged concerning the massive electoral

---

[107] Translator's note: On February 18, 1992, Laurent Gbagbo spearheaded a peaceful march to demand that violators of students' human rights--nightly attacked and raped on their campus--be punished according to Ivorian laws as the result of the findings of a National investigating committee set up by Houphouët himself. Laurent Gbagbo and the peaceful demonstrators were sentenced to two years' imprisonment. Their release after only six months may have been triggered by a letter co-sponsored by Senators Edward Kennedy and Jessy Helms, issued on April 29, 1992, and signed by six U.S. senators and seven U.S. representatives. The letter was sent to President Houphouët-Boigny urging him to swiftly release the demonstrators and their leaders, including Laurent Gbagbo as well as Human Rights'advocate, René Degny Segui, chairman of LIDHO," the Ivorian League for Human Rights.

fraud in the north of the country and the inability of the Independent Electoral Commission to pronounce the winner by the required deadline. The day before, on Friday, December 3, I realized that things could go very wrong. The Constitutional Council had just announced the results, proclaiming me the winner of the election. The same day I received a phone call from Sarko[zy]. He was furious, saying: *"The Constitutional Council shouldn't have done that. No! no! they shouldn't have done it."* He behaved like a crazy man, not like a head of state. How can it be possible that today, in the 21st century, one head of state calls another one to say such a thing? It was at this precise moment, after I hung up the phone, that I got the feeling that everything might spin out of control. I knew they could care less about what institutions in African countries say. For them, it's just a matter of putting their man on the throne... But to trample on the Constitutional Council of a sovereign country whose constitution was modeled on the constitution of France, with such nerve, like that, on the phone, it was like some kind of bad joke. I couldn't believe that I had just spoken on the phone to a head of state...

When I asked Jean-Christophe Notin (close to the official French milieu at that time, even if he didn't have an in-depth knowledge of Africa) why they didn't respect the decision of the Ivorian Constitutional Council, he replied:

"For Paris, it was a puppet Constitutional Council."

Explaining to him that the Ivorian Constitutional Council functioned exactly like the French Constitutional Council, I slipped in the following question:

"By 'puppet,' do you mean 'nigger'?"

All of sudden, it turned to an embarrassed silence. Jean-Christophe Notin, unofficial historiographer of the French Republic, did not continue the discussion. I think, at that moment, he might have had a tiny glimpse into another way of looking at things, different from the viewpoint he had in his role as Licorne's faithful writer-soldier. Gbagbo continues:

On Saturday, a little before my departure for the presidential mansion where the swearing-in ceremony was to take place, in the presence of members of the Constitutional Council, my chief of protocol came to tell me that a message had come in indicating that Nicolas Sarkozy demanded that the ceremony be physically blocked. I decided to go there anyway. I told myself: this guy is acting like a delinquent off the streets. I didn't let it affect me. I thought it was just a bluff or a warning...

On December 6, we formed the new cabinet made up of technocrats, and we started to work. France had cut off our funds at *BCEAO*, hoping that we would not be able to pay the salaries of our civil servants and that we wouldn't be able to honor the Ivorian state's expenditures, which would have turned Ivorians against us.

In a speech delivered in Brussels, Sarkozy all but ordered me to leave. The tone was something like "just get out, you stupid jerk." It wasn't the controlled language of a head of state.

But at the end of the month, despite all this, on December 22, we were able to pay all the salaries. Same thing for January; they understood they couldn't get to us that easily...

And today they blame me...because I just kept doing my work and paying our government employees. Same motive, same punishment, for the measures I took trying to maintain order in the country. I made use of a decree that had been on the books since 1961, which opens up the possibility--not an obligation--of maintaining the Ivorian forces of law and order "on alert," if certain incidents seemed in the offing. In short, I was doing my job to ensure the security of the state and that of the Ivorian population. I was governing. Is that what they want to turn into a crime?

The rebels had introduced armed groups into the heart of Abidjan. It was a fully-fledged army. They were planning to link up with hundreds of rebels, mainly mercenaries from Burkina Faso who were stationed at the Golf Hotel. This hotel is a large complex located on the Lagoon, where the Ouattaras [Ouattara and the rebel leaders] had been living since the month of September.

In the beginning of December, 2010, the attacks against the population and the regular armed forces started in Abidjan. Alassane Ouattara and his aids' strategy of taking power through violent means became clear, coming to a head in a general and concerted attack launched throughout the entire city of Abidjan on December 16, 2010.

The politicians of my party, of my administration, even my son and many others were taken to court and imprisoned, accused of

"undermining the national defense, plotting against the authority of the state, constitutingarmed bands, leading or participating in an armed band, participating in an insurrectionary movement, disturbing the public order, organizing a coalition of civil servants, setting up a

rebellion,   usurping   posts,   and   encouraging   tribalism   and xenophobia." Gbagbo keeps commenting:

Only that? What else more could they add?… All this would just seem absurd, if it hadn't led to so much suffering, to the deprivation of liberty, to so much injustice. They hunted us down like we were animals, and they made us look like criminals. It was the world turned upside down.

The death of Basile Mahan Gahé, a pacifist and union leader, who recently died at sixty years of age due to his ill-treatment in the prisons of Ouattara's regime, affected Laurent Gbagbo deeply, like the other brutal deaths which occurred throughout, and resulted from, the ten years of crisis. Gbagbo continues:

There have been deaths, so many deaths. There have been so many deaths. Isn't it disgraceful to try to make me responsible for those deaths, when all I have been doing is working for reconciliation? I was really afraid that the country would remain split in two. I was so worried that the situation might lead to permanent deep tensions among Ivorians. So I made every effort possible to come to a pacific solution. I accepted all the compromises [I was presented with]. I have often said it: I never possessed an arm. I don't like arms, I don't like war. I have never carried out a coup d'état.

What I have done is write books, *For a Democratic Alternative* or *Acting for Liberties*,[108] and some others. I suggested to the International Criminal Court judges that these books be made available to them because these books can help people know who I am, know what my life is about.

---

[108] Translator's note: Laurent Gbagbo refers here to two of his books: *Côte d'Ivoire, Pour une alternative démocratique* (Ivory Coast, for a Democratic Alternative), published in 1983 and *Côte d'Ivoire, Agir pour les libertés* (Ivory Coast, Acting for Liberties) published in 1991. On the back cover of his 1983 book, Gbagbo notes "Ivory Coast is an under-developed country. So we need to fight against under-development which isn't the result of some spell or quirk. History teaches us that no enslaved people can effectively face human challenges without first breaking their chains. We know that democracy is not a panacea which will magically solve all our problems. But it is a prerequisite." On the back of his 1991 book, Laurent Gbagbo made a statement surprisingly relevant to the failed coup of September 19, 2002: "We want to build a stable state because where there is stability, a state is capable of understanding and following the rules that have been defined in advance--capable of regenerating its institutions without running the risk of destroying them. There is stability when people can lose power without being killed and when others can gain power without killing."

I have always heard contradictory statements about what people think of me. Some of my friends have criticized me for not being hard enough and for trying to negotiate with my adversaries. But for me, politics means talking to everybody! As for my adversaries, they think I'm a dictator. But all my life I have fought for democracy. I spent months in prison and years in exile because of my fight for democracy. I fought the one-party system of government because I thought that the future of Africa could only evolve within a democratic framework. When I was in exile in France, Houphouët-Boigny tried to get me on his side, but I refused all his proposals. I always believed in elections as a way of sorting out issues. I have always believed that it is the people who should decide. And in the end, that's why I am criticized: for being the spokesperson of the people, for wanting to give a voice to the people of Ivory Coast.

How many African leaders represent their people? You can count them on the fingers of one hand. Who allowed people of different political persuasions to express themselves [in Ivory Coast]? Who allowed the rebel groups to have an identity in the Ivorian political landscape? Who integrated the rebels into the government and the army? Who organized the presidential election? Who allowed Ouattara and Bédié to compete for the presidential race even though they didn't meet the criteria in the Constitution? Who made it possible for all the candidates to have the same media time for their campaigns and the same financial means? It seems to me that I have always acted as a true political leader, eager for the well-being of his fellow citizens, eager for the democratic debate to become a reality in Ivory Coast, and eager to listen to others.

I am far, far away from those technocrats without a soul or moral stature, who make up the political personnel of your French Vth Republic. To come back to the maneuvers made to economically stifle my administration in 2011, I decided to break with the *BCEAO* headquarters in Dakar. The boa constrictor technique used to stifle us was undertaken by the boss of the French Treasury in Paris (Rémy Rioux, Deputy Director for International Affairs and the French representative at the *BCEAO*).

Paradox of history: this same Rémy Rioux, certainly commanded from on high to do so, who became one of Gbagbo's tormentors, was the very person who had delivered a glowing report to the French Treasury on the economic management in Ivory Coast. Despite the war which persisted due to rebel activity, Mr. Rioux considered that the country of Ivory Coast…

"...was in a favorable cycle, after Gbagbo was able to have the country integrate the HIPC and in a matter of weeks would have been on the verge of completing the necessary steps allowing for the cancellation of its debt."

Unlike other economic heads, Philippe Henri Dakoury-Tabley, the boss at *BCEAO*, did not give into pressure from Christine Lagarde and was imprisoned. France then enlisted the help of the European Community. They imposed an embargo on everything, including medicines, an embargo which seriously caused the Ivorian population to suffer. They exerted tremendous pressure on economic operators and cocoa exporters with a view to blocking Ivorian ports. Around February 19 and 20, all branches of all the French commercial banks in Ivory Coast were shut down: *BICICI* (BNP Paribas), *SGCI* (The *Société Générale*)... Because of this block, the clients of these private banks were unable to receive their automatically transferred salaries. We responded very quickly by requisitioning all smaller Ivorian banks to automatically deposit the salaries of our civil servants. The boa constrictor was left to bite its own tail...

From that point onward, they became very nasty. I was informed that between late February and mid-March 2011, airplanes were delivering arms to Bouaké to attack us, and this despite the arms embargo issued by the United Nations. The mercenaries who constituted the bulk of the rebel troops had been recruited months beforehand from neighboring countries. ECOWAS announced their army would attack us.

Then the rebels started moving--with the assistance of the French-- on every front. They headed due south towards Abidjan with the help of mercenaries--the Burkinabè and the Malians, the other mercenaries from Niger...The ONUCI and French troops scouted ahead of them and participated in the various battles.

The bombing of the presidential residence, which many confuse with the presidential mansion, started on March 31 [2011]. I could no longer go outside my house. I lived in the armored tunnel built by Houphouët, which was supposed to allow him to reach the residence of the Ambassador of France in case of a coup d'état. What a symbol!

I had the tunnel blocked off. At the moment of the French military intervention, I had people check it. I didn't want to risk an attack on that side. And there was no attack from that side, contrary to what has been written. The truth of the matter is that there were French soldiers stationed at the residence of the Ambassador of France, only a few meters from us. They began shooting at people inside the presidential residence. They just fired shots--it didn't matter who they were shooting at. The people inside were easy targets. Scores of civilians were killed or injured by these snipers. Snipers had also been positioned on the roof of the residence of the president of the National Assembly, Mamadou Koulibaly, who luckily was not inside his home.

We had food supplies, enough to last a long time.

On the night of Saturday, April 9, 2011, Désiré Tagro, General Secretary to the Ivorian president, came to tell me that Gérard Longuet, Sarkozy's Minister of Defence had tried to call me. In fact, the phone call came from Charles Millon, who had asked for my contact number on behalf of Longuet. I went upstairs to my room where I was able to take a shower, shave, and change my clothes. Meanwhile, I told Tagro to call Millon back.

My aide-de-camp informed me that my first Prime Minister and the boss of Petroci (the national oil company of Ivory Coast) wanted to talk to me. I had my Prime Minister on line, and then I spoke to the Ghanaian president, John Atta-Mills. He was a good pal. He reassured me. It was while I was talking on the phone with the Petroci director that a bomb struck the building and exploded exactly above my head. Certainly they were able to locate where I was by tracking my telephone communications. In any case, I never had Longuet on the phone. The strikes were meant to kill me. Undoubtedly, I [my death] would have been presented as collateral damage, not as the victim of a direct hit.

The government forces were fighting. They retook the positions the rebels had gained. Yes, the Ivorian army had the upper hand, but every time they moved forward, every time they made any advance, the French Air Force bombed them. At that time, my former Minister for Foreign Affairs had taken refuge at the Embassy of France. They thought I had sent him to negotiate...

There was not one heavy weapon at my residence in Cocody. Nevertheless, that was the official reason given for bombing the residence, where around a hundred civilians had fled to take refuge. Oh, the poor people! ...my ministers and my friends who thought they would be safer at my house rather than in theirs. And then, there was my family, and old people, and children, and babies and kids in their teens. Among them was the sister of Basile Boli, the Ivorian soccer star. She had headed up a charity for the children of policemen. There were lots and lots of people, as well, outside the residence, and many of them were killed.

During the night of April 2 & 3, 2011, huge French cargo planes landed in Abidjan, carrying tanks and they disembarked soldiers of the Foreign Legion, along with combat material, including armored tanks. The French soldiers went to stay at the French base close to the airport. People called us from their mobile phones to inform us of the movement of the French armored tanks. The number of French combat helicopters also increased.

On the basis of all these different pieces of information, and without trying to politicize the debate and without trying to get people to feel sorry for me, on Tuesday, April 5, by telephone, I was able to provide this information to the French news channel LCI[109]. I told them that France had entered into a war against us in Abidjan. Of course, France was at war with us before, but in an indirect way, transporting rebel troops from one point to another throughout the city, arming them, giving them their weapons and ammunition. I told Vincent Hervouet, the French journalist who interviewed me that my objective was to stay alive. I only wanted the truth of the ballot box to be known. I had called for negotiations. I never called for war:

> *With your back against the wall, are you going to fight?* the journalist asked, again presenting me as *"the one who was clinging to power."*

I responded that I was not fighting, that I was only defending myself, that I had never been, in my entire life, a warmonger, whether in a civil war or in a coup d'état. I told him, for that, you need to look to the other side. I told him how hard it was for me to understand the French authorities' behavior. Why did they have the French army intervene so violently against the Ivorian government forces, while all that was at stake was an electoral dispute, which could have been resolved by a simple recount of the votes?

Why did they have to bomb the residence of a head of state? Why did they have to destroy the headquarters of the Ivorian National Radio-Television Network? I repeated myself, saying, 'All I wanted was the truth about the results of ballot box to be known.' Because that is the heart of the

---

[109] LCI is the acronym of a French channel of information which broadcasts on a 24-hour basis.

question: "who won these elections?" A military cease-fire was still possible. I wanted political dialogue. But it was I alone who wanted it. Those across from me wanted war. As I said, I have never even held a gun in my hand, except during my military service. Ever since the first attacks in 2000, we had never instigated violence.

Meanwhile on the 8th or the 9th, I received a message indicating that French soldiers had taken control of the airport. When they got there, they asked a woman who was working there:

"Are you pro-Gbagbo or pro-Ouattara?"

Luckily that woman was smart enough and informed enough to give them an intelligent answer.

By Sunday April 10, the military officers told me:

"Mr. President, we can't hold out any longer. Our equipment is destroyed, our men are dead." I told them: *"All of you, go find shelter for yourselves."*

Our military head in Plateau, as well as the one in charge at my residence, went to talk to the ONUCI to remind them of their mission which was to protect civilians and their goods. I knew by then it was over.

On the morning of April 11, 2010, a phone call came from Port-Bouët, where the airport and the French military base are located. They told us that around fifty French armored tanks had left that place and were headed in our direction. They arrived soon after and took position around my home. The French helicopters started firing into the residence, with incendiary ammunition. Walls started falling and my library was completely destroyed, my whole collection of classics was reduced to ashes. All of sudden, it became unbearable for the families and the civilians who were grouped together there. There was not a single soldier inside the house. We all went down to the basement which seemed more secure, even if the smoke which was everywhere made the air impossible to breathe.

In a press conference that took place at the Africa House in Paris, Jacqueline Chamois, the French teacher who was the first spouse of Laurent Gbagbo, and who was then fighting for the liberation of her son Michel, reported the testimony of her daughter-in-law who had lived through the siege of the Ivorian presidential residence. Viviane Gbagbo told her that holes had been drilled in the wall that blocked the tunnel linking the Ivorian residence and the French Ambassador's residence in order to infiltrate gas [perhaps tear gas?]. Viviane told her mother-in-law that both she and her husband Michel were beaten and ill-treated, before she was separated from him in the presence of French soldiers on April 11, 2010.

French soldiers arrived in front of the gate [of the residence], and then one of their tanks broke down the gate with repeated cannon fire. Then there was gunfire, machine gun blasts, and through the smoke, I heard:

"We want Gbagbo! We want Gbagbo!"

In the small dark room plunged into darkness, there was with us a ninety year old woman, the mother of my friend, Minister Sangaré, along with a four year old child, a seven year old, and a baby. The rebels came down the stairs, shooting as they came, screaming *"We want Gbagbo!"*

I stood up and said *"I'm Gbagbo."* They grabbed hold of me. I recognized Wattao. He said: *"Don't touch him."* There was also Ouattara Morou, Cherif Ousmane and many other rebel chiefs. Because my shirt was ripped, I asked to be given another one. Wattao's the one who brought it to me. While I was changing my shirt, they filmed me. As I have said, the French army was constantly filming. From beginning to end, the French soldiers filmed everything...

It was Ouattara Morou who got me into a bullet-proof jacket and put on a helmet on my head. At that moment, I knew anything could happen to me, and to any of my family...

Ouattara Morou pushed me into a vehicle which took off at breakneck speed and we drove until we got to the Golf Hotel. They put me in a waiting room where I saw other prisoners lying on the floor. Then they took me up to the fourth floor, it was room 468, I think.

The political heavyweights of the new regime came to see me: [Guillaume] Soro with a little cap on his head and Hamed Bakayoko. Why had they come? They wanted to savor their victory. They stayed for about fifteen minutes--no longer.

I saw Simone arrive and my son, covered in blood. I had seen my close friends beaten, and I saw Tagro assassinated....Then my Minister of Health and my friend Sangaré arrived... They put them in another room...

Alphonse Djédjé Mady, the General Secretary of the PDCI [the party of Konan Bédié] tried to comfort me. I saw Patrick Achi, my former Minister of Economic Infrastructure, who had passed over to the other side...

I slept. No medical exam, no questioning. The next day, on the 12, {Guillaume] Soro came back to see me. He told me I was going to be transferred to Korhogo that very day. I refused.

"If you don't accept, they will move you themselves, and it will be brutal."
"Korhogo, to do what?" I asked him.
"It will be in a house that belongs to me", he replied. *"You will be ok there"*.
"I have a house in Gagnoa", I replied, *"and there is also San Pedro…"*

He didn't want to hear anything about that. Cherif Ousmane arrived. He brutally grabbed me and took me off. They also took my physician Christophe Blé with me. On the road of the Golf Hotel, Christophe Blé nearly got his throat cut by a rebel. And now, here he was being taken off with me for eight months of detention. Christophe Blé is a good man, a competent doctor, a good person. He was nearly killed because he was my personal physician and detained without any arrest warrant. He and I were put into a helicopter that headed for Korhogo.

On the way, I thought of all those who had died and of all those who had suffered. I prayed for them and I wondered what would become of Ivory Coast.

Chapter 25
"They were killing me with a slow death"

Here President Gbagbo describes his feelings as he sits in a closed isolated house in the north of the country, detained for a full eight months, not allowed to go outside, and wondering as he ate the food being brought to him, if he would be poisoned. Along with his physician, Gbagbo is detained without a legal mandate.

With a rebel known for his war crimes as his prison guard, Gbagbo seems to have been forgotten by the International Community as well as by the Ivorian and French authorities.

"They were killing me with a slow death," Gbagbo comments.

Worse, the UN, whose mission it is to ensure proper treatment and rights of prisoners, was not doing its job. While it was their responsibility to oversee the prisoner, they stepped back and let the rebels do the work. When Gbagbo's lawyer Emmanuel Altit tried to see his client, the UN did nothing to help--the lawyer ended up having to find his own aircraft to fly to distant Korhogo--a plane that nearly crashed. When the Prosecutor of the International Criminal Court came to Abidjan during that time period, though informed of the violations of Gbagbo's rights, he made no effort to address the situation.

No one, within the country or without, seems to care that a former president of a sovereign state was deprived of his fundamental rights, in total disrespect of the Geneva Convention.

In Korhogo, which is an important city in the north of Ivory Coast, my physician and I were in a tiny house, a three room shack completely isolated from the rest of the world. I was not allowed to go outside. There was a small living room. Each one has his room. A woman that I did not know used to bring us our meals. They were prepared elsewhere. These meals were meant to weaken us. Had I thought of being poisoned? Yes, I sometimes thought about it. A soldier from ONUCI and a rebel used to watch us eating. Lunch was served around 1PM and dinner about 8:30. That was the only time the door of the house was opened, letting in our meager meal and a tiny bit of light. During each meal, we got a quick glance of the sky. Otherwise, the door of the house was closed. For eight months we lived either in the light of the electric bulbs or in the dark. All the shutters were closed. We were never allowed to go outside, to walk or get exercise. I knew it was raining when I heard the noise of rain on the roof. It wasn't possible to walk--to even take a walk. I turned in circles. This is what it was like for eight months. They were trying to kill me through a slow death.

The real jailers of President Gbagbo were Fofié's men, not the UN soldiers as claimed by the UN, who said they were protecting and taking care of the famous prisoner. To add to the confusion, the UN soldiers also in Korhogo wore uniforms very similar to those worn by the rebels and they were all from the same Sahel regions. But according to Gbagbo's lawyers who visited him during his first detention, the rebels took the place of the ONUCI soldiers, not the opposite. The International Forces were officially in charge of the prisoner but they deliberately abandoned him to his tormenters. Thus they were able to implicitly *de facto* cover up the ill-treatment he received. The fiction fed by the media of a Gbagbo "protected" by ONUCI, fulfilling their real role and mission, was false. But no one came to verify any of this.

On his first trip to Abidjan in June, 2011, Gbagbo's French lawyer, Emmanuel Altit, was able to make his own evaluation of the situation. From the first time he visited him, he predicted that Gbagbo would be transferred to the International Criminal Court before the end of the year. The French lawyer's Ivorian colleagues did not believe it. In June, in Abidjan, Altit met with the team of Jeannot Ahoussou, Ouattara's Minister of Justice and then the officials of ONUCI's Bureau of Human Rights. This was the required procedure for anyone who wanted to see Gbagbo, a necessary step since it was the ONUCI who made the air liaison to Korhogo. But the UN forces were of no assistance to Altit, although they were, in principle, the ones who were supposed to be guaranteeing the rights of the prisoner--the first of which is the prisoner's right to see his lawyer. Laurent Gbagbo pointed out this lapse during his first appearance in the ICC in December of that same year.

Emmanuel Altit had been the defense lawyer of the Bulgarian nurses who were held in Libya from 1999 to 2007 and who were eventually released in a spectacular media event featuring Cécilia Sarkozy, among others. Altit was obliged to go to Korhogo in a small private plane--like a tourist. On board: the pilot, Altit, and his assistant…the aircraft had engine problems and nearly crashed.

Altit returned to Ivory Coast in July and August. The Ivorian Minister of Justice, the Minister of the Interior, and the UN officials in Ivory Coast assured him, each time, that they would do their best to help him see his client as soon as possible. But when it came the time to organize the practical details of his visit, these people disappeared or kept sending him back and forth between the different parties. Especially shocking to Altit was the fact that the services of the ONUCI did not seem concerned about the violations of the rights of the prisoner, who was detained without an arrest warrant. They pretended to ignore certain Ivorian legislative rulings and the very difficult conditions under which Gbagbo was being detained. Yet they all knew President Gbagbo was in the hands of a warlord, one with blood on his hands. They all knew he was being detained in disgraceful conditions. No one cared: not the new Ivorian authorities, nor ONUCI officials, nor the French officials.

On July 14, 2011, the French Prime Minister François Fillon travelled to Abidjan to meet with Alassane Ouattara, to assure him of the support of the French authorities. He appeared at the evening reception celebrating France's Independence Day. At the same time, Emmanuel Altit and his team were in Abidjan. Knowing he had the support of France, the UN, and the U.S., why would Ouattara worry about how President Gbagbo was being treated? Weren't the rebels, at least some of them, hoping he would just die?

Despite the written authorizations he had obtained from Ivorian authorities at the beginning of his mission, Emmanuel Altit was not able to see his client until October. At that time, the Prosecutor of the International Criminal Court, Moreno Ocampo, was in Abidjan for talks with Ivorian authorities. Despite the fact that Emmanuel Altit had officially informed him of the violations of his client's rights, notably the fundamental right to meet with his lawyer, Ocampo didn't seem more concerned than any of the others. At least the trips of the French lawyer and his team were productive, permitting them to meet with key witnesses to move forward with the case.

The meeting between President Gbagbo and Emmanual Altit finally took place in October, 2011, inside the Korhogo courthouse, emptied of all its employees. A few hundred meters away from the courthouse, Fofié's guards moved aside to let the ONUCI soldiers surround the place, to give the impression they were the ones in charge. It was in fact Fofié and his men who, on several occasions, physically prevented Emmanuel Altit from seeing his client, despite the duly stamped authorization papers in the lawyer's hands. At the end of the meeting, Emmanuel Altit and his two Ivorian colleagues were extremely worried: President Gbagbo was visibly worn down by his detention and left at the mercy of the rebels. Anything could happen.

Chapter 26
The ICC: a court solely for Africans?

Exceptionally, this title is not a quote from Laurent Gbagbo, an accusation which certainly would not sit well with the judges at The Hague. But it is a chance for Mattei to give his point of view on the International Criminal Court, put in place by the ratification of the "treaty of Rome" on July 17, 1998, taking effect from July 1, 2002.

What many people don't know is that out of 193 UN members called to vote, only 121 voted for becoming participating members of the ICC and those abstaining are among the most powerful countries in the world: the U.S., Russia, China, India, and Israel. Why did they refuse to vote? They didn't want their own citizens, and especially their leaders, to be called before this Court and be accused of crimes against humanity. Thus from its outset, the ICC has lacked credibility and true backing from the International Community. France, however, is one of its major supporters, paying 10 million out of the ICC's 100 million euro budget.

Within this chapter, Gbagbo gives his account of how he was literally "kidnapped" from his rebel-guarded prison in northern Ivory Coast and whisked away, behind his lawyer's back, to The La Hague--a story which could send chills up the spine of even the least sensitive.

Within these pages, Mattei also reviews many cases actually in progress at The Hague, noting "you don't see too many white faces there," raising the question of a one-sided "prejudicial" justice, which not only targets Africans, but mainly those "vanquished" by more powerful victors. We also hear a profound and thought-provoking quote from French journalist Frederic Taddei who asks:
> *"Can we still call it justice,*
> *when we are so weak towards the strong,*
> *and so strong towards the weak?"*

"To my utter dismay, I learned that the deposed president of Ivory Coast, Laurent Gbagbo, was transferred to the International Criminal Court, on November 29... in total violation of the International Code of procedures and despite conditions needed for peace to be restored in Ivory Coast. The transfer came about so swiftly that it could rightfully be called a kidnapping..." declared Jerry Rawlings, Ghanaian president between 1992 and 2000. Like many others, Rawlings was surprised and shocked by the cursory judicial procedure used in Korhogo.

"This rush to indict Gbagbo and have him transferred (even during the bombing of his home, Laurent Gbagbo did not try to run away) *as a common criminal defies the logic of the quest for a genuine reconciliation and a sustainable peace in Ivory Coast."*

The plot was set up in Paris on November 24, 2011. Alassane Ouattara went there purposely to meet with Nicolas Sarkozy and Luis Moreno Ocampo-- in a meeting which was kept secret. Gbagbo had been ousted. Now they wanted to finish off the job. The ICC Prosecutor had just returned from Libya. The previous day he had been trying to indict the son of Kadhafi. Saif-al Islam was targeted by international justice. Ocampo came back to Europe as soon as he could, because he had heard that the ICC judges had validated the arrest warrant for President Gbagbo. He jumped into a plane heading for Paris to discuss the modalities of President Gbagbo's transfer with the two plotters, the French president [Nicolas Sarkozy] and Ouattara...No "timeout" for him. Gbagbo recounts:

While working on the case in Abidjan, on Friday, November 25, 2010, my lawyers learned that I was going to be auditioned on Monday, November 28 by a judge concerning some purported economic crimes, an illegally concocted case, respecting neither the Ivorian law nor the Ivorian Constitution. The judge was to travel to Korhogo [to question me]. My lawyers stopped what they were doing and immediately jumped into a car and travelled from Abidjan to Korhogo--it's 600 kilometers of hard winding, road, swarming with highway bandits. My lawyers were ready to take the risk.

In the streets of Korhogo, they were surprised to run into judges and law clerks from the Appeals Court of Abidjan. At the time of the audition conducted by a judge at the courthouse, I thought something was

fishy. At first, I refused to answer the judge's questions. I said that all this was illegal. The judge postponed the audition till the next day, Tuesday.

The next day, Tuesday, November 29, 2010, while the audition was taking place, a judge magistrate rushed into the room and announced that the International Criminal Court was asking for my transfer to The Hague. My lawyers objected that only the Court of Appeals is competent to deal with such a request, and if any hearing was to be carried out, it should be done at the Court in Abidjan.

"All the magistrates of the Appeals Court are here," they replied. *"No need to go to Abidjan!"*

Was this a trap? Given the urgency of the situation, Altit e-mailed his defense team including a memo that could be used to ask for a legal postponement, based on the procedures outlined in the Criminal Code, according to international standards. The Ivorian judges refused. I knew then and there that the game was up, and considering how ridiculous this whole comedy was, I just resigned myself. The hearing [for extradition] started.

My Ivorian lawyers--those who were present--wanted to take the floor. The judges hardly even listened to them. But they were very courageous. They insisted and they were able to make their points, evoking clearly and logically what the law stipulated--all to no avail, it wasn't enough to convince the Court.

The judges in Korhogo were in permanent contact with officials at the ICC in The Hague. They updated them minute by minute on the developments in the hearing. Kouakou Fofié and his men were present in the room, armed with Kalashnikovs, making noise, and becoming impatient when they saw the judges were losing their enthusiasm.

This is the way the hearing went, and it had nothing to do with Ivorian law... or anything normal... During the whole day, they didn't even give me anything to eat ... After the hearing, the guards took me with them, telling me I was going back to the house where I had been detained and that I could see my lawyers the next day. My lawyers believed it!

This was the way the transfer to the ICC came about, in a quasi-clandestine manner, with a few quick judicial words thrown together...

As we were going in my jailor's car, I noticed that we had just passed the road to the house where I had been detained. I asked him [Kouakou Kofié] where we were going:

"Aren't we going to stop?"

He replied:

"No, we're going to the airport. The airport is not lit and your plane must take off before it gets dark at 6:30."

"Where am I going?" I asked again.

He didn't have the courage to tell me the truth and he said *"Abidjan."* I laughed. I had understood that he didn't dare answer. I think he was ashamed. So that's what we did: we drove to the Korhogo airport. And then, they put me in one of the two official planes of the Ivorian presidency which headed towards The Hague.

The Paris-based lawyers of President Gbagbo had understood as well. Emmanuel Altit and his team bought their tickets for The Hague. During the night of Tuesday to Wednesday November 30, 2010, the plane which carried Laurent Gbagbo landed in Rotterdam-The-Hague-Airport. From there, the chilled-to-the-bone president was transferred to The Hague. No one had thought to give him a sweater on this cold winter night.

In the patrol wagon, President Gbagbo, in a complete daze, totally worn-out, and dressed in a light flowery shirt made in Abidjan--an African *Pathe'O* shirt made famous around the world, thanks to Mandela--with light trousers and sandals, was heading towards the prison of The Hague. This is how the person who was the president of his country for ten years arrived in the early morning hours at Scheveningen. Gbagbo comments:

Ouattara had sometimes said in interviews that I was more than a friend for him, I was a brother! I can't believe it...

I was the one who made it possible for Ouattara to come back to Ivory Coast after Konan Bédié sent out an international warrant for his arrest, which had sent him into exile for falsification of identity papers. I was the one who made it possible for him to run in the 2010 presidential election, even though the Ivorian Constitution he himself had voted for in 2000 prevented him from doing so. I never blocked his pension. During the ten years I was in office, I made sure that he received his monthly 8 million CFA francs in his capacity as former Prime Minister. I did the same for Bédié and his spouse, who had been President and First Lady of Ivory Coast. For ten years, Bédié received 22 million francs CFA per month and his wife, 8 million CFA francs per month.

But what's worse, I don't believe that any legally elected head of state--and one illegally removed by armed men--had done more than I had to negotiate [for peace].

Like the final spin of a top, events went faster and faster and then abruptly stopped. Gbagbo is "in the bag"--a quick and easy job. The movie's over--or so they believed in Paris, in Washington, in The Hague and in Abidjan.

I told them in The Hague when I appeared before the Court the first time on December 5, 2011, that it didn't do any good to act as they had. They could have just done things normally.

Entering the room, barely able to stand upright on his two legs, Laurent Gbagbo speaks out to the magistrates of the International Criminal Court:

"I am here, and now we are going to get to the end of this.

Madam the Judge, there was no need to use these kinds of methods to transfer me to The Hague. I ran the country of Ivory Coast for ten years. I never did anything like this.

Madam the Judge, please arrange things so that in other countries, in other cases, nothing like this ever happens again. This doesn't help anything. People try to make you believe that people do not want to appear before the ICC. If they accused me, it means they have evidence. When I appear, you will be able to hear my evidence and you can judge for yourself."

To the end, the very end of this flat country where, as Jacques Brel sings *"The sky is so low, a canal was lost, the sky so gray, a canal hung itself,"* the Thalys train travelled, crossing Flanders and entering into the Netherlands, through Amsterdam or Rotterdam before an Inter-city train takes you to The Hague Sport Hall or to the Central stop. From there, by taxi, it takes only about twenty minutes to get to Scheveningen. The prison is a red brick building like all the other houses, villas and high-class buildings in this rich suburb of The Hague, a seaside city on the North Sea.

This is a peaceful, bourgeois neighborhood. In front of the entrance reserved for visitors and staff, there are stone planters filled with holly. The grass is well kept. On the wall near the glass windows, there are signs which read: "no cameras, no phones, no cigarettes, no lighters or matches" [...] and we don't want to forget: "no firearms." The other access to the prison, with a huge black gate, gives way to an ominous and endless wall, overlooking, at a right angle, a big highway full of traffic. You know you are at the entrance of a

251

penitentiary and not a rest home. Last stop for war criminals and those guilty of crimes against humanity.

The militiamen of second class status that the ICC has filed away here are mostly people from African countries, chosen from among the one hundred and twenty-two countries that have, worldwide, recognized the judicial authority of this institution. All the while ignoring many other authors or suspects of mass crimes from other countries and on other continents, the International Criminal Court has done a "triage," seeking out certain geographically "targeted" people. Gbagbo notes:

What is the ICC? Three of the five countries making up the Security Council and who have the right of veto at the UN are not part of the ICC. Only the French and the British have ratified the treaty. As for the Russians, the Americans and the Chinese, none of their citizens run the risk of getting lost in the fog here.

This International Judicial Institution currently has eight investigations under way, exclusively concerning African countries: Uganda, Mali, Democratic Republic of Congo, Central Africa, Sudan, Kenya, Libya and Ivory Coast. But the institution strives to diversify its fields of investigation and eventually its prison population: in Central America and South America, Honduras and Colombia, in Afghanistan, Georgia, Korea… There are a dozen countries that are likely candidates to supply future culprits and prisoners. However, none of these cases has yet been opened… Frederic Taddei, a journalist at France-Television, and anchor of the show *Tonight or Never* which airs on France2 proposed this polemic analysis[110].

"The judges of the International Criminal Court in The Hague are currently examining the evidence collected against Laurent Gbagbo to decide if a trial can be brought against the former Ivorian president for crimes against humanity. Shouldn't we take this opportunity to examine from our vantage point the evidence gathered against the ICC and decide if this court deserves, yes or no, to continue its work? From the outset of its creation, on July 1, 2002, in accordance with the statutes of Rome, the ICC has put only Africans on trial. Is it racism? Is it impotence? Is it blindness? Each one can decide for him- or herself. For the last ten years, according to the ICC, massacres and war crimes have only been committed, as if by chance, in Ivory Coast, Libya, Darfur, Central Africa, the Democratic Republic of Congo and Uganda…

---

[110] Internet Newsring, February 2013.

What about the rest of the world? Nothing to report. What about Iraq and Afghanistan? Cool! What about Tibet and Syria? No problem… Not content with invoking a purported international law which, in reality, does not apply equally to all states, since countries like Russia, China and the United States did not sign or ratify the statutes of Rome, and the member countries of the UN Security Council can veto a submission of a case before the ICC. The truth is that the International Criminal Court never attacks the victors, only the vanquished. Following the example of the International Tribunal created in 1993 for the former Yugoslavia, which condemns all the Serbs they could find and systematically clears all their adversaries (Croatians or Bosnians), the ICC has indicted poor Gbagbo, but it is quite wary of investigating the other side, i.e. the supporters of Alassane Ouattara backed by the great powers. Likewise, they waited until Kadhafi was about to lose the war against the French, the British and the Americans to suddenly accuse him of crimes against humanity. Can we still call it justice when we are so weak towards the strong and so strong towards the weak? For ten years, the ICC has perverted the very concept of crimes against humanity.

ICC was born in the aftermath of the Second World War, with the view to punishing and making imprescriptible crimes of an extreme atrocity, but different types of crimes are currently being confused. As if the concentration camp of Auschwitz, the bombing of Dresden and the Sétif shootings were all the same thing! As if mass genocide and the suppression of a demonstration in front of the Ivorian television network were exactly the same thing! The evidence of the violations of their own guidelines being so numerous and repeated, isn't it time to put an end to this parody of international justice which acts as an instrument of additional domination at the service of the powers in place and ends up bringing disgrace to the 121 countries which have ratified the statutes of Rome?"

Since its creation by the treaty of Rome in 1998, its inauguration on July 1, 2002, and its effective startup in 2003, the ICC has, one could say, specialized in cases located on the African continent. Anyone would believe that the Africa exclusively possesses, among other defects which are commonly ascribed to that continent, the defect of harboring the quasi-totality of all the war crimes on earth. Are Africans the only mass killers and the only fools with blood on their hands?

In any case, all the ICC's trials and investigations have to do with African leaders. The indictment of the president of Sudan, Omar el-Bechir, for acts of violence that took place in Darfur, then that of the president of Kenya, Uhuru Kenyatta, for the suppression of post-electoral troubles, and now the detention of President Gbagbo, have caused Africans to come together to oppose the ICC. During his closing speech for the Fiftieth Summit of the African Union on May 27, 2013, the president of the AU, Ethiopian Prime Minister, Haile Mariam Dessalegen, denounced the ICC's " racist hunt" of Africans,

At the 17th Summit of heads of state of the African Union in June, 2012, in Malabo, Equatorial Guinea, Jean Ping, former Minister of Foreign Affairs of Gabon, railed against the ICC in these terms:

"One has the impression that the International Criminal Court targets only Africans. Does this means that nothing is happening in Pakistan, in Afghanistan, in Gaza, in Chechenia?"

Addressing more directly the former Argentinian diplomat, Luis Moreno Ocampo, the first Prosecutor, viewed at that time as the "star" of the ICC, Ping expressed his mistrust and contempt:

"Don't do politics—Apply the law!"

Quoting one of the heads of state who was present, Jean Ping added without laughing: *"… Ocampo is just a joke."*

Even before the Woody of Mama[111], as Laurent Gbagbo is affectionately known, was arrested and sent to the ICC, that institution has had to struggle to impose its credibility--and that is putting it mildly. Since its birth, that credibility has been weakened by the fact that out of the 193 member states of the UN, only 121 states voted for and became participating members of the ICC. The United States, Russia, China, India, and Israel refused to sign. This weakens the ICC considerably since it cannot deal with any issues involving either the citizens or the leaders of these countries. Thus, the ICC appears as a biased instrument of the Security Council of the UN, given that three eminent members of that Council (US, Russia and China) have not signed or have refused to ratify the treaty of Rome. As for the United States, even if they don't participate in the financing of the functioning of the Court--a budget of 100 million euros, of which France provides 10 million--they are present at the meeting of the annual assessment. In June, 2013, the Danish Judge Harhoff, from the International Tribunal for former Yugoslavia, who belongs to this

---

[111] Woody refers to "a good guy" and Mama is the village where Gbagbo was born.

254

amorphous grouping of international criminal jurisdiction, echoed the African heads of state who criticized the ICC in denouncing that within the institution itself:

> *"Massive and forceful pressures are exerted on international magistrates"... "These international courts are not neutral and obey the orders of the great powers, the U.S. and Israel in particular."*

Americans have warned that they will never accept that one of their nationals be brought before the ICC, while they reserve the right to choose which crimes committed by their troops in Iraq or in Afghanistan will be judged--by themselves. This is the bottom line of a very serious malaise. Such a philosophy undermines the goals of the ICC. It is not surprising that Africans, and before them Asians, perceive in the ICC one of the arms of Western political power, who raises the judicial whip against weak nations. This is ICC's birth mark and its hidden vice which justifies all the growing criticism and resistance leveled against it.

Certainly the project for the creation of an autonomous African Court, often evoked, but difficult to set up for financial reasons, needs to be realized. The handling of the case of the former leader of Chad, Hissène Habré, whose fate was entrusted to the Senegalese Justice by the African Union for crimes committed when he led the country between 1982 and 1990, will be determining. Having taken refuge in Dakar, with complete impunity for the last twenty-three years, Hissène Habré was finally arrested on June 30, 2013. He was supposed to be tried in 2014. If this trial can successfully be carried out, it will show that Africans are beginning to take their destiny into their own hands. Africans will be able to prove that impunity, in Africa, is no longer the rule.

The ICC was also criticized for its very selective and political choice of cases, because most of these cases concern countries in Africa, especially countries considered small and weak on the international scene. The ICC apparently manipulates justice, allowing the victors to send their vanquished for judgment, which at the same time gives them status in the eyes of the International Community, all the while concealing their own crimes. This was the case for the Democratic Republic of Congo (DRC), when Luis Moreno Ocampo brought before the Court a few obscure militia chiefs without bringing to justice the people who were really responsible for the wars and carnage in east DRC--a conflict that saw up to 5 million deaths.

This is the "signature" of Ocampo's management at the ICC: through easy successes he consolidated the status of the institution and, at the same time, his own status. This is actually one of the organic weaknesses of the Court at The Hague. Since the arrest warrants against the Sudanese Omar el-Bechir were released, African leaders reacted, stood together, and stood up against their bogeyman: Ocampo[112]. There is also the scheduled appearance in The Hague of Uhuru Kenyatta as a free defendant. Elected in 2013, he is the sitting president of Kenya. Along with his Vice-president William Ruto, they are accused of having provoked troubles during the presidential election in 2007 which resulted in one thousand deaths. The accusation has been postponed under the pressure of members of the African Union[113]. Some member countries threatened to withdraw from the ICC. Probably these accusations will never be carried out, since those charged are in power, and the witnesses will probably desist, if they haven't already.

When you enter into the Scheveningen prison, you don't come across many white people. In the common rooms reserved for visitors, you might just see a few Serbs, usually families with their tall long-haired girls. There are six tables, separated by screens on wheels, a small kitchenette, a lounge area with a low table, two couches and an armchair, all in red, and a vending machine with sodas and candies. At the opposite end, a wooden elephant trunk serves as a slide for the kids. Beyond, there is also a television playing non-stop cartoons and a huge plastic car. One Saturday afternoon I saw a curly-haired blond angel driving around. Two or three years old, she was being pulled by a Serb with a worn-out face, who had taken off his belt and was using it as a harness, transforming himself into a workhorse. Was it Vojislav Seselj, the Serbian ultra-nationalist leader? I wouldn't be able to say.

Many have been imprisoned in the Netherlands in the context of the Special Tribunal for former Yugoslavia, including Sloboban Milosevic, the former president of Serbia, who passed away in detention in Scheveningen, and

---

[112]Translator's note: South Africa has threatened several times to arrest Omar al-Bashir accused by the ICC of crimes against humanity and genocide for the past six years, including in 2009 prior to Jacob Zuma's inauguration, in 2010 before the soccer world cup and lately during the 25th AU Summit in Johannesburg, on June, 7-15, 2015.
[113] Translator's note: Uhuru Kenyatta was elected president of Kenya in 2013. In March, 2011, he was summoned to appear before the International Criminal Court to answer for crimes against humanity. The initial appearance took place in April, 2011. The charges were confirmed in September and October 2012, and announced on January 23, 2012. Meanwhile, there had been social upheavals across the African continent and reactions to the treatment of Africans at the International Criminal Court. On December 5, 2014, the ICC Prosecutor, the Gambian magistrate, Fatou Bensouda, filed a notice of withdrawal of the charges against the sitting president.

256

Radovan Karadzic or Radko Maldic. As for Charles Taylor, former president of Liberia, he was tried by the Special Court for Sierra Leone. Throughout that trial, he was at The Hague. Sentenced to fifty years imprisonment, he is serving the remainder of his prison sentence in England.

Since the startup of the permanent Court, it has come to replace the different temporary courts: the Special International Court for Rwanda (the SICR), the Special International Court for Yugoslavia (the SICY), and the Special International Court for Sierra Leone (the SICS). Yet most of the prisoners constitute the "war trophies" from Luis Moreno Ocampo's "African safari."

Congolese Thomas Lubanga appears among them. He was sentenced to fourteen years imprisonment for having enlisted child soldiers. Also Congolese officer Germain Katanga was taken to court for massacres in the region of Kivu, in north-eastern Democratic Republic of Congo. Within the prison walls, there is also former Vice-president of the Democratic Republic of Congo, Jean-Pierre Bemba, senator and unlucky candidate against Joseph Kabila for the presidential election of 2006. This gigantic man, more than six foot three inches tall, whom I saw at each time I visited, with his spouse Liliane, his daughters, and his sons who live in Brussels, is accused of crimes, in particular, rapes, committed by the soldiers of his liberation army while they were in Central Africa during the war he lodged against the regime of Désiré Kabila. Kabila had the most to gain, since Jean-Pierre Bemba was his most serious challenger, being also related by marriage through a sister to the family of the late President Mobutu. At the same time Bemba's detention averted attention away from Kabila's own crimes, to the great satisfaction of the United States, his 'godfather.'

Child soldiers in Congo, rapes in Central Africa: these are admittedly very serious accusations. Yet, those accused seem chosen in function of the agendas of certain Non-governmental Organizations (NGOs), serving to legitimize their existence and their budgets.

Laurent Gbagbo is the first president to be held as a prisoner at the International Criminal Court. His transfer was, in extremis, a swift move by Luis Moreno Ocampo as his tenure was coming to a close. As ICC's Prosecutor, Ocampo was in need of a "big case" to provide the last star in his crown.

Fatou Bensouda, formerly his deputy, became his successor. Hers was the job of providing the final touch, the crowing gesture to a spectacular trial, which was to confirm the ICC in its noble mission spelled out at its creation in 2000: to put an end, once and for all, to the impunity of those responsible for mass crimes. Here is the justification and the *raison d'être* of the young judicial institution, short of backers, now heavily defied and highly criticized. On July 4, 2014, *Le Monde* devoted two pages to "The International Court under Pressure." The journalist responsible for this heading's title stressed the "poor grade" given to Bensouda by the judges one month earlier when they noticed that, as the defense team of President Gbagbo had demonstrated, the Prosecutor did not provide convincing evidence in support of her accusations against Gbagbo. For the Parisian newspaper, it was a return to a more reasonable stance after having been clearly in favor of the Prosecutor in articles where there was no shadow of a doubt--until the June sanction of Fatou Bensouda.

Since June 3, 2013, the failure of Fatou Bensouda has become public, as the judges of the ICC asked her, after two years of investigation, to begin her work all over again from the beginning. You don't have to be a staunch supporter of the deposed Ivorian president to see that the plot hatched by the media and the politicians laid a rotten egg.

Chapter 27
"My lawyers had the judges cornered"

This quote from Gbagbo describes the turn-about in the hearing seeking to confirm charges against him. While the International Criminal Court's Prosecutor spent her time giving interviews explaining how her case against the former Ivorian president was watertight, Emmanuel Altit and his team devoted all their time and energy to uncovering all the counter-evidence they needed to undermine the ICC Prosecutor's arguments. It wasn't too difficult, since Fatou Bensouda had not spent too much time or care in developing her case. In her attempt to prove Gbagbo's forces had violently attacked a "peaceful" women's demonstration near Abidjan, the prosecution produced a video of a riot scene filmed in Kenya, nearly 3,000 miles from Abidjan, with those attacking and being attacked speaking Swahili!

That hearing came to an abrupt end on June 3, 2013, when the three ICC judges reviewing the case said that there was not enough evidence to confirm charges against Gbagbo. But instead of granting a 'non-lieu,' closing down the case, and releasing Gbagbo, they gave the Prosecutor another six months to bolster her case.

Part of the latest strategy was then to have Blé Goudé, Gbagbo's stout defender and Abidjan's adored youth leader, transferred from his prison in Abidjan to Scheveningen. Once again the ICC is to hear stories of illegal detention and mistreatment. In a surprise move, the Court has now taken the decision to try together Laurent Gbagbo, Ivory Coast's officially elected president who served the country for ten years, and Blé Goudé, a youth leader named in 2007 as "Ivorian Peace Ambassador" and in 2010, as Minister of Sports and Youth.

When will the world wake up to the series of serious irregularities surrounding what is supposed to be the fair trial of a former head of state?

The budget is worthy of a gigantic future film production. In 2013, the budget of the ICC Prosecutor stood at 28,265,700 euros[114], to which must be added the 2.8 million allowing her to hire new consultants, investigators, and interim staff hired to work especially on the Ivorian case. Dozens of lawyers in The Hague worked round the clock to build up a strong case against President Gbagbo: prosecutors, deputy prosecutors, legal assistants, trial court specialists, appellate court specialists, translators, etc. Added to these are the dozens of investigators from the office of the Prosecutor who were working on the ground in liaison with Ivorian authorities, magistrates and police agents. Ivorian authorities relayed all kinds of evidence to the Prosecutor--all destined to help her drive the final nail into Gbagbo's coffin. Supporting the Ivorian authorities were the French authorities. Counselors Jean-Paul Benoît and Jean-Pierre Mignard, close to François Hollande, played a leading role in this phase of the work. In contrast, against a team of people with so many resources at their disposal, Emmanuel Altit's team only had access to a very limited budget. For the whole duration of the trial, they had been granted only 76,000 euros to carry out their own investigations. This disproportionate imbalance is clear for all to see. Yet, with their experience and legal competence, Gbagbo's lawyers were able to hold in check the Prosecutor and all her international supporters, and, in fact, completely reverse the situation. Prosecutor Fatou Bensouda was now on the defensive and obliged to justify herself before the countries who signed the 'treaty of Rome.'[115]

After several successive postponements, the long-awaited hearing took place February 19-28, 2013. In collaboration with the Ivorian authorities, the prosecution amassed more than 10,000 pages of investigative reports, annexes, and numerous videos, in hopes of providing solid and insurmountable evidence against Gbagbo, which could lead to the confirmation of charges and his indictment. Prosecutor Bensouda attempted to prove that Gbagbo, whom she portrayed as a violent man who would go to any means to stay in power, had commanded his supporters to use terror to intimidate their adversaries during the time period from November, 2010, when the run-off elections took place, until his capture on April 11, 2011. According to the Prosecutor, these purported attacks against Ivorian civilians had left 1,080 dead, all among Gbagbo's adversaries, along with thirty purported cases of rape.

---

[114] The AEP refers to the ICC's 2014 Budget Program for its 12th Session of July 29, 2013 (ICC-ASP/12/10).

[115] The countries which previously signed the 'treaty of Rome' vote each year to provide a budget for the ICC.

What had been the cause of these deaths and rapes? According to the Prosecutor, these terrorist acts were the sole means by which President Gbagbo and his close allies could remain in power. They were, in her judgment, premeditated acts qualifying as crimes against humanity. Gilles Dutertre, Fatou Bensouda's first collaborator, "opened fire" on Gbagbo, followed by Eric MacDonalds and Maria Belikova, giving detailed accounts, including photographs and videos, of 41 criminal acts, the most important of which were the march on the RTI TV station, the massacre of women in Abobo (a northern suburb of Abidjan) as well as the bombing of the market in that same area, and finally the massacres in Yopougon, west of Abidjan. No one could deny it was an impressive set of charges. Everything made it look like the upcoming trial would be a spectacular triumph for Bensouda and one that *"Gbagbo would have wished he would never have to face,"* as noted in *Jeune Afrique*'s May 26, 2012 issue. According to most journalists, Laurent Gbagbo's conviction was 'in the bag.' Today, it's rather the international judicial institution in The Hague whose legs are shaking.

For Altit and his team, every aspect of the defense was well prepared in advance. In the first minutes of the trial, President Gbagbo defense team asks the Prosecutor to account for a number of procedural errors committed on their side. Immediately the Prosecutor is put on the defensive. Never, we were told, had an ICC prosecutor worked so hard to prepare a case and presented it so well. Yet, as the first blows were dealt by President Gbagbo's defense team, the Prosecutor's team is visibly affected.

Having heard the accusations, the defense team takes the floor and for two straight weeks, unleashes everything it possesses. Emmanuel Altit sets the framework for the debate. He begins by expressing his astonishment that it is only President Gbagbo on trial, emphatically reminding the Court that the Prosecutor had proclaimed that all the authors of mass crimes would be pursued, regardless of their camp. *"Is it because the authors of these crimes are unknown [that they are not also appearing here today]?"* asks Altit. On the contrary, he notes, the perpetrators are indeed known by everyone and their crimes documented in detail by the many organizations for the defense of human rights. The lawyer underlines the fact that those who are in power [in Ivory Coast] today are those who

"...since September 19, 2002 have been plundering [the Ivorian population], extorting money [from them] on a huge scale, and carrying out all kinds of trafficking in violation of Ivorian laws." They are the ones who

systematically *"make rape their modus oporendi...using mercenaries and Dozo militias ...who today continue to perpetrate crimes, especially in western Ivory Coast. These people,* Altit continues, *are mentioned in the reports of the United Nations, Amnesty International, Human Rights Watch, the International Crisis Group, Global Witness, and in the reports of the U.S. State Department and of many more [human rights watchdogs]."*

Emmanuel Altit reminds the Court that since the fall of President Gbagbo, these warlords, suspected of the worst possible crimes, are the very people currently running the Ivorian army and police. These different militia have been raised into decision-making positions and have obtained even more power. He notes, as well, that at no time following the runoff of the presidential election had the ICC Prosecutor tried to contact President Gbagbo's government, while she had been in constant contact with the rebels and Alassane Ouattara. Emmanuel Altit expresses his surprise at the good relations the ICC Prosecutor has maintained with the victors of the conflict following the Ivorian crisis. He notes:

> *"In these conditions, how could anyone be surprised that the DCC indictment (Document Containing the Charges) reflects only accusations lodged by chief rebels and the press that is clearly pro-Ouattara during the time of the crisis.* Altit continues: *This document [of indictment] is nothing but a press review--the review of a one-sided politically engaged press."*

Emmanuel Altit especially brings to light the absence of solid evidence to support the accusations:

> *"The Prosecutor does not provide any convincing arguments to support her accusations: it is striking to note the small number of testimonial evidence or documents she has presented, as well as their vague and unclear nature, besides the fact that these are often in contradiction with each other. It is also striking to note that there is no trace whatsoever of an order given by President Gbagbo or by an Ivorian political or military official which would have corroborated, even in part, at least even one of the Prosecutor's allegations..."*
>
> *"The account that the Prosecutor puts forward is fragmented and incomplete for one simple reason: her accusations do not correspond to reality. She is therefore obliged to transform that reality, and to do this, she has to cover up some aspects of the events. But the facts are stubborn and we are*

going to remind the Court of the facts, without omitting any important element so that a full understanding of the events can be reached."

"The account of the Prosecutor is biased for two reasons: first, as we already noted, the account relies totally on information provided by the current Ivorian authorities. Second and more importantly, the account tries to place sole responsibility for the conflict on the shoulders of President Gbagbo. The Prosecutor has adhered to a narrative built up at the time of the crisis with the view to [...] "de-legitimizing [President Gbagbo] and to convincing "the International Community to support [Ouattara]."

Emmanuel Altit continues to argue: "This is what explains the choice of the four events which make up the Prosecutor's indictment charges, which are each fuzzy, contradictory in nature and open to debate. [...] ...These four events [constitute] at the same time, turning points in the Ivorian crisis, and steps in the [attempted] de-legitimization [of the government] of President Gbagbo and simultaneously [in varying degrees] they point to the involvement of certain [world] powers in the [Ivorian] conflict."

"The purported repression during the attack of the RTI TV station in December, 2010, resulted in the condemnation of President Gbagbo's regime at the international level:

"The allegations regarding the women's demonstration in early March, 2011, resulted in the immediate suspension of the ongoing peace talks. The world powers did not want a negotiated peace [...]"

"The alleged bombing of the market in Abobo on March 17, 2011, led, a few days later, to the adoption of the UN Security Resolution 1975 and the launching of the land offensive which had been prepared in secret a long time in advance by the French forces and the ONUCI.

"And what can be said of the accusations regarding the battles in Yopougon after the fall of President Gbagbo? They are intended to hide the pro-Ouattara forces' systematic violations of human rights which they committed after their victory.

Gbagbo's lawyer continues to explain: "The choice of these four events [...] leads people to have a particular reading and to believe a certain narrative" which would legitimize those who are in power in Abidjan today. The "narrative" allows the victors to present an account of the Ivorian conflict that is "acceptable" in the eyes of the International Community. As Emmanual Altit says: This narrative paints "with broad strokes, two distinct camps: one good and one evil."

"Thus, these four events have deep political significance. They construct a reality which tries to 'legitimize,' serving as the foundation for the takeover of power by the Ouattara camp.

"Rather than verifying the truthfulness of this narrative, rather than conducting an investigation to determine the reality [of what really happened], the Prosecutor accepted the narrative as truth. And the problem is that today, the Prosecutor can no longer stray from that narrative, without jeopardizing the whole structure [of her argument]."

"And yet that structure does not hold. As for the attack on the RTI TV station, all the elements available to us prove that it wasn't the pro-Gbagbo forces who attacked [...] unarmed crowds but rather the pro-Ouattara militias who launched a pre-meditated attack targeting government forces of law and order."

"As for the repression of the women's march, the Ivorian press itself echoed the inconsistences of the accusations. But the Prosecutor took as solid truth the version of only one side, "the good camp," without double-checking the facts, without a real investigation, without verifying the different hypotheses."

"As for the bombing of the market in Abobo, the case presented by the Ivorian authorities is not in the least convincing, and the Prosecutor did nothing to shed light on any part of it."

"Besides, how could one not be surprised that the people the Prosecutor presents as the [givers of orders] [...] [the people whose role would have been crucial] in setting up the purported policies [ascribed to President Gbagbo] were immediately promoted and rewarded by Alassane Ouattara?"
[...]

"The Prosecutor preferred to read the Ivorian reality through a simplistic prism. It is easier to see everything in black and white. It is easier to imagine unarmed crowds machine-gunned down, when your goal is to draw a visible line between the camp of good and the camp of evil. It speaks straight to the imagination--it becomes part of the unconscious collective mind."

"Because she herself carried out no investigation, because she relied uniquely on information furnished by the Ivorian authorities, the Prosecutor has not been able to grasp the political reality on the ground, and therefore, she is not able to share this reality with the Chamber."

"We will show, during the course of this hearing, how easy it is to be tempted by what is facile, i.e what is easy and simple, and we will show that this

264

[kind of approach] *can have severe consequences, which have in fact, led the Prosecutor to misinterpret the events being discussed."*

"Thus in attempting to create a scenario that would lead to accuse President Gbagbo before the ICC, the Prosecutor has been obliged to "force" the truth and re-invent a certain reality. Yet, the truth is known to all the experts and to all the inhabitants of Ivory Coast: the fall of President Gbagbo was planned and organized." […]

"The Prosecutor is playing a risky game by buying into a narrative written by others. In fact, if the narrative which she relied on were to be carefully examined, the intellectual and structural arguments built up to accuse President Gbagbo--and simultaneously to legitimize Alassane Ouattara--would simply fall apart. Were this examination to take place, the entire foundation of the accusations would be seen for what it is, namely, the search for a scapegoat who is, in reality, simply a man guilty of wanting liberty [for his country], *rather than bondage."*

"The Prosecutor is truly playing a risky game in emphasizing the importance of the four most mediated incidents of the crisis, those which have had political consequences... in so doing she forgets the countless crimes Ivorian populations have endured."

"The Ivorian people deserve to have […] *their sufferings taken into account. They deserve a different kind of trial--not a political one. They deserve to see a trial accusing those who are responsible for the destruction of the country over the period of an entire decade."*

"And certainly the International Criminal Court deserves to be told what really happened in Ivory Coast during all these years so they themselves can look into the facts. If that should happen, the Court might be able to play a beneficial role in the reconciliation of the nation."

Emmanuel Altit reminded the Court, as well, that the Ivorian crisis is also an issue which involves the French government. This crisis can only be understood in the context of the Franco-African relations. For fifty years, France intervened about forty times in Africa.

After Altit's opening remarks, the remainder of the presentation of defense's team went smoothly. The members of the defense team each took the floor and destroyed one by one, each argument the Prosecutor brought forward. They took each of the elements she presented in support of her allegations and they showed, for each, the pointlessness, the irrelevancy, the lack of clarity, and the contradictions. At the end of the presentations of Professor Jacobs, Agathe

Bahi-Baroan, Jennifer Naouri and Natacha Fauveau, the allegations of the Prosecutor were virtually reduced to nothing. The shock was all the greater, because the hearings were broadcast semi-live by the ICC's internet website and rebroadcast by a certain number of countries. In Ivory Coast, the hearings were passionately followed on the internet.

The defense team took pleasure in revealing the inconsistences of the Prosecutor's arguments, they questioned her long silences [as she was unable to reply], and they showed that several elements of her arguments seemed to have been put forward "for the sake of the cause," and therefore had no bearing on the case. Thus a video that the Prosecutor claimed was an illustration of atrocities that occurred in 2011 in Abidjan was actually footage of events which took place in Kenya in 2009! The defense team pointed out that the exclamations heard during the film were in Swahili!

Because of the professionalism of the defense team and the seriousness with which they led the counter-investigation, the Prosecutor's position seemed more and more fragile. The lack of a genuine investigation was obvious. The fact that she relied mainly on what the Ivorian authorities had decided to tell her or the documents they had chosen to give her was blatant. Her inability to grasp the fundamentals of the situation was more than surprising. It was a huge victory for the defense team, because they succeeded in changing the perception the public had had beforehand. Gbagbo notes:

My lawyers were able to completely reverse the situation. My opponents believed they had won and they were convinced that their manipulation of the International Court was to their advantage. But suddenly it became evident that if the trial moved forward, they were the ones who would have everything to lose. Because a trial would reveal the truth. Now they are cornered. One of the great merits of Emmanuel Altit and his team was to have immediately understood what the realities were on the ground in Ivory Coast and to have made this clear to the judges. They destroyed the evidence of the Prosecutor. Now everyone knows that the elements presented by the Prosecutor to support her allegations cannot stand up to scrutiny. Finally, the Defense team was able to demonstrate the bias of the Prosecutor, who seemed to just follow the wind--wherever the world powers made that wind blow. Why wasn't she indicting the groups and individuals the NGOs were denouncing as mass criminals? Why has she been maintaining her contact, almost on friendly terms, with them? It is probably because she doesn't see them as criminals, because she has been acting on presuppositions and prejudices. My lawyers showed that these

prejudices, conveyed by the media, were pure fabrication. We were able to use the judicial process to show the reality of the Ivorian situation. All the political accusations aimed at preparing the international public opinion to accept my overthrow, proved, after all the contradictory debates, to be false. The defense's team's arguments before the Court showed that the accusations of Ouattara's camp, in conformity to strategies conceived by the French, were a smoke screen aimed at hiding their attempts, over a period of ten years, to seize power through violence from a legitimate government.

As for the Ivorian elections, why doesn't the Prosecutor show any interest in these? After all, it's fairly simple. If I lost the presidential election, we should be able to talk about it. But if I won the election, their arguments would collapse, because the International Community would have supported the loser of the election and would have, through the intervention of France's Licorne force and the UN, put that loser in power through violent means. Why didn't the Prosecutor even envision the hypothesis according to which I could have won the Ivorian presidential election, since everything shows that I did indeed win them? During the post-electoral crisis, why were Ouattara and his French backers so afraid that we would come to an agreement leading to a recount of the votes? Why did they do all in their power to ensure that mediation attempts would fail?

Briefed--and maybe brainwashed--by ONUCI, Jean-Christophe Notin believed to offer the answer in his book. He notes that in December, 2010, *"...once the ballots were counted, they were destroyed."* This argument was never brought forward to Gbagbo [when he asked for a recount], certainly because it is false. If it were to be proven that the ballots were destroyed, it would constitute a clandestine and illegal maneuver, thus proving that fraud was carried out to prevent a recount, a common procedure in all parts of the world whenever there are electoral disputes.

What was supposed to be a triumphant victory march for the Prosecutor turned into something more like going step by step through the Cross stations. While the Prosecutor was busy appearing before the TV cameras, Emmanuel Altit and his team were conducting investigations on the ground. While she was wasting her time meeting with Alassane Ouattara and his deputies, and while she was being encouraged by international leaders, especially the French, the defense team was busy building up its case. While the Prosecutor was spreading the news everywhere, on airwaves and in newspapers, for anyone who wanted to hear, that she had a watertight case, Gbagbo's counselors had already torn everything to shreds. Hence the Prosecutor was surprised, during the two week long hearing in February, to be faced with criticism and lessons about how to be more professional. She came out slightly dazed. At the end of the hearing in February 2013, the victory of President Gbagbo seemed imminent. All the journalists or specialists who had followed the hearing and who had, before the hearing, complacently echoed the affirmations of the Prosecutor, immediately changed sides. After witnessing the demonstration of the defense team, they began writing and talking about how the Prosecutor had been exposed. They noted the dossier in her hands was weak and, for the most part, political.

During each judicial skirmish that preceded the hearing to confirm the charges, Emmanuel Altit continued to present a line of reasoning based on the basics of the law, including the respect of the rights of the defense team: equal "arms" for each party, for the fairness of each procedure, etc., all indispensable elements for the implementation of a trial by fair process of law.

Such a strategy was all the more necessary because the ICC had wanted to be an exemplary Court. During his opening speech on January 20, 2013, and now from a position of strength, it was not too hard for Emmanuel Altit, to denounce the "political cards" the Prosecutor was trying to play. As for Altit, his team played the card of professionalism in the presence of a Prosecutor seemingly forgetful of her duties. The goal was to have the ICC judges step back and look objectively at the Prosecutor's arguments, to prepare them to at least listen to what the defense team had to say. At the end of the fifteen days of hearing, in his closing statement, Emmanuel Altit sent the judges a second message: since the defense team had just demonstrated that the evidence of the Prosecutor was flimsy, inconsistent and contradictory, that the Prosecutor's evidence was based on unchecked elements, and that they had been fabricated to follow a particular political narrative, Emmanuel Altit asked the ICC judges if they were ready to follow the Prosecutor and run the risk of leading the Court into a deadlock. Gbagbo notes:

The way Emmanuel Altit and his associates organized the hearing for the confirmation of the charges made the Prosecutor lose all credibility. My lawyers moved their pawns in such a way as to corner the ICC judges. They asked them to give their opinion on the Prosecutor's evidence which the defense team had just destroyed.

Emmanuel Altit and his associates were obliged to unveil the reality little by little. They had to take care not to affront the prejudices of the judges.

They had to let the facts sink, little by little, into their consciousness. To reconstruct the historical reality took a long time and was not any easy task.

But at the hearing to confirm the charges, the hold the defense team had on the audience was so strong all observers were expecting the charges to be dropped and the trial to not take place. The question the judges had to answer was whether, in fact, the Prosecutor had presented sufficient and credible evidence to warrant a trial.

On June 3, 2013, the judges make their decision known. They noted, as the defense team had demonstrated, that the Prosecutor had brought no convincing and credible evidence to support the proposed narrative of incidents to substantiate her claim that crimes against humanity had been committed. The judges noted, as the defense team had also demonstrated, that the Prosecutor had not carried out a proper investigation. Finally the judges noted that the Prosecutor had not followed the "line of reasoning" which she is normally known for. Thus, the judges refused to confirm the charges. This was a tremendous victory for Gbagbo and his lawyers.

The statutes of the Constitution of the Court make provision for such a case: when charges cannot be confirmed, they are to be annulled, which would have *ipso facto* meant that President Gbagbo would be immediately released. Yet, the judges were split. In fact, one of the judges, the main judge, who had been the Prosecutor's 'right-hand man' for several years, was dead set against dropping the charges. This is perhaps why the judges decided to effect a new reading of the statutes of Rome, and authorize the Prosecutor to start the investigations anew--from scratch--even though the statutes do not make such a provision. Was it a compromise? After noting the devastating failure of the Prosecutor and after having concurred with the demonstration of the defense team, the ICC judges began to wonder if the Prosecutor had perhaps misunderstood her duties. Perhaps she did not understand what was needed to constitute evidence or did not understand what exactly was expected of her at this point in the proceedings, in terms of documentation exhibiting solid proof. The judges even thought that the Prosecutor may have been mistaken in the application of the law. Did this mean, in laymen terms, that the Prosecutor didn't know what she was doing? In any case, it was on this fragile and curious basis that the ICC judges authorized her to start all her inquiries over again on the basis of the charges already formulated. No one had ever seen anything like it! It was indeed a very unusual way to "save" the Prosecutor. Surprisingly she wasn't sanctioned for her professional mistakes. It is rather President Gbagbo who had to pay for the lack of seriousness of the Prosecutor, having himself to stay in prison for several additional months.

It is unusual, to say the least, to give a Prosecutor a second chance--a way for her to 'make up' her mistakes, instead of being sanctioned for professional error, which should have led to the case being dropped. To the surprise of everyone, the ICC seems to tolerate and even encourage the Prosecutor's incompetence, to the detriment of the individual being detained, and all this, at the expense of the international bodies footing the bill. The new masters of Ivory Coast, with their French friends behind them, narrowly escaped: Gbagbo already had one foot out the door, but they pulled him back inside the prison, in extremis.

If the charges had not been confirmed, that would have been heavily significant: it would mean that the ICC judges, who cannot be suspected of being *a priori* favorable to President Gbagbo, estimate that the Prosecutor did not provide conclusive evidence in support of her allegations. It wasn't even a question of conclusive evidence which would be presented during the actual trial. At this stage of the confirmation of charges, prior to any trial, the judges only had to determine if the evidence presented by the Prosecutor had an "appearance of truth," if it had any weight whatsoever. Before the trial itself, the standard of evidence that the Prosecutor must reach is quite low, much lower than the standard needed to obtain a conviction. At that latter stage, the Prosecutor must prove guilt beyond any reasonable doubt. But the Prosecutor didn't reach even the minimum standard of evidence. This meant that the judges considered that nothing supported the Prosecutor's narrative concerning the events occurring during the post-electoral crisis. It means the narrative was not based on reality. Yet, if we admit the defense's team's argument, the "narrative" used by the Prosecutor was nothing but judicial footwork, a remake of the political "narrative" used by the Ouattara camp and his French supporters to legitimize their takeover through violent means. It means that for the ICC judges, the political "narrative" had no basis. And these judges came to this conclusion after a thorough examination of all evidence available to them.

But if President Gbagbo had been released, this would have constituted, from the vantage point of the ICC judges, the proclamation *urbi et orbi* that the intervention of the French army in the Ivorian post-electoral crisis was truly an act of colonial war, serving particular interests. It would have meant that the intervention of the UN peace keepers--who for the first time in their history had actually taken sides in a civil war, —was, in fact, illegitimate.

The Prosecutor immediately appealed the decision. After epic-filled judicial exchanges, the defense team once more gained the upper hand. The appeal of the Prosecutor was rejected.

On January 13, 2014, the Prosecutor submitted a new declaration of charges, the fruit of her new inquiries. Surprise! The Prosecutor had not respected the judges' instructions, and if she preserved the appearance of the former allegations, she changed the tone of the accusations. In fact, she renounced a good number of the ones she had herself formulated in 2012 and 2013. On April 4, 2014, the defense team submitted a document of 320 pages in response to the Prosecutor's declaration of criminal charges, entitled *Modified Public Version of the Second Corrigendum Related to Written Observations of the Defense on the Evidence of the Prosecutor*.

The defense team considered the new arguments of the Prosecutor, took them one by one, and tore them to pieces. When the reading of the defense's team's observations was over, nothing was left of the Prosecutor's accusations. The lawyers of President Gbagbo had done an outstanding job. But the public version is full of crossed out passages. The most crucial parts of their arguments are censured. That's the problem with this kind of procedure, which purports to be exemplary, but is never completely transparent. According to all the observers, the Prosecutor can no longer hope for a clear victory against President Gbagbo's defense team. Chances are slim that she will win in the proceedings against him, if indeed a trial does take place after a hypothetical and unlikely confirmation of charges, which would surprise the majority of observers[116].

Only a few hours after the defense team submitted its observations, the Prosecutor fiercely negotiated with the Ivorian authorities, on the advice of her French lawyers, to transfer Blé Goudé to The Hague. A former leader of Ivorian youth movements, he too was targeted by an arrest warrant. Up to that point, Fatou Bensouda didn't seem interested in Blé Goudé, but maybe she thinks it will be her "last and winning card" in the Gbagbo case.

The request to transfer Blé Goudé was announced on March 20, 2014, three days after President Gbagbo's defense team submitted its conclusions, which were devastating for Fatou Bensouda. Perhaps after reading their observations, the Prosecutor realized how weak her position was and decided to try a final maneuver, by-passing the defense team of President Gbagbo and

---

[116] Translator's note: since this book was published, the charges against Laurent Gbagbo have been confirmed. But after many years behind bars (April 2011- May 2015), Gbagbo has yet to stand trial.

attacking head-on the young political activist. It would seem Blé Goudé was transferred [from Ivory Coast] to the ICC, only after strong pressure was put on the Ivorian authorities, who did not seem too enthusiastic about the move. Blé Goudé had been locked up for more than a year without being able to see his lawyers. Obviously, the Ivorian authorities were not particularly happy to have the horrific conditions of detention to which Ivorian political prisoners are submitted, made public [once again]. But the Ivorian authorities needed to comply with the ICC, to prevent their judges from scrutinizing the "new Ivorian masters" too closely, as several of them are themselves suspected of serious crimes. According to *Jeune Afrique,*

> *"the idea here was to use Blé Goudé as a witness against the one he had so heartily defended--by mobilizing thousands of young people, who took to the streets to defend the cause of the Ivorian president[117].*

It was a timetable set in place to rescue Bensouda, like a lifeline thrown to her. And certainly Blé Goudé will be pressured to render the service they expect from him, that is, to make Gbagbo "dive." In Abidjan, some evoke Blé Goudé's friendly ties to Wattao[118] and negotiations he would have carried out with the Minister of the Interior. But others do not doubt for one second that Blé Goudé will remain loyal to the "Woody of Mama." No matter how Blé Goudé's hearings develop, suspicions will weigh on any deviation in his testimony. Up till now he has been the hero of Abidjan youth[119].

In the end, those who believed what they had read or heard about Laurent Gbagbo had to resign themselves to the fact that after four months of deliberation by the three ICC judges of the Preliminary Chamber, the grievances held against Laurent Gbagbo were estimated insufficient and quasi-inexistent. Therefore going to trial against Gbagbo runs certain risks, since the defense team has shown that the charges lacked depth, cohesion and consistency, and sufficient supporting evidence.

---

[117] N° 2776, 23-29 March 2014.

[118] Translator's note: One of the warlords of the ten-year crisis in Ivory Coast whose real name is Issiaka Ouattara.

[119] Translator's note: As of March 15, 2015, "Trial Chamber I of the International Criminal Court (ICC) granted the Prosecutor's request to join the cases concerning Laurent Gbagbo and Charles Blé Goudé, in order to ensure the efficacy and expeditiousness of the proceedings."

Despite the Prosecutor's efforts at the appeal, she was curtly turned down. On December 16, 2013, the Prosecutor's request was turned down a second time by the ICC institution. The Appellate Chamber which disapproved the appeal was then headed by the institution's current president, the Korean national Song Sang-Hyun, giving the impression of a developing schism between the ICC and Fatou Bensouda. "She's who she is and we are who we are," they seemed to be saying, with the institution not wanting to be part of Bensouda's future "shipwreck." The "African-style Nuremberg" is cut short. Surely one or the other of the protagonists will end up on the floor, a knock-out. Prosecutor Fatou Bensouda has now understood this.

Paradoxically, in its current state of failure, the ICC might be able to make an effort to pull itself up to the level the Treaty of Rome is aiming at--to save itself from disaster and ensure its own credibility. But with the transfer of Charles Blé Goudé, the ICC clearly does not appear to be on the right path.

Chapter 28
"They'll never change"

Gbagbo shakes his head and comments "they'll never change" when he hears how the former French Ambassador Jean-Marc Simon has been busy working to "legitimize" Ivory Coast's new "master," Alassane Dramane Ouattara. All Ambassador Simon wants is for Gbagbo to acknowledge he lost the elections, suggesting that if Gbagbo would just "capitulate," his fate might be different--now or even in the future.

Anyone who knows Gbagbo knows he will never call the fraudulent elections fair, with voters in the north going to the poles under the eye of machine guns and voting stations reporting more favorable votes for his opponent than the number of voters registered on the electoral lists...

Mattei takes this chance to give even more background on events leading up to the war, as rebels were trained in neighboring Burkina Faso—all of which obviously took place with the consent, if not the help, of the then-sitting Burkinabè president, "Beau" Blaise Compaoré. Having come to power in a bloody coup d'etat where his "brother and friend," Thomas Sankara, was assassinated, if not by his own hand, by those he had commandeered, this president, so supported and respected by the International Community, ruled over his country for 27 years (1987-2014). Gbagbo notes with irony that Compaoré always won an overwhelming victory at the polls... as he was "elected" many times over. Following his recent attempt to change his country's Constitution, permitting him to run once more, the populations of "the country of the men of integrity" (the meaning of the name Burkina Faso) took to the street, burned down their National Assembly, and ousted "Beau Blaise" who took immediate refuge under the wing of Alassane Dramane Ouattara in Ivory Coast.

Mattei also describes another chilling incident marking the Ivorian crisis: Dr. Balla Keita, a well-loved minister during Houphouet's era, was assassinated in Ouagadougou in the summer of 2002 under mysterious circumstances, preceding the coup attempt later that year in Ivory Coast. Rumor has it Keita was going to denounce those planning to carry out that destabilization attempt....

275

There was no single confirmed charge. Fatou Bensouda was asked to revise her work. I get an idea of the effect this has on Gbagbo's opponents when the former French Ambassador to Ivory Coast Jean-Marc Simon calls to ask the news. Without hiding his deception, he exclaims: *"No charge? That's not possible!"* At the end of April, he told me over the phone that though he was worried about the disagreements among the ICC judges, he remained hopeful that a final consensus would eventually be reached. Still very active on Gbagbo's case, the former French Ambassador to Ivory Coast had accepted to meet with me for the first time, knowing I saw Gbagbo regularly. After two meetings and several phone conversations interrupted by his frequent trips to Abidjan, Jean-Marc Simon shared with me the thinking of his friends, the new masters in Ivory Coast:

> *"If Gbagbo would only acknowledge he lost the election!! Well, I understand it is difficult. I think I might be able to negotiate with Ouattara for him to give his implicit agreement for the release and the exile of Gbagbo in a host country while waiting for his trial. But the problem is, he would have to talk it over with Hamed Bakayoko* (the Ivorian Minister of the Interior), *with Guillaume Soro* (the president of the Ivorian National Assembly) *whom Gbagbo trusts* [sic]*, with Coulibaly Ngnénéma Coulibaly,* (the Ivorian Minister of Justice), *and with Blaise Compaoré...* (the then-president of Burkina of Faso). *"*

Needless to say, when I reported this extravagant idea to Gbagbo, he put his hands together and looked upwards, with the look of sadness of someone they had underestimated, and sighed: **"They'll never change."**

The former French Ambassador to Ivory Coast couldn't get over the turn of events. Same reaction from *Jeune Afrique*, the mirror and unofficial cog in the machine of the incestuous relationship between France and its former colonies, caught by surprise by the change in the balance of power between the defense team and the Hague. Renown for its unfavorable opinion towards Laurent Gbagbo, the weekly Parisian magazine which treats news on Africa, had headlined before the famous hearing in February, "Presumed guilty." They predicted the office of Prosecutor Fatou Bensouda would crush Gbagbo under a flood of irrefutable facts and send him without discussion to trial. This was the dominant leitmotiv arising from the post-electoral crisis where media hype hostile to Gbagbo prevailed. Any other take on it, even to nuance it slightly, provoked hysterical or skeptical reactions. In the Parisian milieu of that time, no one doubted Gbagbo's guilt, as during the worst moments of the post-electoral crisis or during "the battle for Abidjan." During this time, any reserve expressed about the results of the elections immediately would have the little princes of the world of media turn against you. Some of them, sincere and convinced, nourished what could be called a general "anti-Gbagbo consensus." The majority remained hostile to any critical examination of the French military interference in the Ivorian crisis. Some of them were already gaining points in their favor.

I remember the insults of a colleague working at France 24 TV news channel who entered into a kind of hysteria and indirectly accused me of trying to "intoxicate" him when I tried to share information with him about certain incidents which had marked the vote, that I had hoped to put before him for him to judge for himself. I considered this a simple exchange of information between two journalists. I obviously wasn't aware of the fact that he would go on in 2012 to create a company whose first contract would be the rehabilitation of RTI, the Ivorian Radio and Television Network, which he obtained thanks to his close personal ties with eminent members of Ouattara's team.

We've seen even better since then. A political journalist of an important Parisian weekly journal, a close friend of Dominique Ouattara, was invited and warmly welcomed in Abidjan like a real star, provided with a Mercedes 500 to drive her from the airport to her five star hotel. The Ouattaras really know how to connect with those they need, creating around them a set of notable journalists and other people. There are even some French journalists who act as their advisers and others on the Board of Directors of [Dominique Ouattara's] Children of Africa Foundation, one of the active members is a former founder and boss of one of the most well-known weekly magazines in France.

As for *Jeune Afrique,* it changes its tune after the verdict on June 3, 2013, when it headlines:

"Gbagbo, the thorn in the ICC's flesh."

But this time, the heading appeared in a discrete title block at the top of the magazine's front page to minimize Bensouda's slap in the face and the growing frustration and worry in the anti-Gbagbo camp. In the inside pages, the title "Benefit of Doubt" headed a factual article which, all things considered, was well-researched and well-organized. The magazine acknowledged the damage, but did not exclude a forthcoming surge on the part of the prosecuting attorney during the second round. As the opponents to Alassane Dramane Ouattara say, don't underestimate "Dramanistan," the nickname given to his regime.

The successive headings of the magazine specializing in African Affairs, located on Auteuil Street in the 16th arrondissement in Paris, closely followed the evolution of the power struggle in the battle being waged in The Hague. Even when the news doesn't particularly please their editors, the magazine still is the best indicator of the trends, provided that their stories are properly "decrypted," like reading backwards in a mirror. Thus, on October 27, 2013, the magazine printed full cover-page the unexpected heading:

"And if he [Laurent Gbagbo] *were released?"*

A reaction to the shock wave of what occurred on June 3, even if later there were echoes concerning the divisions among the three judges of the International Criminal Court.

For those who are watching, another alarm signal goes off when Bensouda travels to Abidjan in July, 2013. She makes an urgent trip there to seek out new elements in the preparation of her "catch-up session." The ruling powers in Abidjan, victor of the 2010 crisis, political enemy of Gbagbo, who had ordered his referral before the Court in The Hague, did everything thing they could to assist the Gambian to find evidence. For this magistrate, who was molded by her predecessor, Luis Moreno Ocampo, this was labelled an "investigation."

We know that she was not received either by Alassane Ouattara, president of the Republic, or by Guillaume Soro, president of the National Assembly and former Prime Minister, both major players in the post-electoral crisis. She revised her work with the Minister of Justice, NGnénéma Coulibaly, under pressure to add new testimonies to enrich her case... at the risk of bringing to light more controversial pieces of evidence which would appear "doctored up." We still remember the video showing the violent repression of demonstrations...in Kenya--Fatou Bensouda just doesn't have it. She ends up "hitchhiking." The Rolls Royce of international justice is out of gas.

In Abidjan, as well as elsewhere, people began to have doubts. It prompted the Parisian magazine, *Jeune Afrique*, to publish an issue which stayed on the newsstands for two weeks due to the All Saint's Day long weekend. It was a good commercial manoeuver since Gbagbo is a "good market" but also an imposing figure since the dossier against him at the ICC shows signs of weakening. For *Jeune Afrique* it is important to not be caught off-guard by any breaking news. You can imagine the headaches of the journalists pulled in two directions. Five of them came together to write carefully worded texts which needed to preserve their credibility, and at the same time wouldn't upset Alassane Ouattara, one of the magazine's

278

shareholders. A difficult task but one in which the Auteuil Street magazine excels, as does its founder and boss, Bechir Ben Yahmed, who is as much a passionate journalist as a crafty businessman. When the satirical *Le Canard Enchaîné* points its finger at Ben Yahmed for his contracts with Ben Ali's Tunisia, he confirms in his letter of reply that Ivory Coast's Ouattara is among his generous financial backers.

Alassane Ouattara never hid his link to the boss of *Jeune Afrique*. On November 4, 2013, in Paris, in his speech as he was admitted into the *Académie des Sciences d'Outre-Mer*, Ado greets, among his other guests, Bechir and Danielle Ben Yahmed, those *"who have always been at my side."* The issues of *Jeune Afrique* covering the period of the electoral campaign and post-electoral crisis testify to this friendly and truly deserved homage.

That same day Ado also thanks the former French Ambassador to Ivory Coast, Jean-Marc Simon, his ally and accomplice during the four months of crisis. He thanked him *"for everything he did and continues to do for Ivory Coast"* as well as *"[…] my friend and brother the president of Burkina Faso, Blaise Compaoré."*

"Beau Blaise" ("handsome Blaise" as he is known) is among the most demonic heads of state on the African continent. He seized power through a bloody coup on October 15, 1987, where he is implicated in the assassination of his predecessor and "friend" Thomas Sankara. Sankara was a staunch supporter of the struggle for the independence and dignity of the people of his country, one of the poorest in the world. Sankara's critical stance and his fiery Burkinabè revolution made him anathema to the West and to France. During that time in Africa, you could easily die for less. Sankara was dubbed "the man of integrity" when he re-baptized Upper Volta, the colonial name for his country, Burkina Faso, i.e., *"the country of the men of integrity."* He was the one who replaced the luxury cars of government ministers with lowly Renault 5. He worked hard on behalf of women's rights; he promoted self-sufficiency in food production, to free his people from dependency and economic and financial subjugation. This African-style "Che Guevara" stood up to President Mitterrand during his state visit to Ouagadougou, during a bitter-sweet exchange relating to the official visit in France of the then-president of South-Africa, Pier Willem Botha, proud champion of every version of apartheid. When the team of Jacques Chirac comes back to power with the 1986 shared "Cohabitation" government, with Jacques Foccart serving as "Mister Françafrique," Sankara is killed.

In the meantime, Houphouët-Boigny is delighted to regain his hold over Burkina Faso, Ivory Coast's neighbor to the north, which provides all the immigrant labor, working hand in hand with Foccart and his spiritual son Blaise Compaoré. Houphouet is, in fact, the one who introduces Blaise to the woman who would become his wife.

As soon as he came into power, Blaise Compaoré eliminated his possible opponents: Henri Zongo and Jean-Baptiste Boukari Lingani, accusing them of making plots against him. The journalist, Norbert Zongo, was also suspected and assassinated by the men of the presidential guard. Despite complaints filed by Mariam Sankara, the widow of the murdered Burkinabè president and injunctions from the International Community, Compaoré has always refused to investigate the death of his predecessor. On the one hand, he was condemned in principle by the UN Committee for Human Rights, while on the other, he has seemed to be "cleared" and has entered into the good graces of the West, however contradictory and paradoxical that is. Compaoré's ascension to power offered France and Houphouët-Boigny's Ivory Coast the chance to establish relations more in line with what was hoped in Paris and Abidjan, to the great satisfaction of the West--still in a power struggle with the East as to the fate of the African continent, two years before the fall of the Berlin Wall.

Crowned by his prestigious patrons, the president of Burkina Faso acquires a new stature as mediator in regional conflicts. In 2006, he headed the dialogue between the Togolese government and its opponents. In 2007, he sponsored the peace agreements of Ouagadougou between Laurent Gbagbo and Guillaume Soro. But his role in the Ivorian conflict raises burning questions.

To begin with is the assassination of Doctor Balla Keita, a brilliant Ivorian minister during Houphouët-Boigny's time, which remains unpunished till today, a crime that still sets all of Abidjan buzzing. The secret of who was behind the assassination and who carried it out has not yet been unveiled, On the African continent, there seems to be a congenital lack of will to carry out such investigations, if not pure fear.

In 1987, Dr. Balla Keita, a veterinarian [Animal Doctor] by training, was entrusted by Houphouët, France's man in Africa, with helping Compaoré topple Thomas Sankara who was considered too much of a Marxist. Afterwards, Balla Keita often traveled back and forth from Abidjan to Ouagadougou. During the summer of 2002, having been informed of the coup in the making meant to overthrow Gbagbo, he learned that the operation was being planned so Ouattara, a friend of Compaoré, could seize power, and not his friend, Robert Guéi. Keita was not happy about this. Even more than Alassane, he hated Dominique Ouattara, Ado's French spouse, whom he came to know when she was involved in the private life of Houphouët-Boigny. Balla Keita believed that the Ouattara couple wasn't fit for the top office in the Ivorian state and he made no secret of his feelings. Former leading figures in Houphouët's regime remembered this about Keita and told me about it. In confidence, they give very precise information on Balla Keita's disappearnce. Or they insinuate what they could reveal about the role of those currently in power in the affair, in carefully coded interviews aimed indirectly at those concerned, whenever these want to pick a fight with them…

The raw facts are as follows: In Ouagadougou on one of his trips between the two capitals, Balla Keita was about to return to Abidjan and was planning to 'let the cat out of the bag.' He was assassinated on August 1, 2002 in a villa of "Ouaga 2000," a private neighborhood of the capital city of Burkina Faso, an area guarded around the clock. Till today no one knows how the killers got in…

What we do know is that on September 19, 2002, a military attack was launched from Burkina Faso by rebels who had been housed, trained, and logistically oriented in that country. The rebels swept down through Ivory Coast, while President Gbagbo was on a state visit to Rome. The attack left more than three hundred dead in Abidjan, including the Minister of the Interior, Emile Boga Doudou, assassinated by the rebels who had laid siege to his dwelling as he was trying to escape. Likewise, General Robert Guéi and his wife Rose were also gunned down in conditions which remain mysterious until today.

These tragic events winding through African history are, of course, of no concern to the venerable academicians gathered around Alassane Ouattara in November, 2013, for his enthronement. While all these savage depravities are taking place, aren't we elsewhere, in the very chic 16th arrondissement in Paris, among well-bred people? Wasn't Blaise Compaoré re-elected for his fourth term on November 25, 2010, with more than 80% of the electorate? Gbagbo asks:

Why wasn't I also elected with 80% of the votes, as was the case for Compaoré after he had masterminded a coup d'état? Apparently, for you in the West, as far as Africa is concerned, such a score is more credible than a score in line with democratic standards! In 2003, when Blaise Compaoré had obtained one of his [former] soviet-like presidential results, I was busy fighting to escape from the clutches of the Elysée. Blaise Compaoré had even already threatened that I would be sent to the ICC. I

found that simply amazingly sweet. Anyway, it is true: he was only expressing the secret wishes of his French masters.

Didn't Compaoré play host to Ségolène Royal[120] when she traveled to Ouagadougou in November, 2011, for the General Assembly of the International Association of Francophone Regions? Louise Arbour, president of the NGO International Crisis, which aims at preventing and resolving deadly conflicts, notes:

> *"Mr. Compaoré, who was a military man and who masterminded a coup d'état, is not the most trustworthy individual... to advocate democracy and to promote the power of the people...*

We may not wish to trust the judgment of so idealist a woman as Louise Arbour, who might be allergic to the rough realities of new countries where power is seized rather won at the voting booth, or allergic to politics in general, which Stendhal defines as *"a pistol shot in the middle of a concert."*

Charles Pasqua has a more realistic view, since he was an actor in Françafrique. He told me, while sipping a glass of whisky, in his RPF office on November 23, 2012:

> *"Of course, at the time of Houphouët everything went well. Those who made a big mess were Konan Bédié by acting stupidly and Compaoré who kept an eye on Ivory Coast where many of his fellow citizens went to live. Ivory Coast has always been the envy of its neighbors, the place everybody wanted to grab. Now the Americans have joined the club too... I believe France could have played its cards differently. But in France, there is no one left to invent a new form of African politics... and there is a new generation of Ivorians, different from the ones we knew. It is with this Africa we have to deal."*

That is the way Charles Pasqua summed up the origins of the Ivorian tragedy and the role he believes Compaoré played in destabilizing the country of the elephants. People are talking about Pasqua becoming the head of the OIF

---

[120] Translator's note: Ségolène Royal is a prominent member of the French Socialist Party and currently Minister of Ecology, Sustainable Development and Energy. With President François Hollande, she has four children. Royal was the first female candidate ever to participate in a run-off presidential election in France. She lost to Nicolas Sarkozy, the right-wing candidate.

(International Office of the Francophone region), when the Senegalese Abdou Diouf finishes his third and last term--the best Françafrican reward[121] that exists.

In his address to the *Académie des Sciences d'Outre-Mer*, Alassane Ouattara stressed with cynicism that

> *"... the economic performance in Africa coincides with the progression of democracy on the continent, and with the adoption by the African Union... of regulations expressing the rejection of the coup d'état, under any form, and any illegal means of taking power."*

Ouattara has mastered the art of ellipsis. Wearing his slick presidential suit, he gave his first major interview to *Jeune Afrique* on May 29, 2011, and says without laughing,

> *" I don't owe anything to anybody except to the Ivorians who elected me."*

I can still hear Jean-Marc Simon telling me a year later, without it being a revelation:

> *"It's very simple. We carried him* [Ouattara] *in our arms* [to power]. *"*

At the reception ceremony of Perouse Street, the headquarters of the *Académie des Sciences d'Outre-Mer*, Yamina Benguigui, then entrusted by the Elysée with the task of taking care of "the French overseas and Francophonie," represented François Hollande. Why this minimum service? Hollande's friend, the Franco-Togolese Kofi Yamgnane, former State Secretary for Integration under François Mitterrand had updated François Hollande on the realities and the risks of the Gbagbo's dossier. He had sent the French president a memo, as did Jean-Pierre Mignard, one of Ouattara's advisers at The Hague, but a socialist close to Hollande, in fact the godfather of his sons. Jean-Paul Benoît, the other lawyer at the International Criminal Court close to the actual power in

---

[121] Translator's note: Charles Pasqua failed to get the reward which went to a Canadian national of Haitian origin, Michaëlle Jean. She is the new General Secretary General of the International Organization for French-Speaking countries (OIF). She was designated as the new executive officer of the OIF in Dakar, Senegal in the aftermath of the XVth Summit of that organization, on November 30, 2014.

Ivory Coast is also close to the French president, keeping him abreast of the Gbagbo case. An observer appointed by the embassy of France also attended the debates taking place in the hearing deciding the confirmation charges in February, 2013, as well as all the other important hearings. Nicolas Sarkozy is the one who wove the threads of this story, and François Hollande probably just wants to avoid making a knot. Gbagbo comments:

I am not part of François Hollande's priorities. Today he knows everything about the case, I am sure. It is up to him to assess it.

François Hollande appears very cautious about the Gbagbo case and has not been too hasty in traveling to Ivory Coast. Was it a twist of fate? His first trip to Abidjan scheduled for February 28, 2013, was cancelled because of a surgical procedure Alassane Ouattara had to undergo at the Percy de Clamart Hospital in a Paris suburb. This is a military hospital where the Palestinian Yasser Araft, as well as the ex- Prime Minister Pierre Mauroy both had surgery, where they were treated and later died. François Hollande knows a favorable outcome for Gbagbo will cast France in a bad light, due to its role as the leader of the International Community concerning this affair.

Chapter 29
"Such an operation couldn't have been put together overnight"

This title describes Gbagbo's take on the invasion which occurred in 2002, as Ivorian rebels, trained in Burkina Faso to the north, and foreign mercenaries from many neighboring countries, poured into the south of Ivory Coast. For Gbagbo and the majority of analysts, it is clear such a well-organized and obviously heavily funded operation "couldn't have been put together overnight." This attack had to have backers from the outside and President Compaoré of Burkina Faso had to be "in on the deal." Indeed, the French involvement is clear, including the appointment at that precise moment, of a French General, Emmanuel Beth, as the French Ambassador to Burkina Faso, the first time in France's history a military general had assumed such a post. And it was no coincidence that Emmanuel Beth's brother, Frederic Beth, was on the front lines alongside the rebels.

In this chapter Mattei discusses in quite some detail the evidence brought forward by the ICC Prosecutor Fatou Bensouda, who centers her case against Gbagbo around four incidents which occurred during the post-electoral crisis: (i) the march on the Ivorian TV station, RTI, for which it is claimed Gbagbo ordered a violent repression resulting in several deaths (ii) a women's demonstration in the northern suburb of Abidjan, Abobo, where it is claimed he ordered the use of heavy artillery, (iii) a bombing in the market of that same community of Abobo, which he supposedly ordered, and finally, (iv) a bloody attack on civilians in Yopougon, a heavily populated suburb to the west of Abidjan. Mattei reports how Gbagbo's defense team, point by point, systematically destroyed the evidence on which Bensouda based her arguments.

The inability of the prosecutor's team to stand up to the defense's team's arguments surprised Laurent Gbagbo's adversaries. Gbagbo's opponents had been led to believe the International Criminal Court was infallible. They trusted its professionalism and believed the message the

Prosecutor was circulating via media on the damning evidence she held against Gbagbo.

In the spring of 2013, the charges came very close to not being confirmed. This would have meant the immediate release of Laurent Gbagbo. Understandably, the Office of the French Minister of Foreign Affairs followed the entire process very closely. Just after the hearing to confirm charges, Minister Laurent Fabius even made a trip to the Netherlands, on pretext of supervising a move in location for the French embassy there. In reality he was meeting the French Ambassador to see how the case was evolving. According to our sources, in the last days before the ICC judges delivered their verdict, at the French Foreign Minister's Department, French diplomats were getting nervous, because they wanted to know what the decision would be. President Gbagbo's defense team's arguments had surprised them, and they were now convinced that Emmanuel Altit's team had won the judicial contest. They were themselves convinced of the imminent release of President Gbagbo.

These French diplomats greatly feared the ICC judges' decision, and on June 3, 2013, their fears were confirmed. The ICC judges were split. On the one side, there were the German and Belgian judges. On the other side, there was the Argentinian judge who had been close to the former Prosecutor Moreno Ocampo over the last three years, and thus, *a priori* would be favorable towards the new Prosecutor, Fatou Bensouda. But this judge had to be extremely careful, since in deciding the fate of one of the Court's most famous prisoners, her own career could be at stake. As the hearing closed, anything seemed possible.

But all realized: to release President Gbagbo would mean admitting the ICC Prosecutor was wrong.

On June 3, 2013, even if the judges strove to "save" Prosecutor Bensouda, they nonetheless acknowledged her defeat and her incapacity to offer them convincing elements in support of her accusations. Since these accusations were exactly those that were lodged against President Gbagbo by the pro-Ouattara camp at the time of the post-electoral crisis, it is interesting to come back to the four major incidents which the ICC Prosecutor claimed as evidence to prove Gbagbo had committed crimes against humanity. The ICC judges ruled on June 3, 2013, that the Prosecutor had brought no convincing element to her reading of these four incidents. For the judges, then, her evidence did not constitute proof that Gbagbo had indeed committed crimes against humanity. Even better, the defense's team's ability to "de-construct" Prosecutor Bensouda's narrative of the four incidents in the end allowed the truth to come out. And what does this truth show? It shows that for ten years, the Ouattara camp, supported by the French authorities, repetitively attempted to take hold of power by force. It shows that evidence was fabricated so the international media would accept the narrative. Below are summaries of how information concerning these four incidents was heavily manipulated.

1. March on the RTI TV station

The Prosecutor claimed that a few days after the presidential run-off elections, the security forces of President Gbagbo, with militia and mercenary back-ups, suppressed a peaceful demonstration organized on December 16, 2010, by the pro-Ouattara group, and through violent means, prevented them from reaching the Ivorian TV station.

During the hearing, the defense dteam emonstrated that far from being a peaceful march, the demonstration itself was organized as follows: women and children were put in front, and in the middle of the crowd were hidden rebels, armed with kalashnikovs and rocket-propelled grenades. The lawyers of President Gbagbo displayed photos that leave no room for doubt. According to the defense team, the pro-Ouattara participants in the demonstration belonged to groups who had infiltrated into Abidjan before the presidential election, accompanied and supported by other militants, often delinquents armed with knives and machetes. The defense team showed that

> *"...the purported peaceful demonstration of December 16, 2010, was actually a carefully planned attempt to seize hold of power through violent means. On December 16, 2010, there were simultaneous attacks: armed groups made a surprise attack on police squads in Abobo, a northern suburb of Abidjan, while at the same time rebel soldiers and other armed combatants started out from the Golf Hotel and moved towards the location of the demonstration. It was there they attacked government security forces."*

The defense team based its presentation on irrefutable evidence, notably video clips taken on December 15, 2010, where pro-Ouattara chiefs, including [Guillaume] Soro, were seen actively preparing the assault of the next day, exhorting the rebels--armed to the teeth--to be courageous.

First remark: in the course of the debates, the Prosecutor refused to discuss the evidence presented by the defense team. But in its report, the Emmanuel Altit's team underlined the fact that these elements could have radically called into question

287

"[T]he Prosecutor's theory summarized in her "Document Containing the Charges," according to which 'the demonstration of December 16, 2010, was organized to be carried out in a peaceful manner and the demonstrators were not armed.' The Prosecutor's failure to question these facts was all the more surprising in that it revealed not only that no investigation had been carried out concerning this specific event (contra the instructions of the Chamber), but also her refusal to take the facts presented into account. She preferred to accept and maintain a purely political narrative. It is important to note here the repetitive nature of the Prosecutor's refusals to conduct any investigation concerning the defense's team's evidence and her refusal to even take it into consideration.

Second remark: the attacks conducted by the rebel forces were obviously an attempt by the Ouattara camp to seize power through violent means. Their objective was not only to attack the RTI TV station, but also the Prime Minister's office and the presidential residence. And the *modus operandi* of the operation is worthy of comment: the initiators of the offensive disguise their attack as a peaceful march, and then use the incident they created to denounce the brutality of the government security forces. Their scheme was all the easier to execute since the police forces were in no way expecting such brutal attacks by such professional and well-armed groups. In the ranks of the government security forces, there were numerous dead. They returned fire. To complicate matters, the rebels who were wounded were dressed as civilians. So it was just child's play: all the communicators of Ouattara's camp had to do was claim that government security forces had attacked civilians. And the manipulations got worse: the rebels went so far as to recuperate the bodies of civilians they themselves had killed and attributed these deaths to the government security forces.

2. The demonstration of the women in Abobo on March 3, 2011

"According to the Prosecutor, on March 3, 2011, in Abobo, in violation of human rights, the security forces loyal to Mr. Gbagbo used heavy weapons to suppress the peaceful demonstration of about 3,000 women who were demanding Mr. Gbagbo to step down [as president]. As a result of the attack, seven women were killed and many others seriously injured."

First remark: The defense team showed that the information of the Prosecutor was in all likelihood false. At the time being referred to, there were no longer any government security forces in that area. The presence of armed tanks which had supposedly been put in place at the exact location of the demonstration is also highly unlikely. This is especially true since the leaders of the government security forces had no knowledge of any demonstration that had occurred or was in the process of occurring in that area. They were informed of the purported incidents only *a posteriori*, i.e., only after communiques issued by the rebels were brought to their attention.

Second remark: The defense team was able to show that the demonstration was in no way "spontaneous"—on the contrary, it had been carefully prepared since the rebels had beforehand positioned cameramen right at that location. They were careful, however, to not inform Western journalists. Furthermore, even the location of the demonstration is questionable. There was no reason for the demonstration to be held in this place which was near an important highway crossing the city of Abobo from east to west, a road on which, once every two or three days, two or three vehicles would pass by at breakneck speed to bring supplies to policemen and government soldiers held under siege by the rebels a few kilometers away.

The idea that a "staging" had occurred became more and more likely, reinforced by the fact that the evidence presented by the Prosecutor in support of her accusations was suspect. First of all, the videos presented as evidence turned out to be fabrications. In one of them, a woman, who was supposed to be dead, stood up and walked away. Moreover, the videos show no actual police attack per se. The defense team especially set out to demonstrate that none of the elements presented by the Prosecutor could consolidate her thesis. Even the accusation that a set of individuals had been killed at that particular time was not credible. Worse, the evidence presented seemed to have been fabricated.

3. The bombing of the market of Abobo

"According to the Prosecutor, on March 17, 2011, several mortar shells were deliberately fired from the government Commando Camp, targeting civilians living in a densely populated area of Abobo."

First remark: The defense team demonstrated that the Prosecutor was unable to identify the hit zones. She was unable to prove that a mortar bombing took place and unable to determine the origin and reasons for such a bombing.

Once again, the Ivorian government military leaders seemed unaware of such an attack.

Second remark: The Prosecutor relied on witnesses *"recruited by the Ouattara camp."* Again, the defense team demonstrated that the elements meant to prove that there had been deaths involved seem to have been fabricated.

4. Concerning the events of Yopougon occurring on April 12, 2011

"The Prosecutor claims that on April 12, 2011, in Yopougon (a suburb west of Abidjan), some 'pro-Gbagbo forces' attacked populations of northern origin." However, it is striking to note that the Prosecutor has suddenly become more vague, compared to her previous DCC. She no longer spoke of the precise date of April 12, 2011, but she only indicated that it would have been on or about April 12, 2011.

First remark: The defense team noted that the Prosecutor was unable to provide a precise date, a precise venue and the precise identity of the authors of the incidents she claims carried out the purported acts. For two years, the Prosecutor was unable to provide these basic precisions, and after her last investigation, the details seemed even fuzzier than before.

Second remark: It seemed clear that the accusations were much too uncertain to be retained, especially since President Gbagbo was arrested by French forces on April 11, 2011. Why then were these accusations still made? Many believe this accusation was made to hide the fact that at the same time as the arrest of Laurent Gbagbo, in Yopougon, civilian populations were attacked by rebel soldiers who came--for some, from Abobo and for others, from the north--with the help of the French forces. Thousands of persons went missing. Men, women and children were completely terrorized.

Some events put forth in the accusations may have even been staged during the post-electoral crisis to serve as traps to force sanctions on President Gbagbo. It is on December 16, 2010, the day of the march on the RTI TV station, that the Prosecutor of the ICC, Luis Moreno Ocampo, issued a warning that he would take legal action against anyone responsible for deadly violence in Ivory Coast. Two days earlier, on December 14, 2010, as the rebels were planning the attack for December 16, through the intermediary of his lawyers, Ouattara sent a letter to the judges and the Prosecutor at the ICC in which he recognized the competence of the Court on possible "incidents." But we can ask, which "incidents"? Logically these *incidents* were the attacks which were going to occur on December 16, 2010, which the rebels themselves knew they were going to carry out. Thus it becomes clear that this was pre-meditated crime, with a kind of advanced recognition of guilt by those at the origin of these incidents. It is a Machiavellian scenario almost impossible to imagine. Everyone believed or pretended to believe that President Gbagbo was at the origin of these "incidents" announced in advance.

Curiously, on the evening of December 16, 2010, the UN Security Council threatens all authors of attacks against civilians, stressing that they would be held accountable for their acts and that "legal action" would be taken against them. The Council was targeting the government of President Gbagbo. From then on, that government is publically banned, ostracized from the nations.

Along these same lines was the purported bombing of the civilian population, which it is claimed was purposely carried out by the military leaders of the Gbagbo government. Even if the occurrence of such bombings seemed highly improbable at the time, this "incident" was immediately referred to by the French authorities to convince the members of the UN Security Council to vote in favor of Resolution 1975 which allowed for the use of force in the Ivorian crisis.

The ink on the UN resolution was still fresh when groups of armed rebels made up, as the defense team has shown, of foreign mercenaries, mainly Burkinabè, poured into the south of Ivory Coast. They had been patiently waiting, guns at their sides, equipped and organized by the French army, who took things in hand and opened the way for them. But a certain problem arises: on their way to Abidjan, these rebels commit numerous massacres and serious violations of human rights.

One last word on the usefulness of crushing President Gbagbo and his government…Everyone everywhere admits that the rebels committed numerous massacres. So evoking the purported massacres of the other side is useful: it helps cover the truth that may prove very embarrassing for those who supported and armed the rebels, and France is the one standing in the front row here. But it also allows the memory of the brutality of the French military intervention in the country to fade: the attacks of the French helicopters against the Ivorian military bases, the destruction of Ivorian security forces' relay centers and finally, the destruction of their weaponry. These attacks probably led to the death of scores of Ivorians--soldiers as well as civilians. The attacks conducted against the residence of the Ivorian president by the French forces during the last days before the downfall of Laurent Gbagbo also left scores of civilians dead. The more the French accused President Gbagbo, the more they hoped these other "realities" would be masked. If these facts were revealed, it might lead to legal action against the French military and even to a debate in the French Parliament—if, of course, justice would be allowed to fulfill its mission as provided for in the French Constitution.

On the side of the French, who gave the order to launch the attack from the north towards the south in March, 2011? The rebel troops and the thousands of Dozo's (these traditional hunters immersed in magic and particularly cruel to the Ivorian populations) were champing at the bit to cross the line of demarcation between north and south Ivory Coast. The surge towards Abidjan of the rebel troops and their Dozo auxiliaries, which was the general and final assault, was obviously premeditated and calculated. Gbagbo concludes:

Such an operation couldn't have been put together overnight.

Who then gave the order to launch the attack? What is sure is that the operation was prepared months in advance. The appointment of General Emmanuel Beth as French Ambassador to Burkina Faso was an obvious signal. His brother, Frédéric Beth, was running the Commanding Center for French Special Operations (COS), who appeared on the front lines at each stage of the offensive. As for the rebel troops, they were made up of mercenaries recruited and armed in Burkina Faso and then sent to northern Ivory Coast. Who then paid for their weapons? Who then trained them? Who then organized them? During all this time President Compaoré certainly was "giving his all," "in the service" of his "brother" Ouattara.

Emmanuel Altit explained to the Court: this dossier is not the fruit of a true investigation. It is a collection of second-hand information provided by those in power in Ivory Coast, based on a bunch of newspaper cuttings gathered together and on reports from NGOs providing no formal evidence. During the post-electoral crisis and even after, Luis Moreno Ocampo never once contacted Gbagbo and his close entourage. But he was in constant contact, working with the team of Alassane Ouattara.

Some supporters of Gbagbo may not see too much progress in the "tilt of the balance" achieved by Altit's team. These supporters have been convinced all along that the reason their hero is now standing before the judges at the ICC is not for criminal reasons, but for political ones, a fair counterpart to Gbagbo's opponents who had condemned him in advance. For diametrically opposed reasons, neither group has attached much importance to the trial which is taking place in The Hague. In some way, both critics and supporters of the ICC have taken the same shortcut: they both minimized the importance of the battle being waged at The Hague. Looking at the huge sacrificial ceremony taking place at the ICC, where the great priestess, Fatou Bensouda, reigns, the critics of ICC see the absurdity of the situation, while those favoring the trial think everything is justified. Whatever the case, the "heathen" troops of the defense team were obliged to raise their shields, face their opponents, foil their traps and wage the unequal battle they have been called to fight at The Hague.

Chapter 30
They heartily sang
the Ivorian national anthem: the
Abidjanaise

Despite his lengthy imprisonment, supporters of President Gbagbo have in no way abandoned him. At each hearing, his supporters travel to The Hague, standing outside the courthouse to show their unfailing support. Coming from all over Europe, by car or train, bus or plane, they want Gbagbo to know he is not forgotten. They sing the Ivorian national anthem and chant over and over "Liberate Gbagbo."

In this chapter Mattei describes the Ivorian political scene in the post-crisis era. Various political parties are being formed, such as LIDER under Mamadou Koulibaly, a politician from the North who Gbagbo appointed as the president of the National Assembly as soon as he was elected in 2000. While most supporters of Gbagbo are waiting for the miracle to happen: the release and return of the president to his homeland, others like Koulibaly are thinking "the show must go on."

Mattei evokes the uncertainty of Gbagbo's fate in The Hague and the precariousness of the situation "back home" on the ground.

After the hearing to confirm the charges against him in February, 2013, the release of Laurent Gbagbo from the Scheveningen prison seemed the natural outcome, and the release seemed all the more likely after the defense lawyers submitted their observations on the Prosecutor's presentation of evidence in April, 2014—observations which totally destroyed her arguments. On the judicial front, President Gbagbo's lawyers had gained the upper hand. And their position was strengthened with the submission of their final report in April, 2014, showing once again that Laurent Gbagbo was guilty only of having continued to work as the chief executive of his country, after the Constitutional

Council had proclaimed him president of the Republic. The ICC judges sensed the Prosecutor would risk a great deal if a formal trial were to be held. If a case such as the one against Gbagbo were to be lost, given its importance and its symbolic dimension, the defeat would be proportionately spectacular and seriously affect the credibility of the international institution as a whole. Health reasons could also be evoked and would be another way for the ICC judges to save face. They could thus release Laurent Gbagbo without undermining the credibility of their own institution.

A trial would present serious risks because Emmanuel Altit's team used the preliminary phase of the confirmation hearing to literally destroy the Prosecutor's evidence, but it has yet to unveil all the evidence she has gathered. During this pre-trial period, Fatou Bensouda showed that her game strategy is poor and mediocre. Thus the defense lawyers are in a position of strength and look to the future with serenity. In these conditions, many think that the ICC risks "losing big" if it decides to go to trial. It would give the defense team the chance to play all its cards and unveil truths that no one wants to hear, especially those committed to Françafrique. Not only would the Prosecutor risk being discredited, the Court itself could end up significantly weakened.

Does this mean that people are losing respect for the ICC Prosecutor? Do they think the detainee will be released? In Abidjan, as well as everywhere in France and throughout the world, Gbagbo's supporters crossed that line long ago. They firmly believe in the innocence of 'the Woody of Mama' and believe he will eventually be released. Perhaps too naïve, many rushed to the Netherlands, expecting to bring back their hero--free at last! Buses coming and going, some coming in private cars, groups arriving by plane or train, they all flood into The Hague, each time there is an important hearing. They have not yet stopped coming--not after many months, and still today, not after many years. In December, 2011, at the end of Gbagbo's intervention, in the area around the white concrete and glass Court, they gathered together and heartily sang the Ivorian national anthem, the "Abidjanaise."

In February 2013, during the hearing to confirm the charges against him, hundreds stood paralyzed when, their president, dressed in a blue suit, with little round glasses perched on his nose, appeared on their i-pads. They hadn't seen him since his imprisonment in Scheveningen, except once on Internet, December 5, 2011, when he was first presented to the ICC judges. A relative of Gbagbo who was admitted into the courtroom succeeded in sending pictures from his mobile phone. Outside, the crowds went crazy, huddled around the magic screen. They stand singing, moving with the tom-toms, chanting their unique slogan: *"Liberate Gbagbo."* In Ivory Coast as well, this incantation [Liberate Gbagbo] has become popular and the very watchword of the FPI, Laurent Gbagbo's party and the key point of the program put forth by the FPI.

Even if there are still some 800 political prisoners detained in the Ivorian prisons because of what they believe, numerous Ivorian intellectuals continue every day to express their collective demand (*Le Monde* of December 25-26, 2013, published one of their appeals): the liberation and the return of the Chief, the words on the lips of every leader in the FPI.

Pascal Affi NGuessan[122], the leader of the FPI's fight on the ground, mobilizes crowds, evoking the same theme, and there is always an impressive turn out. People are right there, present, with a common goal. The success of N'Guessan's most recent tour in 2014 clearly shows that the Ivorians who voted for Gbagbo in 2010 continue to support him, and in great numbers. For them, his return to Ivory Coast is the only medicine that can heal the wounds of the collective humiliation they suffered in 2010. They need Gbagbo's return, to alleviate the pain of their president's imprisonment and subsequent deportation to The Hague. The current Ivorian authorities are not unpleased with the situation--rather they are happy that no one is there to provide any alternative to the current government or to oppose them in any way.

Though Mamadou Koulibaly's relations with the FPI are strained since he resigned to create his own political party, this author of several books (including *The War Waged by France against Ivory Coast),* since the defeat of Gbagbo, fiercely militates against Ouattara's regime, to the point of demanding that Ouattara, as well as Guillaume Soro, be brought before the ICC. He notes:

> *I always supported Laurent Gbagbo, even if I did not agree that we should submit to the humiliating demands of Marcoussis and Kleber in 2003. We entered the tunnel that had been prepared beforehand to lead us to where we are today. Now, we must look forward to the future. I personally thought Laurent Gbagbo should have accepted the objective*

---

[122] Translator's note: As of March 5, 2015, two-thirds, that is, 333 out of the 490 members of the Comité Central of the FPI--the decision body pro tempore of this political organization, suspended Pascal Affi NGuessan from acting and speaking on behalf this political organization. Then followed the *Congrès*, the actual decision body of the FPI, held in Gbagbo's home village of Mama on April 30, 2015, which released Affi NGuessan from his duties as president of the FPI while the same *Congrès* inducted Laurent Gbagbo into the presidency of the political party he had to relinquish, in accordance with the Ivorian Constitution because of his rise to the presidency of Ivory Coat when he was elected in October 2000.

failure of our strategy, which would have allowed us to regain power in the next legislative elections. That would have allowed us to implant democracy once and for all."

It isn't sure that a regime full of armed men would have respected the rules of the game. The elections of 2010 have demonstrated this well. Mamadou Koulibaly has created his own party, LIDER (Liberty and Democracy for the Republic), hoping himself to run for president in 2015. He thinks that the empty-chair policy or the chair filled by "the shadow of the great absent" is absurd and would only facilitate the electoral success for Ouattara and his camp. This is one of the differences of opinion which separate him from his former friends.[123]

Some keep hoping for the miracle: the return of Gbagbo. One journalist wrote that it would be a greater event than Didier Drogba[124] bringing back the [World Cup] soccer trophy to Abidjan[125]. Others remain paralyzed as they wait. Mamadou Koulibaly is periodically attacked, if not insulted, by his former political friends. However, the political weight of the prisoner of Scheveningen is such that he constrains his followers to find a way to reconcile the magical nostalgia they feel and the dynamic action they should be taking, even if this action has to deal with uncertainties and surprises linked to forthcoming decisions of the ICC or to the health of Ouattara.

---

[123] Translator's note: On March 19, 2015, Mamadou Koulibaly met with Abou Drahamane Sangaré, the interim president of the FPI, along with several presidential hopefuls from the PDCI Party and other leaders of the Ivorian opposition. The goal of such an encounter was to set up a platform of discussions on various issues to be written down in a charter (the ten-point charter was signed on May 16, 2015) demanding that the upcoming Ivorian presidential election of October 2015 be held under "acceptable" conditions for all parties.

[124] Translator's note: Didier Drogba is an Ivorian world reknown soccer star, who gained fame as a member of the London-based Chelsea soccer team.

[125] Drogba was no longer part of the Ivorian soccer team when it won the 2015 African cup in Malabo, Equatorial Guinea. This was the first time the cup was brought back to Abidjan in 23 years.

Chapter 31
"The French ambassador acted more like a spy than a diplomat"

This chilling chapter reveals in detail the role the French Ambassador to Ivory Coast played in the actual bombing of Gbagbo's residence. Gbagbo thinks himself that Jean-Marc Simon was "more like a spy than a diplomat." Many of these details come from the lips of the Ambassador himself, who seems proud to have been part of such an important part of French history.

The account of the April 11, 2011 bombing of the President Gbagbo's residence and the point blank shooting of the many civilians who flocked there seeking refuge would put chills down anyone's spine. Two incredible passages stand out. In one Mattei recounts his own discussion with the former French Ambassador, Jean-Marc Simon, who describes how he watched the bombing from his own official residence next door. Heartlessly, while taking credit for the operation, he tells Mattei that as the bombs fell, he could hear the prayers, songs, and even the hallelujahs of those inside the residence. Certainly those under fire were praying for deliverance or expecting to die any second.

Mattei also provides the testimony of Sidiki Bakaba, a well-known film producer, who was on the scene when the bombing took place. Having been injured the day before, he was still in the compound when the bombing began on April 11, 2011. Pulled from the rubble, he escaped with his life. His testimony refutes the Ambassador's and all the news accounts which report that French shoulders never entered the compound. They say they were not the ones to capture Gbagbo. However, there is evidence that they broke down the gates of the compound and Bakaba reports seeing white men "on the inside," a version corroborated by many eyewitnesses.

The Ivorian president's residence, originally built by the first president, Félix Houphouët-Boigny, still lays in ruins. The actual president, Alassane Dramane Ouattara, has established a new presidential residence less than one mile from the Golf Hotel, his former war headquarters, from which he commanded various attacks and where he had himself declared president of the Republic of Ivory Coast.

"It was exactly 1:08 PM." I got this chronometric detail from the former Ambassador of France to Ivory Coast, Jean-Marc Simon, who took great care to note the exact time of what he thought was a truly historic moment--the time the French Special Forces launched their brutal attack on the residence of Laurent Gbagbo. The former Ambassador lets me in on this 'secret,' as we sit together in a Parisian café, to underline his role in controlling and maneuvering these events. Of course from his own residence, strategically located right next door to the Ivorian presidential residence, the residence of the president of the National Assembly, and the papal nuncio's home[126], he had a perfect view, all the while being himself completely protected. 1:08 PM signaled the time of the beginning of Gbagbo's downfall, but also for the former French Ambassador, the time of his own "consecration" as the one who gave the orders at this important moment in history. Gbagbo comments:

Ambassador Simon was more a spy than a diplomat. At the Golf Hotel, French advisors and military and political staff were always coming and going. Ouattara's French "messengers," entrusted with the task of manipulating the international media, were always there, along with the great architect of the maneuvers: Jean-Marc Simon, the Ambassador of France,

One year later, for services rendered, Jean-Marc Simon was promoted to the rare and highly sought rank of "life-time Ambassador" of France. And in addition to the honors of the French Republic, he was ensured from then on a life of ease and comfort. This zealous diplomat, who had already become known for his "fine work" in Central African Republic between 2001 and 2003, where he played a role in overthrowing President Ange-Félix Patassé in favor of François Bozizé, was also rewarded for his services by the new Ivorian authorities, in the form of contracts granted to his firm *Eurafrique Strategies* created just after these events and just in time for his retirement. Many times over, Alassane Ouatttara refers to him in public as *"my friend Jean-Marc."* That is the least Ouattara could do to thank the person who, with his ear stuck to his mobile phone, in permanent contact with Nicolas Sarkozy at the Elysée [in Paris] and with Alassane Ouattara and Guillaume Soro in Abidjan, "managed" the end of the ultimate battle which took place in and around Gbagbo's residence in April, 2011.

---

[126] Translator's note: Following France's tradition of diplomatic protocol, the Ambassador of the Vatican is automatically granted the privilege of being the "Dean" of the diplomatic corps in Ivory Coast.

Désiré Tagro, General Secretary of the Presidency of the Ivorian Republic and former Minister of the Interior is no longer among the living, so he is unable tell us what the French diplomat told him over the phone just before he was mortally wounded by the rebels. Others overheard Tagro's last exchange with Jean-Marc Simon. The French Ambassador evidently had given him enough assurance that Gbagbo's advisor left [his refuge at the presidential] residence, white flag in his hand, to organize the surrender of those who had taken refuge therein. Unfortunately for him, the rebels grabbed hold of him and shot a bullet into his mouth, crushing his jaw. He died just a few hours later, at the Golf Hotel, the political and military headquarters of Ouattara and his camp. According to some sources, rather than dying of his wounds, he was "finished off."

Yes, it was Jean-Marc Simon himself who led the assault against the besieged residence of Gbagbo--the president that the rebel army had been unable to bring down. Jean-Marc told me about all this with a visible display of pleasure, as if it were the high point of his career, between a glass of white wine and a mouthful of salmon at Berkeley's, a trendy Parisian restaurant near the Champs Elysées, where Jean-Marc Simon is a frequent visitor. The restaurant is said to be the former hideout of the French "barbouzes" (spies). We often ran into Michou[127] there, settled in with a bottle of champagne, surrounded by men of his "noble court." For businessmen, "people" and pretty women, Berkeley's is the place to be. He cannot hide his feeling of victory:

"It was like a Spanish corrida... First, we tired out the bull, through political, economic and military pressure....then it was time for the kill... I spent a lot of time on the phone with the com'zone leader Koné Zakaria, with Guillaume Soro, with Ouattara, and with the Elysée, to direct all these operations."

He ironically added:

"While we were bombing them, we heard coming out of that place, alleluias, songs and prayers. No doubt they believed heaven would come down to save them... while in fact, the sky was falling on their heads."

---

[127] Translator's note: "Michou" is normally an affectionate nickname for someone named "Michel." It seems here to be a name friends use to call Jean-Marc Simon, though it may refer to some well-known type of spy or "spook."

The unanimity of the West concerning the legitimacy of the action against Gbagbo and the conviction that they had a monopoly on that information, for a long time allowed people to say everything and anything they wanted—without risk. First of all was Nicolas Sarkozy's (2009) speech at Saint-Didier in which the French president declared that France had nothing to do with any intervention in Ivory Coast. It was an astonishing statement, to say the least, given that the French army had been, for decades, one of the heavy weights on the Ivorian political scene (the Licorne force of 900 men would nearly double in 2011). And if we believe Robert Bourgi and the authorized sources mentioned previously, the decision to mobilize the French army against Gbagbo seems to have already been taken even at the time of Sarkozy's speech.

But words from politicians don't carry much weight. Like dead leaves, they fly in the direction the wind takes them. In Pretoria, in February 28, 2008, Sarkozy announced the possible withdrawal of the French army from the entire African continent. Two years later, he prepared the military assault against the government forces of President Gbagbo and three years later, launched an attack of the Licorne force against Ivorian government positions.

Invited for an interview on Radio France International (RFI) on April 11, 2012, Jean-Marc Simon, again feeling nothing was at risk, also contradicts a promise made in confidence to a French woman during a private meeting in his Abidjan office. First, in response to the question concerning the role of the French army in the last hours of the battle for Abidjan, the French Ambassador continues to spread his diplomatic misinformation, which in the light of the raw data, the photos, films, and testimonies, in no way "rings true":

> The French tanks allowed the FRCI to move forward and enter the residence of Laurent Gbagbo."

Jean-Marc Simon denied that the Licorne force actually entered President Gbagbo's residential compound. But the video clips show that the first attacking forces are *white* soldiers, probably the French Special Forces. Sidiki Bakaba, a film director, producer, actor, former director of Abidjan's "Palace of Culture," and the author of a documentary entitled *"Victory without arms"* (La victoire aux mains nues) which praised the resistance of Ivorians against the attacks of the rebels and France, told me that he personally saw French soldiers of the Special Forces all around him inside the residence after the assault on April 11, 2011. Sidika Bakaba had been wounded the previous day by a rocket shot from a French helicopter while he was filming that helicopter shooting on the soldiers defending the residence and also on civilians taking refuge inside.

On April 11, 2011, Sidika Bakaba was found alive in the rubble of the residence. He had been beaten and stabbed by the rebels after they entered the compound following the French commandos. Sidiki is a talented artist, a Muslim and a native from the north like many of those who were with President Gbagbo in the last moments of the siege. Such facts never prevented Ouattara's French communication "messengers" from claiming that this conflict was an ethnic and religious war. As usual adding fuel to the fire…

The narrative of Sidiki can really not be doubted, since later he was, in fact, saved by other French soldiers who intervened when the rebels were about to cut his throat. They slipped him away to a hospital.

"This is the reason why I never wanted to file a suit [against the French]," Sidiki explains.

Other civilians in the presidential residence, who were arrested during the attack, were taken a bit further away and executed point blank. The RFI journalist asks Ambassador Simon:

"But couldn't the pro-Gbagbo forces on the hill of the Plateau area shoot down at the French tanks?" The French diplomat responded: *"Of course, they could have, but they did not…The French column of tanks moved forward without difficulty."*

What Jean-Marc Simon was careful not to say was that several days beforehand Gbagbo had already given instructions to cease all combat to save human lives. At no time had the Ivorian government forces received instructions to attack or counter-attack. At no time were they authorized to shoot at French soldiers or at the UN peace-keeping forces. The instructions given to the Ivorian government forces were clear: protect the civilian population.

The French Ambassador told a French woman residing in Ivory Coast:

"…Looking at you straight in the face, I can swear to you that a French bullet will never hit an Ivorian, except of course, if we are attacked."

That statement was made in March, 2011, barely one month before the French army's assault on the residence of Gbagbo, on pretext of

"destroying heavy weaponry which threatened the civilian population […] a decision taken at the highest level, obviously by Nicolas Sarkozy himself..."

Gbagbo comments:

Heavy weaponry? there was none at the residence.

Sidiki Bakaba, currently living in France, explains:

"There were hundreds of people, civilians, and mainly young people, who came to take refuge on the lawns of the residence and on the road leading there, thinking their presence would protect Gbagbo. When I was arrested and taken away on April 11, 2011, I saw hundreds of bodies; these people were lying dead, killed by the French bombing or by the rebels after the surrender of Gbagbo."

Unfortunately, we will never know the number of those dead.

Chapter 32
When Roland Dumas imposed Vergès

> *This short chapter describes how two very well-known French lawyers were invited to "come on board" to help Gbagbo in the complex post-electoral crisis. In the end, they did little to help the President Gbagbo's cause.*
>
> *In 2005, Gbagbo had called upon Jacques Vergès, a world reknown French lawyer who had defended many anti-colonialist causes, to investigate and shed light on the horrific massacres which had been carried out by the rebels in the West of Ivory Coast. Though well paid, he never finished his assignment and was dismissed.*
>
> *Later in 2011, with his back to the wall, Gbagbo called on his long-time supporter, another French lawyer, the highly respected Roland Dumas, to come to Abidjan to help him. Dumas eventually came, but with Vergès at his side. Gbagbo, never one to hold grudges, accepted Vergès's presence and participation in the new efforts to inform the media--to help the world understand exactly what was happening on the ground in Ivory Coast.*
>
> *As Mattei tells it, in the end, the 2011 visit of the two lawyers, which cost Ivory Coast quite a bit of money, had very little impact, either in France or world-wide.*
>
> *As for the 2005 massacres in the western towns of Guitrozon and Petit Duékoué, very few know anything about it and very few seem to care.*

On the eve of the New Year 2011, two old political "stars" from Paris, Roland Dumas and Jacques Vergès made a trip to Abidjan to support Laurent Gbagbo. But instead of the visit doing some good, the public considered it more as a spectacular media event. The two lawyers were well paid, and Roland Dumas ended up imposing Vergès on Gbagbo despite himself.

In fact, Gbagbo had been displeased with Vergès ever since he had been sent in 2005 by the government to Guitrozon and Petit Duékoué to investigate the massacres which took place on May 31 and June 1. It was a total slaughter: huts and houses had been burned to the ground with their inhabitants inside, heads had been split open with machetes, women had been raped and disemboweled, children had been shot down at point-blank range or knifed to death. All this was like a dress rehearsal of a coming extermination which was going to take place, as the rebels advanced, years later, through the same village in March, 2011. The second massacre occurred 500 meters away from a camp of a French contingent of the Licorne force and the ONUCI military camp in the region.

This wasn't enough horror? Or had the lack of consciousness before the massive death of so many human beings infiltrated into our cultures? Maybe these two massacres didn't have sufficient numbers to reach the ranks of other universal dramas?

For instance, in the Congo in the province of Kivu, since 1999, hundreds of thousands of people have died and some are still dying. Almost 1.5 million refugees had to leave their homes and villages and were forced into exile, without anyone batting an eye. Maybe the famines of Biafra or the massacres in Rwanda have exhausted our capacity to be interested in or feel compassion for Africa....Do events in Africa allow us to get used to the phenomenon of people dying like flies...not here in the West...but "over there"?[128] Or rather, will the careful examination of the reasons creating a context favorable to so many deaths inside this African hell--after more than a century of declared colonialism, followed by total dependency--not bring us to our senses and allow us to accept our share of responsibility?

By the intermediary of a certain Captain B., Jacques Vergès had approached some Ivorians who arranged a meeting for him at the Brussels Hilton with Désiré Tagro, former Ivorian Minister of the Interior. They had discussed the case of the victims' families killed in this massacre in western Ivory Coast with an Ivorian lawyer, Micheline Bamba. Vergès had been entrusted with the task of ensuring the defense of the families in collaboration with the judicial services of the Ivorian government. Vergès had been instructed to work with the Ivorian lawyer Micheline Bamba. The fact that Vergès had been in the entourage of Ouattara a few years beforehand did not seem to bother the Ivorian officials.

Jacques Vergès received an advance of 150,000 euros from the Ivorian state, and Roland Dumas received 67,200 euros. But when Micheline Bamba asked Vergès to provide just 3 million CFA francs (less than 5,000 euros), to launch investigations on the ground, Vergès curtly refused. And he never renewed contact with her. As of July 22, by a simple letter, he was dismissed.

---

[128] Translator's note: Venance Konan, an Ivorian journalist and author notes "Yes, there is now a geo-politics of emotion: what happens in Africa no longer moves the world."

Gbagbo was stunned by the French lawyer's attitude, letting him down in the midst of an agreed deal, but he did not oppose his return to Abidjan in the thick of the post-electoral upheaval at the end of 2010. Roland Dumas vouched for his colleague. Didn't Laurent Gbagbo realize that in 2005, Dumas and Vergès had asked for a big advance, even though all they intended to do was to do a simple evaluation of the situation and increase media awareness on the issue? But that's what Laurent Gbagbo is like. People say he was too easy, far too indulgent. He was lenient toward Vergès and Dumas, as well toward a number of French politicians who benefited from his generous hospitality, but who never returned the favor. He was lenient as well towards his own staff and the many people in his own entourage. President Gbagbo is an intellectual and a statesman. He is someone who provides the broad outlines of his political vision and the main lines of actions to be carried out. He doesn't bother himself with the details. President Gbagbo delegates and trusts that his wishes will be carried out. He counts on the competency and integrity of government and administrative officials. Unlike his counterparts, he does not meddle in any way in the daily intrigues of his entourage, and he does not play "special interest" games.

The only fruit of all the efforts at getting the tragic events of Duékoué in 2005 known was a small booklet released by the Pharos Publishing House, entitled *Crimes against Humanity*, cosigned by Roland Dumas and Jacques Vergès... Yet neither Dumas nor Vergès wrote a single line of this booklet. It was MondioPhonie-Media, also hired to make known overseas the story of the massacres and to archive the evidence, who wrote the book for them.

In the end the impact of the two "old guys'" visit in 2011 was not worth much and perhaps even detrimental to the cause. Upon their return to Paris, the two veteran lawyers participated in a few talks on French TV shows, but their appearances and interviews were ineffective in making known the cause they were supposed to be defending. At least they were able to challenge some of the official takes on the events, which had up till then been completely one-sided.

Roland Dumas, in particular, in his capacity as former president of the French Constitutional Council and former Minister of French Foreign Affairs did do his best to hold back the barrage of media hype against Gbagbo. His sincerity cannot be questioned. From 2002 onwards, he supported Laurent Gbagbo. He was one of the first and among the only ones along with Henri Emmanuelli to show their solidarity towards President Gbagbo.

In January, 2003, Roland Dumas congratulated Mamadou Koulibaly when he walked out on the Linas-Marcoussis talks to show his disgust at what appeared to him to be the hijacking of Ivory Coast's future. Through the intermediary of Koulibaly, before the Linas-Marcoussis talks, Dumas advised Gbagbo not to come to Paris to sign the agreements being imposed on him. Both Dumas and Koulibaly used exactly the same terms to explain what happened:

> *"By coming to Paris, Gbagbo entered a dark tunnel. He has never been able to get out."*

It is true that at the beginning of 2011, Roland Dumas used his experience, his charm and his oratory skills to help Gbagbo. Vergès played the role of the "provocateur": that's what he was there for. But he overdid it. This would be his last glorious act. The two old guys seemed to have a little too much fun, as they said themselves, *"stirring things up"*[129] in their last big stand-off...

Dumas and Vergès ended up cosigning and publishing a "public report," but basically it had no effect, since the anti-Gbagbo "machine" had already been launched and was rolling at high speed... Jacques Vergès, the fierce anti-colonialist, finally understood this before he died in August, 2013.

---

[129] Translator's note: the French expression used here ("foutre le bordel") is quite vulgar.

Chapter 33
"Yesterday is not so far away"

As life moves on in Ivory Coast, Laurent Gbagbo sits in his prison cell waiting for his trial, accused of committing crimes against humanity. This is not the first time he is being held prisoner. He was a political prisoner under the regime of Félix Houphouët-Boigny, the first president of Ivory Coast. He was imprisoned for his nonviolent fight against a one party system. He was imprisoned because he believed in democracy.

Back at home in Ivory Coast, the country appears to be flourishing, as Madam Ouattara flies in her guests for international charity galas and Ouattara flaunts figures attesting to a high growth rate. But behind the glitter, there is poverty. Behind the appearance of democracy, there are still political prisoners, still thousands in exile, still night-time abductions of the opponents the sitting president fears.

In this brief and final chapter, Mattei brings forward experts who question the announced growth rates and ask who is benefitting from the apparent prosperity. Mattei seems to be saying, beware of appearances. Beware of false rumors. Beware of wavering governments, like the U.S. who called Ouattara a champion and now views him with concern. Mattei tells all to beware because, as he notes, Ivory Coast has become what France and the International Community have made it to be: "a time bomb."

It's said by those who were with him during his first imprisonment that Laurent Gbagbo did not sit idle in prison nor did he let others sit idly by. He sat down to write a play, the Lion of Manding, *with a perhaps predictable three-part plot: a "complication," an exile experience, and a triumphal return. Ever the leader, he set the student-prisoners with him to the task of performing his play. The lines from the play are haunting, and though they speak of an "unhappy world," they announce a better one: "Yesterday is not so far away... tomorrow is deep, of a deepness full of hope..."*

From his prison cell, Gbagbo speaks and his supporters listen. They listen and wonder if the play will have a happy ending. Whether it does or not, Gbagbo will continue to speak and we will continue to hear:

Listen to my word: it can only move forward.

Listen to my word: history is truth.

Ivory Coast disappeared from French television screens as if nothing had happened, as if everything had been said, as if the media had finished writing that country's history. At tremendous expense, Madam Ouattara began chartering planes--full of personalities--invited to charity galas in Abidjan. Ado is busy taking care of his health problems, while Guillaume Soro, number two of the regime and Hamed Bakayoko, the Minister of the Interior (known around Paris thanks to the "Alizée" night club located in the 15th arrondissement) watch each other from out of the corner of their eyes, ready to pull the trigger.

After all the drama, life still goes on in the country of the elephants, where not even one of the issues dividing Ivorians has been resolved. Several supporters of Gbagbo are in prison, others are in exile, and the inhabitants who fled the country are still afraid to return. Their houses and all of their assets have been taken away by the rebels.

In Washington, the situation in Ivory Coast now evokes some criticism and Alassane Ouattara's regime is now viewed with some caution--Alassane Ouattara who used to be their champion. This change in the U.S. attitude persists despite the announced growth rate of 8%[130] due to the return of investors after ten years of war and the division of the country into two. However, it is a growth which impoverishes.

"Money is working but is not in circulation" says Ouattara ironically.

The truth is, as Ahoua Don Mello explains, that this is a fictitious growth rate:

> *"Ivory Coast is an agricultural country. Yet, progress in this sector has only been 0.2% for the announced GDP. The population in rural areas has increased, with a corresponding increase in poverty. The growth is solely concentrated in the sector of the BTP (Public and Private Buildings) and, in addition, it is done in an artificial way. The project for the 3rd bridge in Abidjan was estimated at 60 million euros under Laurent Gbagbo. Now it is up to 180 million euros under Ouattara. This over-invoicing is what renders the growth rate fictitious. The fact is that the economy is actually free-falling. Cocoa production was reduced by 10% in 2012, oil and gas products have fallen by 22%. Why is this the case? It is not because there is less production of cocoa or oil and gas. It is because all these raw materials are stolen and diverted to the 'black market' where they are sold."*

---

[130] According to Mamadou Koulibaly the growth rate was 9.8% as of May 31, 2014.

310

In any case, the growth officially stated did not prevent the new Ivorian authorities from asking for a loan of 75 billion CFA francs (114 million euros) from the European Union. It did not prevent them from requesting France to cancel their debt, and most astonishing of all, asking for a loan of 100 billion CFA francs (152 million euros) from Congo-Brazzaville, as revealed by *Jeune Afrique* in its issue of October 27, 2013.

France released an emergency fund of 400 million euros in order to ensure the salaries of Ivorian civil servants and the running of the Ivorian state. Since he came to power, Ado has sought loans totaling 15 billion. And he has spent more time in France, in his Mougins[131] residence and in his private plane than in Ivory Coast. These costly trips and all the expense accompanying this lifestyle, during such a period of financial difficulties at home, seems ill-adapted to the situation. The fact is most Ivorians are finding they have to "tighten their belts." To ensure that the resources of the country are not squandered by others, Alassane Ouattara at least was careful to put the Ministry of Mines under his own control. The mines are, after all, the backbone of war and the key to Ouattara's power.

Deprived of speaking publicly since his arrest in Abidjan on April 11, 2011, and his detention in Korhogo in the north of the country, Laurent Gbagbo has not confided in anyone during the last three years, except for his lawyers, and two or three friends who were allowed to visit him in prison at The Hague after his transfer to the ICC. Some thought they could take advantage of his being absent from the Ivorian political scene or his being precluded from communicating. Thus some people claimed to have received confidential information from him, even though they never saw or spoke to him, hoping certainly to make their articles or books a little "richer."

So, there has been much said, as if coming from Gbagbo: indirect comments spread by intermediaries or invented information. Ivory Coast deserves better than this dishonest hodge-podge of journalistic charlatanism. It is essential for people to hear what Laurent Gbagbo is saying and what he has said, he who, in the eyes of many Africans, has become the hero of their emancipation. In Paris, people in high places now know that things are not going "well" at The Hague, and according to Jean-Christophe Notin, who still has connections with some of his eminent informants, everything could

---

[131] Translator's note: Located in southeastern France, Mougins is 15-minute drive from Cannes in the middle of the French Riviera.

"explode" again—if, for example, Alassane Ouattara should suddenly die or be removed.

The recent announcement of his illness and surgery threw his followers into a panic. The requests for visas multiplied incessantly, suggesting there might be a massive escape abroad if the worst happened. Were Alassane Ouattara to die, the whole tragic game of conquest of power in Abidjan, which started with the death of Houphouët-Boigny in 1993, would start all over again. Unfortunately, this is not an impossible scenario, as each protagonist keeps his private army militia close at hand. The importation of populations from northern countries by the tens of thousands in order to secure the victory of Ouattara in the forthcoming 2015 presidential election and to provide a counter weight to the strength of southern Ivory Coast, worries the experts. Hardly four years after the "victory of democracy"--with missiles--Ivory Coast has again become what Nicolas Sarkozy and the International Community made of it: a time-bomb.

Laurent Gbagbo, the president who always counted on his own means and strength, didn't see how the world powers were joining together against him. His stormy face-off with France was skillfully transformed in 2010 by Sarkozy and his camp into a clash between an African president and the International Community. Confronted by the "war machine" put together by the French authorities which attacked from all sides--political, diplomatic, financial, and military--Laurent Gbagbo found himself nearly isolated and quasi-disarmed until the fatal blow…

The great voices of Africa of these last fifty years have disappeared: we no longer hear the voices of Nasser, Sékou Touré, Thomas Sankara, Patrice Lumumba, and Nelson Mandela. The West fought all of them or despised them--like the Senegalese president, Léopold Senghor, poet and lover of the French language, who was buried in December 2001 in the absence of the president of the French Republic, Jacques Chirac, and the then-Prime minister, Lionel Jospin. In *Le Monde* of January 5, 2002, Eric Orsenna, former adviser to Mitterrand, comments on this state of affairs in an article he entitled "I am ashamed."

Throughout his life, Laurent Gbagbo has often been imprisoned, but he has always made his voice heard through those prison walls. In 1972, jailed for political reasons in a military camp in the north of Ivory Coast[132], he wrote in a

---

[132] The military camp was actually located in Seguéla, in central-northern Ivory Coast.

play he called *The Manding Lion* (*Le Lion du Manding*)[133] the following lines of which today still ring in Africa's ears:

> *"The world is unhappy*
> *Yet yesterday is not so far away*
> *And tomorrow is deep*
> *Of a deepness full of hope*
> *Listen to my word: it can only move forward*
> *Listen to my word: history is truth."*

---

[133] This is a quote offered by Guy Labertit in his book mentioned above in footnote 34. Labertit quotes therein the black African poet and musician, Mamdou Kouyaté, known as the "messenger of legend."

Glossary:
List of Acronyms

ADO: Nickname of Alassane Dramane Ouattara. Ouattara was the Prime Minister under Houphouet-Boigny, from November 11, 1990 until the death of the president on December 7, 1993.

AICI: *Agence immobilière de la Côte d'Ivoire, or the* Real Estate Agency of Ivory Coast, a company run by Dominique-Folloroux-Ouattara.

AFP: *Agence France Presse.* Along with Reuters and Associated Press (AP), AFP is considered one of the top news agencies in the world. Many other news agencies base their news reports on their data.

BAE: *Brigade anti-émeute* or Anti-Riot Brigade.

BCEAO: *Banque Centrale des Etats de l'Afrique de l'Ouest* is the Central Bank of the States of West Africa (CBSWA).

BEAC: *Banque des Etats d'Afrique Centrale* or the Bank of Central African States (BCAS).

BICICI: *Banque internationale pour le commerce et l'industrie de la Côte d'Ivoire* or the International Bank for Trade and Industry of Ivory Coast.

BMCE: *Banque du Maroc pour le commerce extérieur*, the Bank of Morocco for Foreign Trade (BMFT).

BCRA :   *Bureau central de renseignements et d'action,* the French Central Bureau of Intelligence and Operations, created in 1940 and the off-shoot of a former military intelligence agency which was founded in 1871.

BTP: *Bâtiment et travaux publics,* an economic enterprise encompassing private and public buildings from conception to construction.

CCDO: *Centre pour la coordination des décisions   opérationnelles,* the Center for the Coordination of Operational Decisions (CCOD).

CEDEAO: *Communauté économique des Etats de l'Afrique de l'Ouest*, known in English as **ECOWAS** or the *Economic Community of West African States*. This body plays an economic as well as political role in the region, sending peace-keeping forces to troubled areas, issuing sanctions, etc. Citizens belong to the countries which make up the CEDEAO (Benin, Burkina Faso, Ivory Coast, Gambia, Ghana, Guinea, Guinea-Bissau, Liberia, Mali, Niger, Nigeria, Senegal, Sierra Leone, Togo, and CapeVerde) can travel across borders within this region without visas.

CEI: *Commission électorale indépendante* or the Independent Electoral Commission (IEC).

CFA: Also known as the the CFA franc, this is the currency used in the francophone region. From 1945-1958, it was called *Franc des colonies françaises d'Afrique.* In 1958 this currency took on the name *Franc des communautés françaises* d'Afrique.

COS: Commanding Center for Special Operations.

CTK: *Commandant de la compagnie territoriale de Korhogo,* i.e. Commander of the Territorial Company of Korhogo. The CTK is also known as Com'zone or Zone Commander or Region Commander, the region of Korhogo in this particular case.

DCC: *Document contenant les charges*, a legal document which lists charges agaisnt a group or individual.

DGSE: *Direction générale de la sécurité extérieure* or "General Direction for External Security

DOZO: a traditional hunters' association whose members live in northern Ivory Coast, southeast Mali and Burkina Faso. They played a major role in the civil war and are still today throughout the "occupied" zone. They are distinguished by their physical appearance: traditional clothing, amulets and fetishes, and local-made rifles.

ECOWAS: *Economic Community of West African States*. See **CEDEAO**.

FANF: *Nouvelles forces armées des forces nouvelles* or New Armed Forces created in the aftermath of the Linas-Marcoussis talks of January 2003. They became FRCI (see below) during the post-electoral crisis (a presidential decree issued by Alassane Ouattara on March 17, 2011.

FDS: *Forces de défense et de sécurité* or Defense and Security Forces. This is the name for the armed forces of the Republic of Ivory Coast before Alassane Ouattara changed the name to **FRCI**. See below.

FPI: *Front populaire ivoirien* or "Ivorian People's Party", the political party founded by Laurent Gbagbo and a handful of other committed intellectuals in the early 1980s.

FMI: *Fonds monétaire international*, i.e., International Monetary Fund or IMF.

FRCI: *Forces républicaines de Côte d'Ivoire* or the Republican Forces of Ivory Coast.

FSECI: *Fédération scolaire et estudiantine de Côte d'Ivoire* or Federation of Ivorian Students' Union. Two main political players headed FSECI: Soro Guillaume and Charles Blé Goudé.

DGSE: *Direction générale de la sécurité extérieure* or General Directorate for External Security.

IHAAA: *Institut d'histoire, d'art et d'archéologie africaine*. The Institute of African Art and Archeology, based in Abidjan.

MACA: *Maison d'arrêt et de correction d'Abidjan,* i.e. "Arrest and Correction Facility of Abidjan." In the southern part of the country, the MACA is the main prison for convicted criminals as well as for political prisoners.

MJP: *Mouvement pour la Justice et la Paix.* Along with the MPCI and the MPIGO, this Movement for Justice and Peace is the third branch of the rebel movement.

MNLA: *Movement national de liberation de l'Azawad* or the National Movement for the Liberation of Azwaad (the northern territories of Mali).

MPCI: *Mouvement patriotique de Côte d'Ivoire* or the "Patriotic Movement of Ivory Coast." Created in 2005 and led by Guillaume Soro Kigbafori, this is one of the branches of the armed rebellion.

ONUCI: French acronym for *Opération des Nations Unies en Côte d'Ivoire,* United Nations Operation in Ivory Coast.

PDCI: *Parti démocratique de Côte d'Ivoire* or "Democratic Party of Ivory Coast" is the political party of Houphouet-Boigny, created in April, 1946. Before the multiparty system, it was the only party in Ivory Coast. Today the head of the party is Henri Konan Bédié.

PETROCI: *Compagnie pétrolière de Côte d'Ivoire* is the "National Oil Company of Ivory Coast."

PS Parti socialiste or the Socialist Party (in France)

PIT: *Parti ivoirien des travailleurs* is the "Ivorian Labor Party."

PPTE: *Pays pauvres très endettés* refers to Heavily Indebted Poor Countries (**HIPC**), an initiative of the International Monetary Fund and the World Bank to provide debt relief and low-interest loans.

RTI: *Radio télévision ivoirienne* is the Ivorian Radio and Television Network.

SAC: *Service d'action civique* is the Civic Action Service, De Gaulle's militia force founded by Jacques Foccart in January, 1960.

SDECE: *Service de documentation extérieure et de contre-espionnage* is the External Documentation and Counter-Espionage Service (of France)

SFIO: *Section française de l'international ouvrière* was the name of the French socialist party created in 1904. In 1969, it was replaced by the current socialist party (**PS**).

RFI: *Radio France Internationale,* a French Public radio which broadcasts worldwide, parallel to BBC World Service, Voice of America and Deutsche Welle.

RDR: *Rassemblement des républicains* or the "Rally for Republicans", an Ivorian political party created in 1994 by the late Georges Degny Kobina. This is the party of Allassane Ouattara.

317

RPR: *Rassemblement pour la République*, "Rally for the Republic" founded by former French president Jacques Chirac, in December, 1976 with a view to restoring Gaullist policies.

SGBCI *Société générale de banques en Côte d'Ivoire* or General Society of Banks in Ivory Coast.

UEMOA: *Union économique et monétaire ouest africaine* or the West African Economic and Monetary Union (**WAEMU**).

UMP: *Union pour un movement populaire,* i.e., "Union for a popular movement", a right-wing French political party, to which Nicholas Sarkozy belongs. Its new name is "Les Républicains" or the Republicans.

UPC: *Union populaire du Cameroun* or the People's Union of Cameroon.

BIBLIOGRAPHY

Agbohou, Nicolas. *Le Franc CFA et l'euro contre l'Afrique*, Solidarité Mondiale, 2000.

Adler, Laure. *L'Année des adieux*, Flammarion, 1995.

Deltombe, Thomas, Domergue, Manuel, and Tatsisa, Jacob. *Kamerun! Une guerre cachée aux origines de la Françafrique, 1948-1971,* La Découverte, 2011.

Duval, Philippe. *Fantômes d'Ivoire,* Editions du Rocher, 2003.

Glaser, Antoine et Smith, Stephen. *Comment la France a perdu l'Afrique,* Editions Calmann-Lévy, 2005.

Guisnel, Jean (ed.) and Faligot, Roger (ed.). *Histoire secrète de la Ve République*, La Découverte 2007.

Hugueux, Vincent. *Reines d'Afrique : le roman vrai des premières dames,* Perrin, 2014.

Kahn, Jean-François. *L'Horreur médiatique,* Plon, 2014.

Konan, Bédié Henri. *Les Chemins de ma vie,* Plon, 1999.

Koudou, Kessié Raymond. *Laurent Gbagbo, au centre d'un complot*, L'Harmattan, 2013.

Koulibaly, Mamadou. *La Guerre de la France contre la Côte d'Ivoire,* L'Harmattan, 2003.

Labertit, Guy. *Adieu, Abidjan-sur-Seine! Les coulisses du conflit ivoirien,* Autres Temps Editions, 2008.

Neyrac, Georges. *Ivoire nue,* Editions Jacob-Duvernet, 2005.

Notin, Jean-Christophe. *Le Crocodile et le scorpion: La France et la Côte d'Ivoire (1999-2013)*, Editions du Rocher, 2013.

Péan, Pierre. *La République des malettes,* Fayard, 2011.

Sehoué, Germain. *Le Commandant invisible raconte la bataille d'Abidjan,* L'Harmattan, 2012.

Soro, Guillaume. *Pourquoi je suis devenu un rebelle,* Hachette, 2005.

Yamgnane, Kofi. *Afrique, introuvable démocratie*, Editions Dialogues, 2013.